TRAVELS WITH
HERODOTUS

Ryszard Kapuściński

TRANSLATED FROM THE POLISH BY
Klara Glowczewska

PENGUIN BOOKS

PENGUIN BOOKS

Published by the Penguin Group
Penguin Books Ltd, 80 Strand, London WC2R ORL, England
Penguin Group (USA), Inc., 375 Hudson Street, New York, New York 10014, USA
Penguin Group (Canada), 90 Eglinton Avenue East, Suite 700, Toronto, Ontario, Canada M4P 2Y3
(a division of Pearson Penguin Canada Inc.)
Penguin Ireland, 25 St Stephen's Green, Dublin 2, Ireland (a division of Penguin Books Ltd)
Penguin Group (Australia), 250 Camberwell Road, Camberwell, Victoria 3124, Australia
(a division of Pearson Australia Group Pty Ltd)
Penguin Books India Pvt Ltd, 11 Community Centre, Panchsheel Park, New Delhi – 110 017, India
Penguin Group (NZ), 67 Apollo Drive, Rosedale, North Shore 0632, New Zealand
(a division of Pearson New Zealand Ltd)
Penguin Books (South Africa) (Pty) Ltd, 24 Sturdee Avenue, Rosebank, Johannesburg 2196, South Africa

Penguin Books Ltd, Registered Offices: 80 Strand, London WC2R ORL, England

www.penguin.com

Originally published in Poland as *Podróże z Herodotem* by Znak, Kraków 2004
First published in the United States of America by Random House, Inc. 2007
First published in Great Britain by Allen Lane 2007
Published in Penguin Books 2008

1

Copyright © Ryszard Kapuściński 2007
Translation copyright © Klara Glowczewska 2007

Portions of this book originally appeared in *Condé Nast Traveller*, *The New Yorker* and *The Paris Review*

Grateful acknowledgement is made to Oxford University Press for permission to reprint excerpts of
The Histories by Herodotus, translated by Robin Waterfield, translation copyright © 1988 by
Robin Waterfield. Reprinted by permission of Oxford University Press.

The moral right of the author and translator has been asserted

The Herodotus map of the world from the sixth century, from E. H. Bunbury's
A History of Ancient Geography among the Greeks and Romans (1879).

Printed in Great Britain by Clays Ltd, St Ives plc

A CIP catalogue record for this book is available from the British Library

978-0-141-02114-0

www.greenpenguin.co.uk

Mixed Sources
Product group from well-managed
forests and other controlled sources
www.fsc.org Cert no. SA-COC-1592
© 1996 Forest Stewardship Council

Penguin Books is committed to a sustainable future
for our business, our readers and our planet.
The book in your hands is made from paper
certified by the Forest Stewardship Council.

PENGUIN BOOKS

TRAVELS WITH HERODOTUS

'This is both a rattling good read, and a superior work on reflective instruction . . . a massive achievement' Paul Cartledge, *Independent*

'A gifted descriptive writer . . . Like all the best travel writers he has an eye for the telling detail, selecting the fertile fact from the accumulated millions, and for the glittering setpiece' Sara Wheeler, *Guardian*

'Kapuściński could be trusted to tell the truth about complex and difficult events . . . What drove him on was his endless curiosity about humanity, in all its forms. Like Herodotus, he listened and recorded, but did not blame' Margaret Atwood

'Like Herodotus, Ryszard Kapuściński was a reporter, a historian, an adventurer and, truly, an artist' Matthew Kaminski, *Wall Street Journal*

'A fine testament to his genius' Iain Finlayson, *The Times*

'One of the twentieth century's finest foreign correspondents . . . He writes spare, characterful prose that is a pleasure to read . . . an engaging running commentary with kernels of wisdom, insights, shared sympathies and eminently human observations on the people and places he encounters' Justin Marozzi, *Sunday Telegraph*

'Extraordinary . . . His observations are anthropological but punctuated by wonder' Elizabeth Speller, *Financial Times*

'By the time you finish *Travels with Herodotus*, you'll be shaking your own gnawed fingernails from its pages . . . you'll be pleasantly surprised by how much satisfaction, as well as salience, there is to be found in this perfect discomfort read' Stephen Smith, *Observer*

Ryszard Kapuściński was born in Poland in 1932. As a foreign correspondent for PAP, the Polish news agency, until 1981 he was an eyewitness to revolutions and civil wars in Africa, Asia and Latin America. His books include *The Shadow of the Sun*, *The Emperor*, *Shah of Shahs* and *Another Day of Life*, all of which are published by Penguin. He won dozens of major literary prizes all over the world, and in 1999 was made 'journalist of the century' in Poland. He died in January 2007.

I am like one of those old books that ends up moldering for lack of having been read. There's nothing to do but spin out the thread of memory and, from time to time, wipe away the dust building up there.

—SENECA

All memory is present.

—NOVALIS

We are, all of us, pilgrims who struggle along different paths toward the same destination.

—ANTOINE DE SAINT-EXUPÉRY

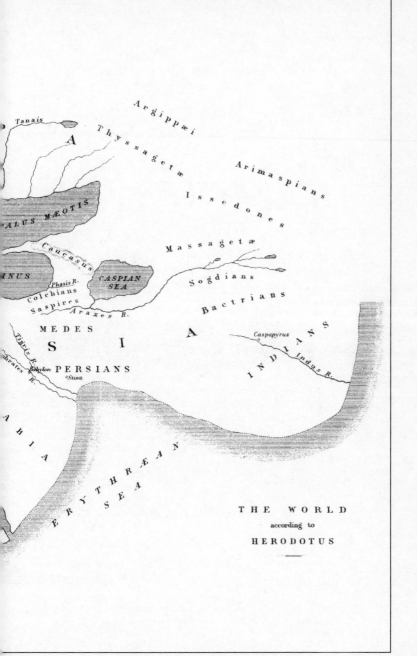

THE WORLD

according to

HERODOTUS

CONTENTS

CONTENTS

TRAVELS WITH HERODOTUS

CROSSING THE BORDER

Before Herodotus sets out on his travels, ascending rocky paths, sailing a ship over the seas, riding on horseback through the wilds of Asia; before he happens upon the mistrustful Scythians, discovers the wonders of Babylon, and plumbs the mysteries of the Nile; before he experiences a hundred different places and sees a thousand inconceivable things, he will appear for a moment in a lecture on ancient Greece, which Professor Bieżuńska-Małowist delivers twice weekly to the first-year students in Warsaw University's department of history.

He will appear and just as quickly vanish.

He will disappear so completely that now, years later, when I look through my notes from those classes, I do not find his name. There are Aeschylus and Pericles, Sappho and Socrates, Heraclitus and Plato; but no Herodotus. And yet we took such careful notes. They were our only source of information. The war had ended six years earlier, and the city lay in ruins. Libraries had gone up in flames, we had no textbooks, no books at all to speak of.

The professor has a calm, soft, even voice. Her dark, attentive eyes regard us through thick lenses with marked curiosity. Sitting at a high lectern, she has before her a hundred young people the majority of whom have no idea that Solon was great, do not know the cause of Antigone's despair, and could not explain how Themistocles lured the Persians into a trap.

If truth be told, we didn't even quite know where Greece was or, for that matter, that a contemporary country by that name had a past so remarkable and extraordinary as to merit studying at university. We were children of war. High schools were closed during the war years, and although in the larger cities clandestine classes were occasionally convened, here, in this lecture hall, sat mostly girls and boys from remote villages and small towns, ill read, undereducated. It was 1951. University admissions were granted without entrance examinations, family provenance mattering most—in the communist state the children of workers and peasants had the best chances of getting in.

The benches were long, meant for several students, but they were still too few and so we sat crowded together. To my left was Z.—a taciturn peasant from a village near Radomsko, the kind of place where, as he once told me, a household would keep a piece of dried kielbasa as medicine: if an infant fell ill, it would be given the kielbasa to suck. "Did that help?" I asked, skeptically. "Of course," he replied with conviction and fell into gloomy silence again. To my right sat skinny W., with his emaciated, pockmarked face. He moaned with pain whenever the weather changed; he said he had taken a bullet in the knee during a forest battle. But who was fighting against whom, and exactly who shot him, this he would not say. There were also several students from better families among us. They were neatly attired, had nicer clothes, and the girls wore high heels. Yet they were striking exceptions, rare occurrences— the poor, uncouth countryside predominated: wrinkled coats from army surplus, patched sweaters, percale dresses.

The professor showed us photographs of antique sculptures and of Greek figures painted on brown vases—beautiful, statuesque bodies, noble, elongated faces with fine features. They belonged to some unknown, mythic universe, a world of sun and silver, warm and full of light, populated by slender heroes and dancing nymphs. We didn't know what to make of it. Looking at the photographs, Z. was morosely silent and W. contorted himself to massage his aching knee. Others looked on, attentive yet indifferent. Before those future prophets proclaiming the clash of civilizations, the collision was taking place long ago, twice a week, in the lecture hall where I learned that there once lived a Greek named Herodotus.

I knew nothing as yet of his life, or about the fact that he left us a famous book. We would in any event have been unable to read *The Histories*, because at that moment its Polish translation was locked away in a closet. In the mid-1940s *The Histories* had been translated by Professor Seweryn Hammer, who deposited his manuscript in the Czytelnik publishing house. I was unable to ascertain the details because all the documentation disappeared, but it happens that Hammer's text was sent by the publisher to the typesetter in the fall of 1951. Barring any complications, the book should have appeared in 1952, in time to find its way into our hands while we were still studying ancient history. But that's not what happened, because the printing was suddenly halted. Who gave the order? Probably the censor, but it's impossible to know for certain. Suffice it to say that the book finally did not go to press until three years later, at the end of 1954, arriving in the bookstores in 1955.

One can speculate about the delay in the publication of *The Histories*. It coincides with the period preceding the death of Stalin and the time immediately following it. The Herodotus manuscript arrived at the press just as Western radio stations began speaking of Stalin's serious illness. The details were murky, but people were afraid of a new wave of terror and preferred to lie low, to risk nothing, to give no one any pretext, to wait things out. The atmosphere was tense. The censors redoubled their vigilance.

But Herodotus? A book written two and a half thousand years ago? Well, yes: because all our thinking, our looking and reading, was governed during those years by an obsession with allusion. Each word brought another one to mind; each had a double meaning, a false bottom, a hidden significance; each contained something secretly encoded, cunningly concealed. Nothing was ever plain, literal, unambiguous—from behind every gesture and word peered some referential sign, gazed a meaningfully winking eye. The man who wrote had difficulty communicating with the man who read, not only because the censor could confiscate the text en route, but also because, when the text finally reached him, the latter read something utterly different from what was clearly written, constantly asking himself: What did this author *really* want to tell me?

And so a person consumed, obsessively tormented by allusion reaches for Herodotus. How many allusions he will find there! *The Histories* consists of nine books, and each one is allusions heaped upon allusions. Let us say he opens, quite by accident, Book Five. He opens it, reads, and learns that in Corinth, after thirty years of bloodthirsty rule, the tyrant called Cypselus died and was succeeded by his son, Periander, who would in time turn out to be even more bloodthirsty than his father. This Periander, when he was still a dictator-in-training, wanted to learn how to stay in power, and so sent a messenger to the dictator of Miletus, old Thrasybulus, asking him for advice on how best to keep a people in slavish fear and subjugation.

Thrasybulus, writes Herodotus, *took the man sent by Periander out of the city and into a field where there were crops growing. As he walked through the grain, he kept questioning the messenger and getting him to repeat over and over again what he had come from Corinth to ask. Meanwhile, every time he saw an ear of grain standing higher than the rest, he broke it off and threw it away, and he went on doing this until he had destroyed the choicest, tallest stems in the crop. After this walk across the field, Thrasybulus sent Periander's man back home, without having offered him any advice. When the man got back to Corinth, Periander was eager to hear Thrasybulus' recommendations, but the agent said that he had not made any at all. In fact, he said, he was surprised that Periander had sent him to a man of that kind—a lunatic who destroyed his own property—and he described what he had seen Thrasybulus doing.*

Periander, however, understood Thrasybulus' actions. He realized that he had been advising him to kill outstanding citizens, and from then on he treated his people with unremitting brutality. If Cypselus had left anything undone during his spell of slaughter and persecution, Periander finished the job.*

And gloomy, maniacally suspicious Cambyses? How many allusions, analogies, and parallels in this figure! Cambyses was the king of a great contemporary power, Persia. He ruled between 529 and 522 B.C.E.

Everything goes to make me certain that Cambyses was completely mad ... His first atrocity was to do away with his brother Smerdis ... and the second was to do away with his sister, who had come with him to Egypt. She was also his wife, as well as being his full sister ... [and] on another occasion he found twelve of the highest-ranking Persians guilty of a paltry misdemeanour and buried them alive up to their necks in the ground. ... These are a few examples of the insanity of his behaviour towards the Persians and his allies. During his time in Memphis he even opened some ancient tombs and examined the corpses.

Cambyses ... set out to attack the Ethiopians, without having requisitioned supplies or considered the fact that he was intending to make an expedition to the ends

---

*All quotations in italics throughout the text are from Herodotus, *The Histories*, translated by Robin Waterfield, with an introduction and notes by Carolyn Dewald (Oxford and New York: Oxford University Press, 1998).

of the earth ... so enraged and insane that he just set off with all his land forces ... However, they completely ran out of food before they had got a fifth of the way there, and then they ran out of yoke-animals as well, because they were all eaten up. Had Cambyses changed his mind when he saw what was happening, and turned back, he would have redeemed his original mistake by acting wisely; in fact, however, he paid no attention to the situation and continued to press on. As long as there were plants to scavenge, his men could stay alive by eating grass, but then they reached the sandy desert. At that point some of them did something dreadful: they cast lots to choose one in every ten men among them—and ate him. When Cambyses heard about this, fear of cannibalism made him abandon his expedition to Ethiopia and turn his men back.

As I mentioned, Herodotus's opus appeared in the bookstores in 1955. Two years had passed since Stalin's death. The atmosphere became more relaxed, people breathed more freely. Ilya Ehrenburg's novel *The Thaw* had just appeared, its title lending itself to the new epoch just beginning. Literature seemed to be everything then. People looked to it for the strength to live, for guidance, for revelation.

I completed my studies and began working at a newspaper. It was called *Sztandar Młodych* (The Banner of Youth). I was a novice reporter and my beat was to follow the trail of letters sent to the editor back to their points of origin. The writers complained about injustice and poverty, about the fact that the state took their last cow or that their village was still without electricity. Censorship abated and one could write, for example, that in the village of Chodów there is a store but that its shelves are always bare and there is never anything to buy. Progress consisted of the fact that while Stalin was alive, one could not write that a store was empty—all of them had to be excellently stocked, bursting with wares. I rattled along from village to village, from town to town, in a hay cart or a rickety bus, for private cars were a rarity and even a bicycle wasn't easily to be had.

My route sometimes took me to villages along the border. But this happened infrequently. For the closer one got to a border, the emptier grew the land and the fewer people one encountered. This emptiness increased the mystery of these regions. I was struck, too, by how silent the border zone was. This mystery and quiet attracted and intrigued me. I was tempted to see what lay beyond, on the other side. I wondered what one experiences when one crosses the border. What does one feel? What does one think? It must be a moment of great emotion, agitation, tension. What is it like, on the other side? It must certainly be—different. But what does "different" mean? What does it look like? What does it resemble? Maybe it resembles nothing that I know, and thus is inconceivable, unimaginable? And so my greatest desire, which gave me no peace, which tormented and tantalized me, was actually quite modest: I wanted one thing only—the moment, the act, the simple fact of *crossing the border*. To cross it and come right back—that, I thought, would be entirely sufficient, would satisfy my quite inexplicable yet acute psychological hunger.

But how to do this? None of my friends from school or university had ever been abroad. Anyone with a contact in another country generally preferred not to advertise it. I was even cross with myself for this bizarre yen; still, it didn't abate for a moment.

One day I encountered my editor in chief in the hallway. Irena Tarłowska was a strapping, handsome woman with thick blond hair parted to one side. She said something about my recent stories, and then asked me about my plans for the near future. I named various villages to which I would be going, the issues that awaited me there, and then summoned my courage and said: "One day, I would very much like to go abroad."

"Abroad?" she said, surprised and slightly frightened, because in those days going abroad was no ordinary matter. "Where? What for?" she asked.

"I was thinking about Czechoslovakia," I answered. I wouldn't have dared to say something like Paris or London, and frankly they didn't really interest me; I couldn't even imagine them. This was only about *crossing the border*—somewhere. It made no difference which one, because what was important was not the destination, the goal, the end, but the almost mystical and transcendent act. *Crossing the border.*

A year passed following that conversation. The telephone rang in our newsroom. The editor in chief was summoning me to her office. "You know," she said, as I stood before her desk, "we are sending you. You'll go to India."

My first reaction was astonishment. And right after that, panic: I knew nothing about India. I feverishly searched my thoughts for some associations, images, names. Nothing. Zero. (The idea of an Indian trip originated in the fact that several months earlier Jawaharlal Nehru had visited Poland, the first premier of a non-Soviet-bloc country to do so. The first contacts were being established. My stories were to bring that distant land closer.)

At the end of our conversation, during which I learned that I would indeed be going forth into the world, Tarłowska reached into a cabinet, took out a book, and handing it to me said: "Here, a present, for the road." It was a thick book with a stiff cover of yellow cloth. On the front, stamped in gold letters, was Herodotus, THE HISTORIES.

It was an old twin-engine DC-3, well-worn from wartime forays along the front lines, its wings blackened by exhaust fumes and patches on its fuselage. But it flew, and headed, with only a few passengers, almost empty, to Rome. I sat by the window, excitedly looking out to see the world from a bird's-eye view for the first time. Until then I hadn't even been to the mountains. Beneath us slowly passed multicolored chessboards, motley patchwork quilts, gray-green tapestries, as if stretched out on the ground to dry in the sun. But dusk came quickly, then darkness.

"It's evening," my neighbor said in Polish, but with a foreign accent. He was an Italian journalist returning home, and I remember only that his name was Mario. When I told him where I was going and why, that this was my first trip abroad and that I really knew nothing, he laughed and said something to the effect of "Don't worry!" and promised to help. I was secretly overjoyed and felt slightly more confident. I needed that, because I was flying west and had been taught to fear the West like fire.

We flew in darkness; even inside the cabin the lights were barely shining. Suddenly, the tension which afflicts all parts of the plane when the engines are at full throttle started to lessen, the sound of the engines grew quieter and less urgent—we were approaching the end of our journey. Mario grabbed me by the arm and pointed out the window: "Look!"

I was dumbstruck.

Below me, the entire length and breadth of the blackness through which we were flying was now filled with light. It was an intense light, blinding, quivering, flickering. One had the impression of a liquid substance, like molten lava, glimmering down below, with a sparkling surface that pulsated with brightness, rising and falling, expanding and contracting. The entire luminous apparition was something alive, full of movement, vibration, energy.

It was the first time in my life I was seeing an illuminated city. What few cities and towns I had known until then were depressingly dark. Shop windows never shone in them, there were no colorful advertisements, the street lamps had weak lightbulbs. And who needed lights anyway? In the evenings the streets were deserted: one encountered few cars.

As we descended, this landscape of lights drew nearer and assumed enormous proportions. Finally the plane thumped against the tarmac, crunched and creaked. We had arrived. The Rome airport—a great, glassed-in lump full of people. We drove into the city on a warm evening through busy, crowded streets. Bustle, traffic, lights, and sounds—it worked like a narcotic. I became disoriented at moments—where was I? I must have looked like a creature of the forest: stunned, a little fearful, wide-eyed, trying to take in, understand, distinguish things.

In the morning I overheard a conversation in the adjoining room and recognized Mario's voice. I would find out later that it was a discussion about how to dress me, seeing as how I had arrived sporting fashions à la Warsaw Pact 1956. I had a suit of Cheviot wool in sharp, gray-blue stripes—a double-breasted jacket with protruding, angular shoulders and overly long, wide trousers with large cuffs. I had a pale-yellow nylon shirt with a green plaid tie. Finally, the shoes—massive loafers with thick, stiff soles.

The confrontation between East and West took place not only in the military realm but in all other spheres of life as well. If the West dressed lightly, then the East, according to the law of opposites, dressed heavily; if the West wore closely fitting clothes, then the East did the reverse—everything had to stick out by a mile. One did not have to carry one's passport around:—one could see at a distance who was from which side of the Iron Curtain.

We started making rounds of the shops, accompanied by Mario's wife. For me, these were expeditions of discovery. Three things dazzled me the most. First, that the stores were full of merchandise, were actually brimming with it, the goods weighing down shelves and counters, spilling out in towering, colorful streams onto sidewalks, streets, and squares. Second, that the salesladies did not sit, but stood, looking at the entrance doors. It was strange that they stood in silence, rather than sitting and talking to one another. Women, after all, have so many subjects in common. Troubles with their husbands, problems with the children. What to wear, one's health, whether something burned on the stove yesterday. And here I had the impression that they did not know each other at all and had no desire to converse. The third shock was that the salesclerks answered the questions posed to them. They responded in complete sentences and then at the end added *"Grazie!"* Mario's wife would ask about something and they would listen to her with sympathy and attention, so focused and inclined forward that they looked as if they were about to start in a race. And then one heard that oft-repeated, sacramental *grazie!*

In the evening I summoned the courage to go out alone. I must have been living somewhere in the center, because Stazione Termini was nearby, and from there I walked along Via Cavour all the way to Piazza Venezia, and then through little streets and alleys back to Stazione Termini. I did not notice the architecture, the statues, the monuments; I was fascinated only by the cafés and bars. There were tables everywhere on the sidewalks, and people sat at them, drinking and talking, or just simply looking at the street and the passersby. Behind tall, narrow counters the barmen poured drinks, mixed cocktails, brewed coffee. Waiters bustled about, delivering glasses and cups with a magician's legerdemain, the likes of which I had seen only once before, in a Soviet circus, when the performer charmed a wooden plate, a glass goblet, and a screeching rooster out of thin air.

One day I spotted an empty table, sat down, and ordered a coffee. After a while I became conscious that people were looking at me. I had on a new suit, an Italian shirt white as snow, and a most fashionable polka-dotted tie, but there must still have been something in my appearance and gestures, in my way of sitting and moving, that gave me away—betrayed where I came from, from how different a world. I sensed that they took me for an alien, and although I should have been happy, sitting there beneath the miraculous skies of Rome, I began to feel unpleasant and uncomfortable. I had changed my suit, but I apparently could not conceal whatever lay beneath it that had shaped and marked me as a foreign particle.

CONDEMNED TO INDIA

Astewardess dressed in a light, pastel-colored sari was greeting passengers in the doors of the four-engine Air India International colossus. The subdued hues of her outfit suggested that a peaceful, pleasant flight awaited us. Her hands were arranged as if in prayer; the anjali, I would soon learn, was a Hindu gesture of greeting. In the cabin was a strong and unfamiliar aroma—surely, I thought, the scent of some eastern incense, Hindu herbs, fruits, and resins.

We flew by night, only a small green light twinkling at the tip of the wing visible through the window. This was still before the population explosion, when air travel was comfortable, with planes often carrying but a few passengers. So it was this time. Passengers slept, stretched out across several seats.

I felt that I wouldn't be able to shut my eyes, so I reached into my bag and took out the book that Tarłowska had given me. *The Histories* of Herodotus is a lengthy tome of several hundred pages. I found such thick books alluring, and I began with the introduction, in which the translator, Seweryn Hammer, describes Herodotus's life and introduces us to the meaning of his work. Herodotus, writes Hammer, was born in 485 B.C.E. in Halicarnassus, a port city in Asia Minor. Around 450 he moved to Athens, and from there, several years later, to the Greek colony of Thurii, in southern Italy. He died around 425 B.C.E. He traveled extensively during his life. And he left us a book—one can assume it is the only one he wrote.

Hammer tried to bring to life a man who lived two and a half thousand years ago, about whom we know little, and whose appearance is difficult to imagine. Even the one thing he left behind was, in its original version, accessible to only a handful of specialists who, in addition to possessing a knowledge of ancient Greek, had to know how to decipher a very specific kind of notation: the text looked like one unending, undifferentiated word stretching across dozens of rolls of papyrus. "Individual words or sentences were not demarcated," wrote Hammer, "just as chapters and books were unknown; the text was as densely woven as a tapestry." Herodotus concealed himself behind this verbal fabric as behind a screen, which we are even less well equipped to penetrate than his contemporaries were.

The night ended and day came. Looking through the little window, I was able to gaze for the first time on an enormous expanse of our planet. The sight brought thoughts of infinity to mind. The world I had known until then was perhaps five hundred kilometers in length and four hundred in width. And here we were, flying seemingly forever, while the earth, very far below us, kept changing colors—for a while it was burnt, brown; then green; and then, for a long while, dark blue.

It was late evening when we landed in New Delhi. I was instantly awash in heat and humidity, and stood dripping with sweat. The people with whom I had been flying suddenly vanished, swept away by the colorful, animated crowd of friends and relatives that had been waiting for them.

I was left alone and had no idea what to do. The airport building was small, dark, and deserted, a far cry from Rome's. It stood all by itself cloaked in night, and I didn't know what lay beyond, in the depths of the darkness. After a while an old man in a white, loose knee-length garment appeared. He had a gray beard and an orange turban. He said something I did not understand, although I assume he was asking why I was standing there alone, in the middle of the empty airport. I had no idea what to answer and looked about me, pondering—what next? I was quite unprepared for this journey. I had neither names nor addresses in my note-book. My English was poor. I was not entirely to blame, though: my sole desire had been to achieve the unachievable—*to cross the border*. I wanted nothing more. But in expressing that wish I'd started the chain of events that had now deposited me all the way here, on the far side of the world.

The old man thought for a while, then motioned with his hand for me to follow him. To one side of the entrance stood a scratched-up, dilapidated bus. We got in, the old man started the motor, and we set off. We had covered only several hundred meters when the driver slowed down and began honking vio-lently. Before us, where the road should have been, I saw a broad, white river vanishing somewhere in the thick blackness of the sul-try, sweltering night. The river was of people sleeping out in the open, some on wooden plank beds, others on mats, on blankets, but most directly on the bare asphalt and the sandy banks stretch-ing on each side of it.

I thought that the crowds, awakened by the roar of the horn resounding directly over their heads, would fall upon us in a rage, beat us, perhaps lynch us even. Far from it! As we inched forward, they rose one by one and moved aside, taking with them children and pushing along old women barely able to walk. In their ardent compliance, in their submissive humility, there was something apologetic, as if sleeping here on the road were some crime whose traces they were quickly trying to erase. And thus we inched our way toward the city, the horn blaring, people stirring and giving way—on and on and on. Once we reached town, its streets turned out to be equally difficult to navigate: it too seemed just one enormous camp of white-clad, somnambular phantoms of the night.

In this fashion we arrived at a place illuminated by a red light-bulb: HOTEL. The driver left me at reception and disappeared without a word. The man at the desk, this one sporting a blue turban, led me upstairs to a little room furnished with only a bed, a table, and a washstand. Without a word he pulled off the bedsheet, on which scurried panicked bugs, which he shook off onto the floor, muttered something by way of good night, and departed.

Left alone, I sat down on the bed and started to consider my situation. On the negative side, I didn't know where I was. On the positive, I had a roof over my head; an institution (a hotel) had given me shelter. Did I feel safe? Yes. Uncomfortable? No. Strange? Yes. I could not define precisely wherein lay this strangeness, but the sensation grew stronger in the morning, when a barefoot man entered the room bearing a pot of tea and several biscuits. Nothing like this had ever happened to me before. He placed the tray on the table, bowed, and, having uttered not a word, softly withdrew. There was such a natural politeness in his manner, such profound tactfulness, something so astonishingly delicate and dignified, that I felt instant admiration and respect for him.

Something more disconcerting occurred an hour later, when I stepped out of the hotel. On the opposite side of the street, on a cramped little square, rickshaw drivers had been gathering since dawn—skinny, stooped men with bony, sinewy legs. They must have learned that a sahib had arrived in the hotel. A sahib, by definition, must have money, so they waited patiently, ready to serve. But the very idea of sprawling comfortably in a rickshaw pulled by a hungry, weak waif of a man with one foot already in the grave filled me with the utmost revulsion, outrage, horror. To be an exploiter? A bloodsucker? To oppress another human being in this way? Never! I had been brought up in a precisely opposite spirit, taught that even living skeletons such as these were my brothers, kindred souls, near ones, flesh of my flesh. So when the rickshaw drivers threw themselves upon me with pleading encouragement, clamoring and fighting amongst themselves for my business, I began to firmly push them away, rebuke them, protest. They were astounded—what was I saying, what was I doing? They had been counting on me, after all. I was their only chance, their only hope—if only for a bowl of rice. I walked on without turning my head, impassive, resolute, a little smugly proud of not having allowed myself to be manipulated into assuming the role of a leech.

Old Delhi! Its narrow, dusty, fiendishly hot streets, with their stifling odor of tropical fermentation. And this crowd of silently moving people, appearing and disappearing, their faces dark, humid, anonymous, closed. Quiet children, making no sound. A man stares dully at the remains of his bicycle, which has fallen apart in the middle of the street. A woman sells something wrapped in green leaves—what is it? What do those leaves enfold? A beggar demonstrates how the skin of his stomach is plastered to his spinal cord—but is this even possible? One has to walk carefully, to pay attention, because many vendors spread their wares directly on the ground, on the sidewalks, right on the edge of the road. Here is a man who has laid out two rows of human teeth and some old pliers on a piece of newspaper, thereby advertising his dental services. His neighbor—a wizened, shrunken fellow—is hawking books. I rummage through the carelessly arranged, dusty piles and settle on two: Hemingway's *For Whom the Bell Tolls* (useful for learning English) and the priest J. A. Dubois's *Hindu Manners, Customs, and Ceremonies.* Father Dubois arrived in India as a missionary in 1792 and stayed for thirty-one years, and the fruit of his studies of Hindu ways of life was the book I had just purchased, which was published in England in 1816 with the assistance of the British East India Company.

I returned to the hotel, opened the Hemingway to the first sentence: "He lay flat on the brown, pine-needled floor of the forest, his chin on his folded arms, and high overhead the wind blew in the tops of the pine trees." I understood nothing. I had a small English-Polish pocket dictionary, the only one that had been available in Warsaw. I managed to find the word "brown," but none of the others. I proceeded to the next sentence: "The mountainside sloped gently ..." Again—not a word. "There was a stream alongside ..." The more I tried to understand this text, the more discouraged and despairing I became. I felt trapped. Besieged by language. Language struck me at that moment as something material, something with a physical dimension, a wall rising up in the middle of the road and preventing my going further, closing off the world, making it unattainable. It was an unpleasant and humiliating sensation. It might explain why, in a first encounter with someone or something foreign, there are those who will feel fear and uncertainty, bristle with mistrust. What will this meeting bring? How will it end? Better not to risk it and to remain in the cocoon of the familiar! Better not to stick one's neck out of one's own backyard!

On first impulse, I might have fled India and returned home, if not for my having bought a return ticket on the passenger ship *Batory*, which in those days sailed between Gdańsk and Bombay.

The Egyptian president Gamal Abdel Nasser had just nationalized the Suez Canal, prompting England and France to respond with armed intervention; as war broke out, the canal was blocked, and the *Batory* was stuck somewhere on the Mediterranean Sea. Cut off from home, I was condemned to India.

Cast into deep water, I didn't want to drown. I realized that only language could save me. I started to think about how Herodotus, wandering the world, had dealt with foreign languages. Hammer writes that Herodotus knew only Greek, but because Greeks at the time were scattered over the entire planet, had their colonies, ports, and factories everywhere, the author of *The Histories* could avail himself of help offered by the countrymen he encountered, who served as his translators and guides. Moreover, Greek was the lingua franca of those days, and many people in Europe, Asia, and Africa spoke the language, which was later replaced by Latin, and then French and English.

I began cramming words, night and day. I placed a cold towel on my temples, feeling my head was bursting. I was never without the Hemingway, but now I skipped the descriptive passages I couldn't understand and read the dialogues, which were easier:

> "How many are you?" Robert Jordan asked.
> "We are seven and there are two women."
> "Two?"
> "Yes."

I understood all of that! And this, too:

> "Augustín is a very good man," Anselmo
>   said....
> "You know him well?"
> "Yes. For a long time."

I walked around the city, copying down signboards, the names of goods in stores, words overheard at bus stops. In movie theaters I scribbled blindly, in darkness, the words on the screen, and noted the slogans on banners carried by demonstrators in the streets. I approached India not through images, sounds, and smells, but through words; furthermore, words not of the indigenous Hindi, but of a foreign, imposed tongue, which by then had so fully taken root here that it was for me an indispensable key to this country, almost identical with it. I understood that every distinct geographic universe has its own mystery and that one can decipher it only by learning the local language. Without it, this universe will remain impenetrable and unknowable, even if one were to spend entire years in it. I noticed, too, the relationship between naming and being, because I realized upon my return to the hotel that in town I had seen only that which I was able to name: for example, I remembered the acacia tree, but not the tree standing next to it, whose name I did not know. I understood, in short, that the more words I knew, the richer, fuller, and more variegated would be the world that opened before me, and which I could capture.

During all those days after my arrival in Delhi I was tormented by the thought that I was not working as a reporter, that I was not gathering material for the stories that I would later have to write. I hadn't come as a tourist, after all. I was an envoy, engaged to render an account, to transmit, relate. But I found myself empty-handed, and feeling incapable of doing anything, at a loss even to know where to begin. I knew nothing about India, after all, and hadn't asked for it. *Crossing the border*—that was it. Nothing more. But now, since the Suez war made returning impossible, I could only move forward. I decided to travel.

The receptionists in my hotel advised me to go to Benares: "Sacred town!" they explained. (I had noticed already how many things in India are sacred: the sacred town, the sacred river, millions of sacred cows. It is striking, the degree to which mysticism permeates life, how many temples there are, chapels and various little altars at every step, how many fires and how much incense is burning, how many people have ritual markings on their foreheads, how many are sitting motionless, staring at some transcendent point.)

I heeded the receptionists and took a bus to Benares. One drives there through the valley of the Jamuna and the Ganges, through flat, green countryside dotted with the white silhouettes of peasants wading in rice paddies, digging in the ground with hoes, or carrying bundles, baskets, or sacks on their heads. But this view outside the window was mutable, and frequently an immense expanse of water filled the landscape. It was the season of the autumn floods, and rivers metamorphosed into broad lakes, veritable seas. On their shores camped barefoot flood victims. They fled before the rising water but maintained their contact with it, escaping only as far as was necessary and returning immediately when the floodwaters started to recede. In the ghastly heat of the dying day, the water vaporized and a milky, still fog hovered over everything.

We reached Benares in late evening, at night really. The city seemed to have no suburbs, which normally prepare one gradually for the encounter with downtown; here one emerges all of a sudden out of the dark, silent, and empty night into the brightly lit, crowded, and noisy city center. Why do these people flock and swarm together so, clamber all over one another while all around, just beyond, there is so much free space, so much room for everyone? After getting off the bus I went for a walk. I reached the outskirts of Benares. To one side, in the darkness, lay the still, uninhabited fields, and to the other rose the buildings of the city, densely peopled, bustling, brilliantly illuminated, throbbing with loud music. I cannot fathom this need for a life of congestion, of rubbing against one another, of endlessly pushing and shoving— all the more so when right over there is so much free space.

The locals advised me not to go to sleep at night, so that I would get to the banks of the Ganges while it was still dark and there, on the stone steps that stretch along the river, await the dawn. "The sunrise is very important!" they said, their voices resounding with the promise of something truly magnificent.

It was indeed still dark when people began converging on the river. Singly and in groups. Entire clans. Columns of pilgrims. The lame on crutches. Aged virtual skeletons, some carried on the backs of the young, others—twisted, exhausted—crawling with great difficulty on their own along the asphalt. Cows and goats trailed alongside the people, as did packs of bony, malarial dogs. I too joined this strange mystery play.

Reaching the riverside steps is not easy, because they are preceded by a thicket of narrow, airless, and dirty little streets tightly packed with beggars, who nudge the pilgrims importunately all the while raising a lament unbearably terrible and piercing. Finally, passing various passages and arcades, one emerges at the top of the stairs that descend straight down to the river. Although dawn has barely touched the sky, thousands of the faithful are already there. Some are animated, pushing their way who knows where and why. Others sit in the lotus position, stretching their arms up toward the heavens. The bottom rungs of the stairs are occupied by those performing the purification ritual—they wade in the river and now and then submerge themselves completely in the water. I see a family subjecting a stout grandmother to the purification rite. The grandmother doesn't know how to swim and sinks at once to the bottom. The family rush in and bring her back up to the surface. The grandmother gulps as much air as she can, but the instant they let her go, she goes under again. I can see her bulging eyes, her terrified face. She sinks once more, they search for her again in the murky waters and again pull her out, barely alive. The whole ritual looks like torture, but she endures it without protest, perhaps even in ecstasy.

Beside the Ganges, which at this point is wide, expansive, and lazy, stretch rows of wooden pyres, on which are burning dozens, hundreds of corpses. The curious can for several rupees take a boat over to this gigantic open-air crematorium. Half-naked, soot-covered men bustle about here, as do many young boys. With long poles they adjust the pyres to direct a better draft so the cremation can proceed faster; the line of corpses has no end, the wait is long. The gravediggers rake the still-glowing ashes and push them into the river. The gray dust floats atop the waves for a while but very soon, saturated with water, it sinks and vanishes.

THE TRAIN STATION
AND THE PALACE

If in Benares one finds cause for hope—a cleansing in the holy river, and with it the improvement of one's spiritual condition, the promise of drawing closer to the infinite—Sealdah Station in Calcutta has the opposite effect. I arrived in Calcutta from Benares by train, a progress, as I was to discover, from a relative heaven to an absolute hell.

The conductor at the Benares station looked me over and asked:

"Where is your bed?"

I understood what he was saying but apparently looked as if I didn't, for a moment later he repeated his question, this time more insistently:

"Where is your bed?"

It turns out that even the moderately wealthy, not to mention members of a chosen race like the European, travel the rails with their own beds. They arrive at the station accompanied by servants carrying rolled-up mattresses on their heads, as well as blankets, sheets, pillows, as well as, of course, other luggage. Once aboard (there are no seats in the train cars) the servant arranges his master's bed, then vanishes without a word, as if dissolving into thin air. Raised as I was in the spirit of brotherhood and individual equality, this situation, in which one walks empty-handed while another walks behind, laden with a mattress, suitcases, and a basket of food, seemed offensive in the extreme, a cause for protest and objection. But upon entering the train car I quickly reevaluated my position, as voices of clearly astonished people resounded from every direction.

"Where is your bed?"

I felt idiotic to have nothing with me except my hand luggage. But how could I have known that I would need a mattress in addition to a ticket? And even if I had known, and had bought a mattress, I couldn't have carried it by myself and would have had to engage a servant. But what would I have done with the servant later? Or with the mattress, for that matter?

I had noticed already that a different person is assigned here to every type of activity and chore, and that this person vigilantly guards his role and his place—this society's equilibrium seems to depend upon it. One person brings tea in the morning, another shines shoes, another still launders shirts, an altogether different one cleans the room—and so on ad infinitum. Heaven forbid that I ask the person who irons my shirt to sew a button on it. For me, of course, raised as I was in the manner foregoingly described, it would be simple just to sew on the button myself, but then I would be committing a terrible error, for I would be depriving someone burdened with a large family and obliged to make his living by sewing buttons on shirts of his livelihood. This society was a pedantically, meticulously woven fabric of roles and assignments, classifications and purposes, and a great deal of experience, a profound knowledge and a keen intuition were required to penetrate and decipher the delicacies of its structure.

I passed a sleepless night on the train, for those old cars, dating back to colonial times, shook, hurled you about, rumbled, and you were even pelted with rain, which came in through windows that could not be shut. It was a gray, overcast day by the time we pulled into Sealdah Station. On every square inch of the enormous terminal, on its long platforms, its dead-end tracks, the swampy fields nearby, sat or lay tens of thousands of emaciated people—under streams of rain, in the water and the mud; it was the rainy season, and the heavy tropical downpour did not abate for a moment. I was struck at once by the poverty of these soaked skeletons, their untold numbers, and, perhaps most of all, their immobility. They seemed a lifeless component of this dismal landscape, whose sole kinetic element was the sheets of water pouring from the sky. There was of course a certain, albeit desperate, logic and rationality in the utter passivity of these unfortunates: they sought no shelter from the downpour because they had nowhere to go—this was the end of their road—and they made no exertion to cover themselves because they had nothing to cover themselves with.

They were refugees from a civil war, which ended but a few years earlier, between Hindus and Muslims, a war which saw the birth of independent India and Pakistan and which resulted in hundreds of thousands, perhaps millions of dead and many millions of refugees. The latter wandered about for a long time, unable to find succor, left to their own fate, vegetating for a while in places like Sealdah Station before eventually dying there of hunger or disease. But there was more to this. These columns of postwar vagabonds encountered throngs of others along the way—the legions of flood victims evicted from villages and small towns by the waters of India's powerful and unbridled rivers. And so millions of homeless, indifferent people shuffled along the roads, dropping from exhaustion, often never to rise. Others tried to reach the cities hoping to get a sip of water there, and perhaps a handful of rice.

. . .

Just getting out of the train car was difficult—there was no room for me to place my foot on the platform. Usually, a different color skin attracts attention here; but nothing distracts the denizens of Sealdah Station, as they seem already to settle into a realm on the other side of life. An old woman next to me was digging a bit of rice out of the folds of her sari. She poured it into a little bowl and started to look around, perhaps for water, perhaps for fire, so that she could boil the rice. I noticed several children near her, eyeing the bowl. Staring—motionless, wordless. This lasts a moment, and the moment drags on. The children do not throw themselves on the rice; the rice is the property of the old woman, and these children have been inculcated with something more powerful than hunger.

A man is pushing his way through the huddled multitudes. He jostles the old woman, the bowl drops from her hands, and the rice scatters onto the platform, into the mud, amidst the garbage. In that split second, the children throw themselves down, dive between the legs of those still standing, dig around in the muck trying to find the grains of rice. The old woman stands there empty-handed, another man shoves her. The old woman, the children, the train station, everything—soaked through by the unending torrents of a tropical downpour. And I too stand dripping wet, afraid to take a step; and anyway, I don't know where to go.

From Calcutta I traveled south, to Hyderabad. The south was very different from the north and all its pains. The south seemed cheerful, calm, sleepy, and a little provincial. The servants of a local rajah must have confused me with someone else, because they greeted me ceremoniously at the station and drove me straight to a palace. A polite, elderly man welcomed me, sat me down in a wide leather armchair, and was surely counting on a longer and deeper conversation than my primitive English could allow. I stuttered something or other, felt myself turning red, sweat was pouring down my forehead. The elderly man smiled kindly, which gave me some courage. It was all rather dreamlike. Surrealistic. The servants led me to a room in one of the palace wings. As the guest of the rajah I was to live here. I wanted to call the whole thing off, but didn't know how—I lacked the words with which to explain that there had been some misunderstanding. Perhaps just the fact of my being from Europe conferred some prestige on the palace? I don't know.

I crammed vocabulary words daily, doggedly, feverishly. What shone in the sky? *The sun.* What fell on the earth? *The rain.* What swayed the trees? *The wind.* Etc., etc., twenty to forty words daily. I read Hemingway, and in the book by Father Dubois I tried to make sense of the chapter on castes. The beginning actually wasn't difficult: There are four castes. The first and highest are the Brahmans—priests, people of the spirit, thinkers, those who show the way. The second, lower down, are the Kshatriyas—warriors and rulers, people of the sword and of politics. The third, lower still, are the Vaisyas—merchants, craftsmen, and farmers. The fourth and final caste are the Sudras—laborers, peasants, servants, workers for hire. Here's where the problems started, because it turns out that these castes are divided into hundreds of subcastes, and these in turn into dozens of sub-subcastes, and so on into infinity. India is all about infinity—an infinity of gods and myths, beliefs and languages, races and cultures; in everything, and everywhere one looks, there is this dizzying endlessness.

At the same time I felt instinctively that that which I perceived all around me were merely external signs, images, symbols, of a vast and varied world of hidden beliefs, ideas about which I knew nothing. I wondered, too, whether this realm was inaccessible to me because I lacked theoretical, book knowledge about it, or whether there was a more profound reason, namely that my mind was too fully imbued with rationalism and materialism to be able to identify with and grasp a culture as saturated with spirituality and metaphysics as Hinduism.

In such a state, and further overwhelmed by the richness of the details I found in the work of the French missionary, I would put down the book and go into town.

The rajah's palace—all glassed-in verandahs, maybe a hundred of them, which when the panes were opened allowed a light and bracing breeze to waft through the rooms—was surrounded by lush, well-tended gardens, in which gardeners constantly bustled, pruning, mowing, and raking. Further on, beyond a high wall, the city began. One walked there along little streets and alleyways, narrow and always crowded, passing countless colorful shops, stalls, and stands selling food, clothing, shoes, cleaning products. Even when it wasn't raining, the streets were always muddy, because all waste gets poured into the middle of the street here— the street belongs to no one.

There are speakers everywhere, and emanating from them a piercing, loud, continuous singing. It's coming from the local temples. These are small structures, often no larger than the one- or two-story houses surrounding them, but they are numerous. They look alike: painted white, dressed in garlands of flowers and glittering decorations, bright and festive like brides going to their wedding. The atmosphere in these little temples is somehow at once serene and joyful. They are full of people, whispering amongst themselves, burning incense, rolling their eyes, stretching out their hands. Some men (sacristans? altar boys?) distribute food to the faithful—a piece of cake, marzipan, or candy. If one holds out one's hand a little longer, one can receive two, maybe even three portions. One must eat what one gets or place it on the altar. Admission to each temple is free: no one asks who you are, or of what faith. Everyone worships individually, on his own, without a collective rite, and as a result there is an atmosphere of ease, freedom, even a bit of disorder.

There are so many of these places of worship because the deities in Hinduism are infinite in number; no one has been able to make a complete inventory. Furthermore, the deities do not compete with one another, but rather coexist harmoniously and peacefully. One can believe in one or in several at once, even exchange one for another depending on place, time, mood, or need. The ultimate worldly ambition of any given deity's followers is to erect a dedicated sanctuary, to build a temple. One can imagine the material consequences of this, bearing in mind that this liberal polytheism has lasted thousands of years already. How many temples, chapels, altars, and statues have been raised over the years, and how many have been destroyed by floods, fires, typhoons, wars with Muslims. If all the ones ever constructed were still to exist, simultaneously, they would surely cover half the surface of the globe.

In my wanderings I happened upon the temple of Kali. She is the goddess of destruction and represents the ruinous workings of time. I do not know if she can be propitiated, because after all one cannot stop time. Kali is tall, black, sticks out her tongue, wears a necklace of skulls, and stands with her arms outstretched. She is a woman, but into her embrace it is better not to fall.

The way to the temple leads between two rows of stalls selling pungent scents, colorful powders, pictures, pendants, all manner of kitschy bric-a-brac. A dense, slowly moving line of perspiring, excited people snakes its way to the goddess's statue. Inside the sanctuary, an overpowering airless odor of incense, heat, darkness. A symbolic exchange takes place before the statue—you give the priest a previously purchased pebble, and he hands back another one. I suppose you leave the unconsecrated one and receive one that's been blessed. But I'm not certain.

The palace of the rajah is full of servants. You see no one else, really, and it's as if the entire estate had been given over to their absolute rule. Countless butlers, footmen, waiters, maids and valets, specialists in brewing tea and frosting cakes, clothes pressers and messengers, exterminators of mosquitoes and spiders, and many more whose duties and roles it is impossible to fathom, course continually through the rooms and salons, pass by along the corridors and on the stairs, dusting rugs and furniture, beating pillows, arranging armchairs, cutting and watering the flowers.

All of them move about in silence, fluidly, cautiously, giving a slightly fearful impression. But there is no visible nervousness, no running about or gesticulating. It's as if a Bengal tiger were circling around here somewhere; one's only chance is to make no sudden movements. Even during the day, in the glare of the shining sun, the servants resemble anonymous shadows, moving about without uttering a word, always in such a way as to remain on the periphery, careful not to catch anyone's gaze, let alone cross anyone's path.

They are variously dressed, according to function and rank: from golden turbans pinned with precious stones to simple dhotis—bands worn around the hips by those at the bottom of the hierarchy. Some are attired in silks, embroidered belts, and glittering epaulettes, while others wear ordinary shirts and white caftans. They have one thing in common: all are barefoot. Even if they are adorned with embroideries and tassels, brocades and cashmeres, they have nothing on their feet.

I noticed this detail right away, owing to personal experience. It started during the war, under German occupation. I remember that the winter of 1942 was approaching and I had no shoes. My old ones had fallen apart, and my mother had no money for a new pair. The shoes available to Poles cost 400 złoty, had tops of a thick denim coated with a black, water-repellent paste and soles made of a pale linden wood. Where could one get 400 złoty?

We were living in Warsaw then, on Krochmalna Street, near the gate to the ghetto, in the apartment of the Skupiewskis. Mr. Skupiewski had a little cottage industry making bars of green bathroom soap. "I will give you some bars on consignment," he said. "When you sell four hundred, you will have enough for your shoes, and you can pay me back after the war." People then still believed that the war would end soon. He advised me to work along the route of the Warsaw–Otwock railway line, frequented by holiday travelers; vacationers will want to pamper themselves a little, he counseled, by buying a bar of soap. I listened to him. I was ten years old, and I cried half the tears of a lifetime then, because in fact no one wanted to buy the little soaps. In a whole day of walking I would sell none—or maybe a single bar. Once I sold three and returned home bright red with happiness.

After pressing the buzzer I would start to pray fervently: God, please have them buy something, have them buy at least one! I was actually engaged in a form of begging, trying to arouse pity. I would enter an apartment and say: Please, madam, buy a soap from me. It costs only one złoty, winter is coming and I have no shoes. This worked sometimes, but not always, because there were many other children also trying to get over somehow—by stealing something, swindling someone, trafficking in this or that.

Cold autumn weather arrived, the cold nipped at the soles of my feet, and because of the pain I had to stop selling. I had 300 złoty, but Mr. Skupiewski generously threw in another hundred. I went with my mother to buy the shoes. If one wrapped one's leg with a piece of flannel and tied newspaper on top of that, one could wear them even in the worst frosts of winter.

I returned to Delhi, where my return ticket home was due to arrive any day. I found my old hotel, and even got the same room as before. I explored the city, went to museums, tried to read the *Times of India*, studied Herodotus. I do not know whether Herodotus reached India; given the difficulties of such a passage at that time, it seems highly unlikely, although one cannot rule it out definitively. After all, he came to know places so very far from Greece! He did describe twenty provinces, called satrapies, of what was then the greatest power on earth, Persia, and India was the most populous of those. *Indians ... are by far the most numerous people in the known world,* he asserts, and then talks of India, its location, society, and customs. *The Indians live further east in Asia than anyone else—further east than any other known people about whom there is reliable information—because beyond them the eastern part of India is sandy and therefore uninhabitable. There is a large number of Indian tribes, and they do not all speak the same language. Some, but not all, are nomadic; some live in marshes formed by the river and eat raw fish which they catch from cane boats. . . . These marsh Indians wear clothes made out of rushes; first they cut the plant down and gather it from the river, and then they weave it as one would a basket and wear it like a breastplate.*

Another tribe of Indians, called the Padaei, who live to the east of these marsh Indians, . . . are said to have the following customs. If any of their compatriots—a man or a woman—is ill, his closest male friends (assuming that it is a man who is ill) kill him, on the grounds that if he wasted away in illness his flesh would become spoiled. He denies that he is ill, but they take no notice, kill him, and have a feast. Exactly the same procedure is followed by a woman's closest female friends when it is a woman who is ill. They sacrifice and eat anyone who reaches old age, but it is unusual for anyone to do so, because they kill everyone who falls ill before reaching old age.

There is another Indian tribe, however, with different habits: they do not kill any living thing or grow crops, nor is it their practice to have houses. They eat vegetables, and there is a seed . . . which they collect, cook . . . and eat. If any of them falls ill, he goes and lies down in some remote spot, and no one cares whether he is dead or ill.

All the Indian tribes I have described have sexual intercourse in public, as herd animals do. Also, they are almost as black in colour as Ethiopians. The semen they ejaculate into their women is as black as their skin, not white like that of other men; the same goes for the semen Ethiopians ejaculate too.

Later I traveled to Madras and Bangalore, to Bombay and Chandigarh. In time I grew convinced of the depressing hopelessness of what I had undertaken, of the impossibility of knowing and understanding the country in which I found myself. India was so immense. How can one describe something that is—and so it seemed to me—without boundaries or end?

I received a return ticket from Delhi to Warsaw via Kabul and Moscow. I landed in Kabul just as the sun was setting. An intensely pink, almost violet sky cast its last light onto the dark navy-blue mountains surrounding the valley. The day was dying, sinking into a total and profound silence—it was the hush of a landscape, a region, a world that could be disturbed neither by the bell on a donkey's neck nor by the fine patter of a flock of sheep passing by the airport barracks.

The police detained me because I had no visa. But they could not send me back because the plane on which I'd arrived had already flown off and there was no other aircraft on the runway.

They conferred among themselves before driving off to town. Two of us remained, the airport guard and I. He was an enormous, broad-shouldered fellow with an anthracite beard, gentle eyes, and an uncertain, shy smile. He wore a long military coat and carried a Mauser rifle from army surplus.

Night descended suddenly and at once it grew cold. I was trembling; I had flown here straight from the tropics and had only a shirt on my back. The guard brought some wood, kindling, and dry grasses and started a fire on a slab of concrete. He gave me his coat and wrapped himself up to the eyes in a dark camel-hair blanket. We sat facing one another without uttering a word. Nothing was happening around us. Some crickets awoke in the distance and later, farther still, a car engine growled.

In the morning the policemen returned with an elderly man, a merchant who bought cotton in Kabul for the factories in Łódz. Mr. Bielas promised to see about a visa; he'd been here for some time already and had connections. Indeed, he not only secured a visa, he also invited me to his villa, pleased to have some company for a while.

Kabul is dust upon dust. Winds blow through the valley where the city lies, carrying clouds of sand from the nearby deserts. A pale brown, grayish particulate matter hangs in the air, coating everything, pushing its way in everywhere, settling only when the winds die down. And then the air grows transparent, crystal clear.

Every evening the streets look as if a spontaneous, improvised mystery play were being staged on them. The all-pervasive darkness is pierced only by oil lamps and torches burning on the street stalls, whose feeble and wavering flames illuminate the cheap and meager goods laid out by the vendors directly on the ground, on patches of road, on the thresholds of houses. Between these rows of lights people pass silently—hunched, covered figures whipped on by the cold and the wind.

When the plane from Moscow started to descend over Warsaw, my neighbor trembled, squeezed the arms of his chair with both hands, and closed his eyes. He had a gray, ravaged face, covered in wrinkles. A musty, cheap suit hung loosely on his thin, bony frame. I looked at him furtively, out of the corner of my eye. Tears were flowing down his cheeks. And a moment later I heard a suppressed but nevertheless distinct sob.

"I'm sorry," he said to me. "I'm sorry. But I didn't believe that I would return."

It was December 1956. People were still coming out of the gulags.

RABI SINGS THE UPANISHADS

India was my first encounter with otherness, the discovery of a new world. It was at the same time a great lesson in humility. Yes, the world teaches humility. I returned from this journey embarrassed by my own ignorance, at how ill read I was. I realized then what now seems obvious: a culture would not reveal its mysteries to me at a mere wave of my hand; one has to prepare oneself thoroughly and at length for such an encounter.

My initial reaction to this lesson, and to the implied necessity of an enormous amount of work on my part, was to run back home, to return to places I knew, to my own language, to the world of already familiar signs and symbols. I tried to forget India, which signified to me my failure: its enormity and diversity, its poverty and riches, its mystery and incomprehensibility had crushed, stunned, and finally defeated me. Once again I was glad to travel only around Poland, write about its people, talk to them, listen to what they had to say. We understood each other instantly, were united by common experience.

But of course I remembered India. The more bitter the cold of the Polish winter, the more readily I thought of hot Kerala; the quicker darkness fell, the more vividly resurfaced images of Kashmir's dazzling sunrises. The world was no longer uniformly cold and snowy, but had multiplied, become variegated: it was simultaneously cold and hot, snowy white while also green and blooming.

When I had free time (slivers only, as there was much work at the paper) and some spare change (unfortunately, an even rarer commodity), I searched for books about India. But my expeditions to ordinary bookstores and antiquarian dealers ended fruitlessly most often. In one used-book shop I found *Outlines of Indian Philosophy*, by Paul Deussen, published in 1907. Professor Deussen, a great German specialist on India and friend of Nietzsche's, thus explained the essence of Hindu philosophy: "This world is mâyâ, is illusion ... All is illusive, with one exception, with the exception of my own Self, of my Atman ... [man] feels himself everything,— so he will not desire anything, for he has whatever can be had;— he feels himself everything,—so he will not injure anything, for nobody injures himself."

Deussen reproaches Europeans. "European idleness," he complains, "tries to escape the study of Indian philosphy"—though perhaps "despair" is the more accurate motive since, in the course of four thousand years of uninterrupted development, this philosophy has evolved into a system so immense and immeasurable as to intimidate and paralyze all but the hardened daredevil and enthusiast. Furthermore, in Hinduism the sphere of the unfathomable is boundless, and the rich variety of what lies within it is characterized by the most bewildering, mutually contradictory, and stark contrasts. Everything here turns in the most natural way into its opposite, the boundaries between material things and mystical phenomena are fluid and fleeting, one becomes the other or, simply, eternally is the other; being is transformed into nothingness, disintegrates and metamorphoses into the cosmos, into a celestial omnipresence, into a divine way that disappears into the depths of bottomless nonbeing.

There is an infinite number of gods, myths, and beliefs in Hinduism, hundreds of the most varied schools of thought, orientations, and tendencies, dozens of roads to salvation, paths of virtue, practices of purity, and rules of asceticism. The world of Hinduism is so great that it has space enough for everyone and everything, for mutual acceptance, tolerance, harmony, and unity. It is impossible to count all the holy books of Hinduism: one of them alone, the Mahabharata, numbers some 220,000 sixteen-syllable verses, which is eight times the *Iliad* and the *Odyssey* combined!

One day at an antiquarian bookshop I found a dog-eared, disintegrating work by Yogi Ramacharaka, published in 1905 and entitled *The Hindu-Yogi Science of Breath: A Complete Manual of the Oriental Breathing Philosophy of Physical, Mental, Psychic and Spiritual Development.* Breathing, explains the author, is the most important activity performed by man, because through it we communicate with the world. If we stop breathing, we stop living. Therefore the quality of our breathing determines the quality of our life, and whether we are healthy, strong, and wise. Unfortunately, says Ramacharaka, most people, especially in the West, breathe poorly, and that is why there is so much disease, disability, sickliness, and depression.

I was especially interested in the exercises for developing the creative powers, because of my own great difficulties with this objective. "Lying flat on the floor or bed," the yogi recommended, "completely relaxed, with hands resting lightly over the Solar Plexus (over the pit of the stomach, where the ribs begin to separate), breathe rhythmically. After the rhythm is fully established *will* that each inhalation will draw in an increased supply of prana or vital energy from the Universal supply, which will be taken up by the nervous system and stored in the Solar Plexus. At each exhalation will that the prana or vital energy is being distributed all over the body...."

I had barely finished reading *The Hindu-Yogi Science of Breath* when *Glimpses of Bengal* by Rabindranath Tagore, published in 1923, fell into my hands. Tagore was a writer, a poet, a composer, and a painter. He was compared to Goethe and Jean-Jacques Rousseau. He was awarded the Nobel Prize for Literature in 1913. When he was a child, little Rabi—as he was called at home—the descendant of a princely family of Bengali Brahmans, distinguished himself, he writes, by his obedience toward his parents, his good grades in school, and his exemplary piety. He recalls that in the morning, while it was still dark, his father woke him to memorize Sanskrit declensions. After a while, he continues, dawn would break, and his father, having said his prayers, would help him finish the morning milk. Finally, with Rabi by his side, his father would turn once more to God and sing the Upanishads.

I tried to imagine this scene: it is dawning, and the father and small, sleepy Rabi stand facing the rising sun and singing the Upanishads.

The Upanishads are philosophical songs dating back three thousand years, but still vibrant, still present in India's spiritual life. When I realized this, and thought about the small boy greeting the morning star with stanzas from the Upanishads, I doubted whether I could ever comprehend a country in which children start the day singing verses of philosophy.

Rabi Tagore was a child of Calcutta, born in that monstrously huge city in which the following thing happened to me. I was sitting in a hotel room reading Herodotus when through the window I heard the wailing of sirens. I ran outside. Ambulances were screeching by, people were running into doorways to shelter, a group of policemen burst out from around a corner, thrashing the fleeing pedestrians with long sticks. One could smell the odor of gas and of something burning. I tried to find out what was going on. A man sprinting by with a stone in his hand yelled, "Language war!" and rushed on. Language war! I did not know the details, but had been made aware earlier that linguistic conflicts could assume violent and bloody forms in this country: demonstrations, street clashes, murders, even acts of self-immolation.

Only in India did I realize that my unfamiliarity with English was meaningless—insofar as only the elite spoke it here. Less than 2 percent of the population! The rest spoke one of the dozens of other languages. In this sense, my not knowing English helped me feel closer, more akin to the ordinary folk in the cities or the peasants in the villages I passed. We were in the same boat—I and half a billion of India's inhabitants!

While this thought gave me comfort, it also troubled me—why, I wondered, am I embarrassed that I don't know English but not that I don't know Hindi, Bengali, Gujarati, Telugu, Urdu, Tamil, Punjabi, or any of the many other languages spoken in this country? The argument of accessibility was irrelevant: the study of English was at the time as rare a thing as that of Hindi or Bengali. So was this Eurocentrism on my part? Did I believe a European language to be more important than those languages of this country in which I was then a guest? Deeming English superior was an offense to the dignity of Hindus, for whom the relationship to their native languages was a delicate and important matter. They were prepared to give up their lives in the defense of their language, to burn on a pyre. This fervor and resolve stemmed from the fact that identity here is determined by the language one speaks. A Bengali, for example, is someone whose mother tongue is Bengali. Language is one's identity card, one's face and soul, even.

Which is why conflicts about something else entirely—about social and religious issues, for instance—can assume the form of language wars.

Searching for books on India, I would ask if there was anything about Herodotus. Herodotus had started to interest me—I took a downright fancy to him, in fact. I was grateful for his being by my side in India during moments of uncertainty and confusion, for helping me with his book. Judging by how he wrote, he seemed a man kindly disposed toward others and curious about the world. Someone who always had many questions and was ready to wander thousands of kilometers to find an answer to any one of them.

When I immersed myself in various sources, however, I learned that we know little about Herodotus's life, and that even the few facts we do have are not entirely reliable. For in contrast to Rabindranath Tagore—or, for instance, his contemporary Marcel Proust, both of whom meticulously parsed every detail of their childhoods—Herodotus, like the other great men of this epoch—Socrates, Pericles, Sophocles—tells us next to nothing about his. Was it not customary? Was childhood considered irrelevant? Herodotus says only that he came from Halicarnassus. Halicarnassus lies above a calm bay shaped like an amphitheater, in a beautiful part of the world, where the western shore of Asia meets the Mediterranean Sea. It is a land of sun, warmth, and light, of olive trees and vineyards. One instinctively feels that someone born here must naturally have a good heart, an open mind, a healthy body, a consistently cheerful disposition.

Biographers tend to agree that Herodotus was born between 490 and 480 B.C.E., perhaps in 485. These are greatly important years in the history of world culture. Around 480 B.C.E., Buddha departs for the other world; a year later, in the Lu principality, Confucius dies; Plato will be born fifty years later. Asia is the center of the world; even insofar as the Greeks are concerned, the most creative members of their society—the Ionians—also live in Asia. There is no Europe yet; it exists as myth only, in the name of a beautiful girl, Europa, daughter of the Phoenician king Agenor, whom Zeus, transformed into a white bull, will carry off to Crete to have his way with her.

The parents of Herodotus? His siblings? His house? All of this is in deep shadowland uncertainty. Halicarnassus was a Greek colony on land subject to the Persians, with a non-Greek native population—the Carians. His father was called Lyxes, which is not a Greek name, so perhaps he was a Carian. It was his mother who most probably was Greek. Herodotus was therefore a Greek Carian, an ethnic half-breed. Such people who grow up amid different cultures, as a blend of different bloodlines, have their worldview determined by such concepts as border, distance, difference, diversity. We encounter the widest array of human types among them, from fanatical, fierce sectarians, to passive, apathetic provincials, to open, receptive wanderers—citizens of the world. It depends on how their blood got mixed, what spirits settled in it.

What sort of child is Herodotus? Does he smile at everyone and willingly extend his hand, or does he sulk and hide in the folds of his mother's garments? Is he an eternal crybaby and whiner, giving his tormented mother at times to sigh: Gods, why did I give birth to such a child! Or is he cheerful, spreading joy all around? Is he obedient and polite, or does he torture everyone with questions: Where does the sun come from? Why is it so high up that no one can reach it? Why does it hide beneath the sea? Isn't it afraid of drowning?

And in school? With whom does he share a bench? Did they seat him, as punishment, next to some unruly boy? Or, the gods forbid, a girl? Did he learn quickly to write on the clay tablet? Is he often late? Does he squirm during lessons? Does he slip others the answers? Is he a tattletale?

And toys? What did a little Greek living two and a half thousand years ago play with? A scooter carved out of wood? Did he build sand castles at the edge of the sea? Climb trees? Make himself clay birds, fish, and horses, which we can study today in museums?

Which aspects of his childhood will he remember for the rest of his life? For little Rabi, the most exalted moment was the morning prayer at his father's side. For little Marcel, it was waiting in a dark room for his mother to come and hug him good night. Which experience did little Herodotus anticipate in this way?

What did his father do? Halicarnassus was a small port town lying on the trade route between Asia, the Near East, and Greece proper. Phoenician merchant ships from Sicily and Italy stopped here, as did Greek ships from Piraeus and Argos, and Egyptian ones from Libya and the Nile delta. Might Herodotus's father have been a merchant himself? Perhaps it was he who kindled in his son a curiosity about the world. Did he disappear from home for weeks and months at a time, leaving his wife, questioned by her child, to answer that "Father is in ..."? And here one can imagine a list of place-names from which he drew one lesson—that somewhere, far away, there exists an omnipotent world which could take his father away from him forever, but also (thank the gods!) can bring him back again. Is that how the temptation to get to know this world was born? The temptation and the resolve?

From the few facts that have reached us, we know that little Herodotus had an uncle whose last name was Panyassis, and that he was the author of various poems and epics. Did this uncle perhaps take him on walks, instruct him in the beauties of poetry, the arcana of rhetoric, the art of storytelling? Because *The Histories* is the product of natural talent but also an example of writerly craft, of technical mastery.

While still a young man—and it seems for the first and only time in his life—Herodotus gets embroiled in politics, thanks to his father and uncle, who take part in the revolt against the tyrant of Halicarnassus, Lygdamis. The tyrant succeeds in suppressing the rebellion. The mutineers take refuge on Samos, a mountainous island two days of rowing to the northwest. Herodotus spends years here, and perhaps it is from here that he sets forth around the world. If he reappears now and then in Halicarnassus, it is only briefly. What would he do that for? To see his mother? We do not know. One can probably assume that he did not return here again.

It is the middle of the fifth century B.C.E.; Herodotus arrives in Athens. The ship reaches the Athenian port of Piraeus; it is eight kilometers from here to the Acropolis, a distance traversed on horseback or, as was often the case, on foot. Athens is then a world metropolis, the most important city on the planet. Herodotus is provincial, a non-Athenian, and thus something of a foreigner, and while such individuals are treated better than slaves, they are not treated as well as native Athenians. Athenian society was highly sensitive to race, with a strongly developed sense of superiority, exclusivity, arrogance even.

But it appears that Herodotus adapts quickly to his new city. The thirty-something-year-old man is open, friendly, a hail-fellow-well-met. He gives lectures, appears for meetings, author evenings—he probably makes his living that way. He establishes important contacts—with Socrates, Sophocles, Pericles. This isn't that difficult. Athens, with a population of one hundred thousand, isn't large in those days, and is tightly, even chaotically built up.

Two places only stand out and distinguish themselves: the center of religious cults, the Acropolis, and the center of meetings, events, commerce, politics, and social life—the Agora. People gather here from the early morning. The square of the Agora is always crowded, full of life. We would surely find Herodotus here as well. But he does not stay in the city for long. At approximately the time of his arrival, Athenian authorities pass a draconian law, according to which only those both of whose parents were born in Attica, the region immediately surrounding Athens, are entitled to political rights. Herodotus is unable to obtain Athenian citizenship. He sets off once again, and finally settles permanently in southern Italy, in the Greek colony of Thurii.

Opinion differs as to what happens later. Some believe that he did not budge from there again. Others claim that he later visited Greece once more, that he was sighted in Athens. Even Macedonia is mentioned. But in point of fact nothing is certain. He dies at age sixty, perhaps—but where? Under what circumstances? Did he spend his last years in Thurii, sitting in the shade of a sycamore tree and writing his book? Or maybe he could no longer see well enough and dictated it to a scribe? Did he have notes or was he able to rely on memory alone? People in those days had great powers of recall. He could well have remembered the stories of Croesus and Babylon, of Darius and the Scythians, of Persians, Thermopylae, and Salamis. And so many of the other tales that constitute *The Histories*.

Or perhaps Herodotus dies on board a ship sailing somewhere across the Mediterranean? Or perhaps he is walking along a road and sits down on a stone to rest, never to get up again? Herodotus vanishes, leaves us twenty-five centuries ago in a year that is impossible to pinpoint precisely and in a place we do not know.

.   .   .

The newspaper office.

Field trips.

Assemblies. Meetings. Conversations.

In my free moments I sit amidst dictionaries (a proper English one has finally been published) and various books about India (the imposing work of Jawaharlal Nehru, *The Discovery of India,* has just come out, the great autobiography of Mahatma Gandhi, and the beautiful *Panchatantra, or the Wisdom of India, Five Books.* After Stalin's death, censorship had eased and books that for years had been kept under lock and key started to appear).

With each new title I read, I felt as if I were undertaking a new journey to India, recalling places I had visited and discovering new depths and aspects, fresh meanings, of things which earlier I had assumed I knew. These journeys were much more multi-dimensional than my original one. I discovered also that these expeditions could be further prolonged, repeated, augmented by reading more books, studying maps, looking at paintings and photographs. What is more, they had a certain advantage over the actual trip—in an iconographic journey such as this, one could stop at any point, calmly observe, rewind to the previous image, etc., something for which on a real journey there is neither the time nor the chance.

So here I am, becoming increasingly engrossed in India's extraordinariness and riches, thinking that with time this country will become my thematic homeland, when one day in the fall of 1957 our omniscient secretary, Krysia Korta, called me out of my office at the newspaper and, looking mysterious, agitated, whispered to me:

"You're going to China."

CHAIRMAN MAO'S
ONE HUNDRED FLOWERS

Autumn 1957

I reached China on foot. Well, I flew to Hong Kong via Amsterdam and Tokyo. In Hong Kong, a local train took me to a small station in an open field—where, I had been told, I would be able to cross into China. In reality, however, when I stepped down onto the platform, it was only to be approached by a conductor and a policeman, who gestured toward a bridge on the far horizon.

"China!" the policeman said.

He was a Chinese man in a British police uniform. He walked with me a ways along the asphalt road, then wished me a good journey and turned back for the station. I continued on alone, carrying my suitcase in one hand and a bag full of books in the other. The sun beat down mercilessly, the air was hot and heavy, flies buzzed aggressively.

The bridge was short, with a diagonal metal grating, and below it flowed a half dried-up river. Further on stood a tall gate covered in flowers, with signs in Chinese and on top a coat of arms—a red shield and five yellow stars, four small and one large. Guards stood near the gate. They carefully inspected my passport, wrote the relevant data down in a big ledger, and told me to keep walking—toward a train which was visible perhaps half a kilometer away.

I walked on in the heat, with great effort, perspiring, amidst swarms of flies.

The train was empty. The cars resembled those on the train from Hong Kong—seats arranged in rows, no separate compartments. Finally, we were on our way. The landscape we traversed was sunny and green, the air coming in through the windows felt warm and humid and smelled of the tropics. It all reminded me of India, the India from the area around Madras and Pondicherry. Through these subcontinental analogies, I began to feel at home. I was among landscapes I knew and liked. The train stopped frequently and more and more people got on at the little stations. They were dressed alike, the men in dark blue denim jackets buttoned up to their chins, the women in flowery dresses identically cut. They sat straight-backed, silent, facing forward.

At one of the stations, when the train was already full, three people in uniforms of bright indigo came on board—a young woman and her two male helpers. The girl delivered a rather long speech in a decisive stentorian voice, after which one of the men handed everyone a cup and the second one poured out green tea from a metal pot. The tea was hot; the passengers blew on it to cool it and drank in small gulps, slurping loudly. Other than that, the silence continued. No one spoke so much as a word. I tried reading the passengers' faces, but they were frozen, seemingly without expression. Plus, I didn't want to scrutinize them too intently, for fear that this would be deemed rude or perhaps even arouse suspicion. Certainly no one was looking at me, although among all these work jackets and flowery percales I must have cut quite a queer figure in my elegant Italian suit purchased a year earlier in Rome.

I reached Peking after a three-day journey. It was cold and a chill dry wind was blowing, covering the city and its inhabitants in clouds of gray dust. Two journalists from the youth newspaper *Chungkuo* were waiting for me at the barely illuminated station. We shook hands, and one of them, standing stiffly, almost at attention, declaimed:

"We are pleased about your arrival because it is proof that the politics of One Hundred Flowers, announced by Chairman Mao, is bearing fruit. Chairman Mao recommends that we collaborate with others and share our experiences, and that is precisely what our respective editorial offices are doing in exchanging their permanent correspondents. We greet you as the permanent correspondent of *Sztandar Młodych* (The Banner of Youth) in Peking, and in exchange our own permanent correspondent will, at the appropriate time, travel to Warsaw."

I listened, trembling from the cold, for I had neither a jacket nor a coat, and looked about in vain for someplace warm. Finally we piled into a Pobieda and drove to the hotel. We were met there by a man whom the reporters from *Chungkuo* introduced to me as Comrade Li. He was to be my permanent translator, they explained. We all spoke Russian to one another, which from now on would be my language in China.

Here is how I had imagined it: I would get a room in one of the little houses hidden behind the clay or sand walls that stretched without end along Peking's streets. There would be a table in the room, two chairs, a bed, an armoire, a bookshelf, a typewriter, and a telephone. I would visit the editorial offices of *Chungkuo*, get the news, read, go out into the field, gather information, write and send articles, and all the while, of course, study Chinese. I would visit museums, libraries, and architectural monuments, meet professors and writers, in general encounter countless interesting people in villages and in cities, in shops and in schools; go to the university, to the marketplace, and to the factory; to Buddhist temples and to Party committees—and to dozens of other places worth knowing and investigating. China is an immense country, I told myself, joyfully thinking that besides my work as a correspondent and reporter I would have the opportunity to gather an infinite number of impressions and experiences, one day to depart from here enriched by new insights, discoveries, knowledge.

Full of these high hopes, I followed Comrade Li upstairs to my room, while he entered one directly across the hall from mine. I went to close my door and at that moment noticed that it had neither doorknob nor lock, and, moreover, that its hinges were so positioned as to force the door to remain permanently open onto the hallway. I noted, too, that the door to Comrade Li's room was similarly ajar and allowing him always to keep an eye on me.

I pretended not to notice anything and started to unpack my books. I took out Herodotus, near the top in my bag, then three volumes of the *Selected Works* of Mao Tse-tung, *The True Classic of Southern Florescence* by Chuang Tzu, and several titles I had purchased in Hong Kong: *What's Wrong with China,* by Rodney Gilbert; *A History of Modern China,* by K. S. Latourette; *A Short History of Confucian Philosophy,* by Liu Wu-chi; *The Revolt of Asia; The Mind of East Asia,* by Lily Abegg; as well as textbooks and dictionaries of the Chinese language, which I decided to start learning at once.

The following morning Comrade Li took me to *Chungkuo*'s editorial offices. For the first time I saw Peking by day. In every direction stretched a sea of low houses hidden behind walls. Above the walls protruded the tops of dark-gray roofs, whose tips curled upward like wings. From a distance they resembled a gigantic flock of motionless black birds awaiting the signal to take flight.

I was given a warm welcome at the paper. The editor in chief, a tall, thin young man, said that he was happy at my arrival, for in this way we jointly fulfilled Chairman Mao's prescription—let a hundred flowers bloom!

I answered that I, too, was very glad to be here, that I was aware of the tasks awaiting me, and that I wished to add that in my free time I intended to study the *Selected Works* of Mao Tse-tung, which I had brought with me in a three-volume edition.

This was greeted with great satisfaction and approval. The entire conversation, in fact, throughout which we also sipped green tea, came down to such exchanges of pleasantries, as well as to praising Chairman Mao and his politics of One Hundred Flowers.

After a while, my hosts suddenly fell silent, as if following an order. Comrade Li rose and looked at me—I sensed that the visit was at an end. Everyone said his farewells with great warmth, smiling and with wide open arms.

The entire visit was arranged and conducted in such a fashion as to accomplish nothing in its course—not one single concrete subject was touched upon, let alone discussed. They had asked me nothing and had given me no opportunity to inquire how my sojourn and my work were to be structured.

But, I reasoned, perhaps such are local customs. Perhaps it is considered impolite to get to the point quickly? I had certainly read, more than once, that in the East the rhythm of life is slower than what we westerners are used to, that there is a time for everything, that one must be calm and patient, one must learn to wait, grow internally calm and tranquil, that the Tao values not motion but stillness, not activity but idleness, and that all haste, passion, and frenzy arouse distaste here and are interpreted as symptoms of bad upbringing and a lack of refinement.

I was also well aware that I was but a mote of dust in the face of the vastness that is China and that I, as well as my work, meant nothing when compared to the great tasks facing everyone here, including the staff of *Chungkuo*, and that I simply had to wait until the time was right for arranging my affairs. Meantime, I had a hotel room, food, and Comrade Li, who did not leave me alone for even a moment; when I was in my room, he sat by the door of his, observing me all the while.

I sat and read the works of Mao Tse-tung. This effort coincided nicely with the decree of the moment: huge banners all over town proclaimed DILIGENTLY STUDY THE IMMORTAL THOUGHTS OF CHAIRMAN MAO! I was reading a lecture delivered by Mao in December of 1935, during a meeting of the Party's hard core in Wayaopao, in which he discussed the effects of the Long March, "the first of its kind in the annals of history," as he called it. "For twelve months we were under daily reconnaissance and bombing from the skies by scores of planes, while on land we were encircled and pursued, obstructed and intercepted by a huge force of several hundred thousand men, and we encountered untold difficulties and dangers on the way; yet by using our two legs we swept across a distance of more than twenty thousand *li* through the length and breadth of eleven provinces. Let us ask, has history ever known a long march to equal ours? No, never." Thanks to this march, in which Mao's army "cross[ed] perpetually snow-capped mountains and trackless grasslands," it escaped the forces of Chiang Kai-shek and was later able to mount a counteroffensive.

Sometimes, tired of reading Mao, I would pick up Chuang Tzu's book. Chuang Tzu, a fervent Taoist, scorned all worldliness and held up Hui Shi, a great Taoist sage, as an example. "When Jao, a legendary ruler of China, proposed that he should assume power, he washed his ears, which had been defiled by such a notion, and took refuge on the desolate mountain of K'i-Shan." For Chuang Tzu, as for the biblical Kohelet, the external world was nothing, mere vanity: "In conflict with things or in harmony with them, they pursue their course to the end, with the speed of a galloping horse which cannot be stopped;—is it not sad? To be constantly toiling all one's lifetime, without seeing the fruit of one's labor, and to be weary and worn out with his labor, without knowing where he is going to: is it not a deplorable case? Men may say, 'But it is not death'; yet of what advantage is this? When the body is decomposed, the mind will be the same along with it: must not the case be pronounced very deplorable?"

Chuang Tzu is beset by doubts and uncertainties: "Speech is not only the exhaling of air. Speech is meant to convey something, but what that is has not been fully determined. Is there really something like speech, or is there nothing at all like it? Can one see it as distinct from the warbling of birds, or not?"

I wanted to ask Comrade Li how a Chinese would interpret these fragments, but I was afraid that they might sound too provocative in the face of the ongoing campaign to study the sayings of Mao. So I picked something innocent, about a butterfly: "Once Chuang Tzu dreamt he was a butterfly, a butterfly flitting and flittering about, happy with himself and doing as he pleased. He didn't know he was Chuang Tzu. Suddenly he woke up and there he was, solid and unmistakable Chuang Tzu. But he didn't know if he was Chuang Tzu who had dreamt he was a butterfly, or a butterfly dreaming he was Chuang Tzu. Between Chuang Tzu and a butterfly there must be *some* distinction! This is called the Transformation of Things."

I asked Comrade Li to explain the meaning of this story to me. He listened, smiled, and carefully noted it down. He said he would have to consult someone and then would give me the answer.

He never did.

I finished volume one of Mao Tse-tung and started on volume two. It is the end of the 1930s, the Japanese army already occupies a large portion of China and is advancing further into the interior. The two adversaries, Mao Tse-tung and Chiang Kai-shek, enter into a tactical alliance in order to make a stand against the Japanese invader. The war drags on, the occupier is savage, and the country devastated. In Mao's opinion, the best tactic in the struggle against a prevailing enemy is an adroit elasticity and ceaseless tormenting of the opponent. He speaks and writes about this constantly.

I was reading a lecture about the lengthy war with Japan which Mao delivered in the spring of 1938 in Yunnan when Comrade Li, having finished a telephone conversation in his room, put down the receiver and came in to announce that tomorrow we would be going to the Great Wall. The Great Wall! People come from the ends of the earth to see it. It is one of the wonders of the world, a unique, almost mythical, and in some sense unfathomable creation. The Chinese constructed it, with interruptions, over the course of two thousand years. They commenced when the Buddha and Herodotus were alive and were still building it when Leonardo da Vinci, Titian, and Johann Sebastian Bach were at their labors in Europe.

The wall is variously estimated as being from three to ten thousand kilometers long. Variously, because there is no single Great Wall—there are several of them. And they were built at different times, in different places, and from different materials. They had one thing in common, however: the originating impulse. As soon as one dynasty came to power, it immediately set about erecting the Great Wall. The idea of a wall possessed China's rulers. If they ceased construction for a while, it was only because of a lack of means—they were right back at it the instant their finances improved.

The Chinese built the Great Wall to defend against invasions by the restless and expansionist nomadic tribes of Mongolia. These tribes, in great armies, hordes, legions, emerged from the Mongolian steppes, from the Altai mountains and the Gobi desert, and attacked the Chinese, constantly menacing their nation, sowing terror with the threat of slaughter and enslavement.

But the Great Wall was only a metaphor—a symbol and a sign, the coat of arms and the escutcheon of what had been a nation of walls for millennia. The Great Wall demarcated the empire's northern borders; but walls were also erected between warring principalities, between regions and even neighborhoods. The structures defended cities and villages, passes and bridges. They guarded palaces, government buildings, temples, and markets. Barracks, police stations, and prisons. Walls encircled private homes, separated neighbor from neighbor, family from family. If one assumes that the Chinese built walls uninterruptedly for hundreds, even thousands of years, and if one factors in the population—enormous throughout the national history—their dedication and devotion, their exemplary discipline and antlike purposefulness, then one reckons with hundreds upon hundreds of millions of hours spent building walls, hours which in this poor country could have been spent learning to read, acquiring a profession, cultivating new fields, and breeding robust cattle.

That is how the world's energy is wasted. In complete irrationality! Complete futility! For the Great Wall—and it is gigantic, a wall-fortress, stretching for thousands of kilometers through uninhabited mountains and wilderness, an object of pride and, as I have mentioned, one of the wonders of the world—is also proof of a kind of human weakness, of an aberration, of a horrifying mistake; it is evidence of a historical inability of people in this part of the planet to communicate, to confer and jointly determine how best to deploy enormous reserves of human energy and intellect.

In these parts, the idea of coming together was but a chimera: The very first reflex in the face of potential trouble was to build a wall. To shut oneself in, fence oneself off. Because whatever comes from without, from over there, can only be a threat, an omen of misfortune, a harbinger of evil—perhaps the most genuine evil there is.

And the wall is not merely motivated by exterior considerations. Protecting against foreign menaces, it also allows one to control what is happening internally. There are passages in the wall, doors and gates, and guarding them, of course, one could control who entered and exited. One could question, one could check for valid papers, one could take down names, look at faces, observe, commit to memory. And thus such a wall is simultaneously a shield and a trap, a veil and a cage.

The worst aspect of the wall is to turn so many people into its defenders and produce a mental attitude that sees a wall running through everything, imagines the world as being divided into an evil and inferior part, on the outside, and a good and superior part, on the inside. A keeper of the wall need not be in physical proximity to it; he can be far away and it is enough that he carry within himself its image and pledge allegiance to the logical principles that the wall dictates.

The Great Wall is one hour's drive north of Peking. At first, we pass through parts of the city. An ice-cold wind is blowing. Pedestrians and bicyclists lean forward, struggling with the gale. There are rivers of bicyclists everywhere. Each of these rivers halts when the lights turn red, as if a lock had suddenly been closed, then resumes its flow until the next set of lights. Only the wind disrupts this otherwise monotonous, laborious rhythm: If it picks up too violently, the river begins to surge and billow, spinning some bicyclists around and forcing others to stop and dismount. Confusion and chaos erupt in the ranks. But as soon as the wind subsides, everything continues once again in its proper place and dutiful movement forward.

The sidewalks in the center of the city are full of people and one frequently sees columns of schoolchildren clad in school uniforms. They walk in pairs waving little red flags, and the one at the head of the procession carries either a red banner or a portrait of the Good Uncle—Chairman Mao. The children enthusiastically call, sing, or cry out in unison. What are they saying? I ask Comrade Li. "They want to study the thoughts of Chairman Mao," he replies. The policemen, whom one sees on every corner, always give these processions the right-of-way.

The city is all yellow and navy blue. The buildings fronting the streets are yellow and the clothes everyone wears are navy. "These uniforms are an achievement of the Revolution," explains Comrade Li. "Before, people had nothing to wear and died of cold." Men have their hair cut like military recruits, and women, be they girls or old ladies, wear theirs in a short pageboy style with bangs. One has to look closely to distinguish one individual from another—an awkwardness, since it is considered impolite to stare.

If someone is carrying a bag, then that bag is identical to all the rest. What happens when there is a large gathering and everyone must leave their caps and bags in a cloakroom? How do they distinguish their belongings from those of thousands of others? I have no idea—and yet they appear to do so. It is proof that real differences can indeed dwell not only in large things, but in the smallest of details—in the way, for instance, that a button has been sewn on.

One mounts the Great Wall through one of its abandoned towers. The wall is bristling with massive crenellations and turrets, and wide enough for ten people to walk along it side by side. From our vantage point, the wall serpentines into infinity, each end disappearing somewhere beyond mountains and forests. It is deserted, not a soul around, and the wind tears at us. I take it all in, touch the boulders dragged here centuries ago by people dropping from exhaustion. To what end? What sense does it make? Of what use is it?

With each passing day I thought of the Great Wall more and more as the Great Metaphor. I was surrounded by people with whom I could not communicate, encircled by a world I could not fathom. I was supposed to write—but about what? The press was exclusively in Chinese, so I understood nothing of it. At first I asked Comrade Li to translate for me, but every article, in his translation, began with the words: "As Chairman Mao teaches us," or "Following the recommendations of Chairman Mao," etc., etc. Is that what was actually written? My only link to the outside world was Comrade Li, and he was the most impenetrable barrier of all. To my every request for a meeting, a conversation, a trip, he responded, "I will convey this to the newspaper." And I would hear nothing more on the matter. Nor could I go out alone, without Comrade Li. But where could I have gone anyway? To see whom? I did not know the city, I knew no one, I had no telephone (only Comrade Li had one).

Above all, I did not know the language. Yes, I did try studying it, right from the start. I attempted to tear my way through the thickets of hieroglyphs and ideograms only to come up against the dead end of each character's maddening multiplicity of meanings. I had just read somewhere that there exist more than eighty

English translations of the Tao Te Ching (the bible of Taoism), all of them competent and reliable—and all utterly different! My legs buckled beneath me. No, I thought to myself, I cannot cope with this, I cannot manage. The characters flickered before my eyes, shimmered and pulsated, changed shape and position, relations and connections, proportions and patterns; they multiplied and divided, formed rows and columns, exchanged places, the shapes for "ao" appeared who knows how in the character for "ou," or suddenly I confused the notation for "eng" with the notation for "ong"—which was a truly horrendous error.

CHINESE THOUGHT

I had a lot of time on my hands and spent much of it reading the books about China which I had purchased in Hong Kong. They were so absorbing that I would momentarily forget about Herodotus and the Greeks.

I still believed that I would be working here, and therefore wanted to learn as much as possible about this country and its people. I didn't realize that the majority of correspondents reporting on China were based in Hong Kong, Tokyo, or Seoul, that they were either Chinese or at least fluent in the language, and that there was something impossible and unreal about my situation in Peking.

I constantly felt the presence of the Great Wall; not the one I had seen several days ago in the mountains to the north, but the much more formidable and insurmountable one for me—the Great Wall of Language. How desperately I yearned for my gaze to alight on some recognizable letter or expression, to hold on to it, breathe a sigh of relief, feel at home. All in vain. Everything was illegible, obscure, inscrutable.

It was actually not dissimilar to how I had felt in India. There too I could not penetrate the thicket of the local Hindu alphabet. And were I to travel farther still, would I not encounter similar barriers?

Where did this linguistic-alphabetical Tower of Babel come from, anyway? How does a particular alphabet arise? At some primal point, at the very beginning, it had to start with a single sign, a single character. Someone made a mark in order to remember something. Or to communicate something to someone else. Or to cast a spell on an object or a territory.

But why do different people describe the same object with so many completely different notations? All over the world a man, a mountain, or a tree look much alike, and yet in each alphabet different symbols, images, or letters correspond to them. Why is it that the very first individual who wanted to describe a flower made a vertical line in one culture, a circle in another culture, and in a third decided on two lines and a cone? Did these first scribblers make these decisions on their own, or collectively? Did they talk them over beforehand? Discuss them around the fire at night? Request endorsement during a family council? At a tribal gathering? Did they seek counsel from the elders? From charlatans? From soothsayers?

It would be good to know, because later, once the die has been cast, one cannot turn back. Matters acquire their own momentum. From that first, simplest decision—to make one line to the left and one to the right—all the rest will follow, increasingly ingenious and intricate, because by the alphabet's fiendish evolutionary logic the alphabet with time grows more and more complex, less and less legible to the uninitiated, even to the point of finally becoming, as has occurred more than once, utterly indecipherable.

Although the Hindi and the Chinese writing systems caused me equal difficulty, the behavior of people in the two countries could not have been more different. The Hindu is a relaxed being, while the Chinese is a tense and vigilant one. A crowd of Hindus is formless, fluid, slow; a crowd of Chinese is formed before you know it into disciplined marching lines. One senses that above a gathering of Chinese stands a commander, a higher authority, while above the multitude of Hindus hovers an Areopagus of innumerable and undemanding deities. If a throng of Hindus encounters something interesting, it stops, looks, and begins discussing. In a similar situation, the Chinese will walk on, in close formation, obedient, their eyes fixed on a designated goal. The Hindus are significantly more ritualistic, mystical, religious. The realm of the spirit and its symbols is always close at hand in India, present, perceptible. Holy men wander along the roads; pilgrimages head for temples, the seats of the gods; masses gather at the feet of holy mountains, bathe in holy rivers, cremate the dead on holy pyres. The Chinese appear spiritually less ostentatious, significantly more discreet and closed. Instead of paying homage to gods, they concern themselves with observing proper etiquette; instead of holy men, works march along the roads.

Their faces, too, I found are different. The face of a Hindu contains surprise; a red dot on a forehead, colorful patterns on cheeks, or a smile that reveals teeth stained dark brown. The face of a Chinese holds no such surprises. It is smooth and has unvarying features. It seems as if nothing could ruffle its still surface. It is a face that communicates that it is hiding something about which we know nothing and never will.

One time Comrade Li took me to Shanghai. What a difference from Peking! I was stunned by the immensity of this city, by the diversity of its architecture—entire neighborhoods built in the French style, or the Italian, or the American. Everywhere, for kilometers on end, shaded avenues, boulevards, promenades, arcades.

The scale and energy of urban development, the metropolitan bustle, the cars, the rickshaws, the untold multitudes of pedestrians. Many stores and even the occasional bar. It is much warmer here than in Peking and the air is gentle—one senses the proximity of the sea.

As we drove one day through a Japanese neighborhood, I noticed the heavy, squat columns of a Buddhist temple. "Is this temple open?" I asked Comrade Li. "Here, in Shanghai, certainly so," he answered, with a mixture of irony and scorn, as if Shanghai were China but not 100 percent so, not fully a China according to Mao Tse-tung.

Buddhism did not flower in China until the first millennium of our era. For some five hundred years prior to that time, two parallel spiritual currents, two schools, two orientations dominated the region: Confucianism and Taoism. Master Confucius lived from 560 to 480 B.C.E. There is no consensus among historians as to whether the creator of Taoism—Master Lao-tzu—was older or younger than Confucius. Many scholars even maintain that Lao-tzu did not exist at all, and the only little book which he is said to have left behind him—the Tao Te Ching—is simply a collection of fragments, aphorisms, and sayings gathered by anonymous scribes and copyists.

If we accept that Lao-tzu did exist and was older than Confucius, then we can also believe the story, often repeated, about how young Confucius made a journey to where the wise man Lao-tzu lived and asked him for advice on how to conduct his life. "Rid yourself of arrogance and desire," the old man answered, "rid yourself of the habit of flattery and of excessive ambition. All this causes you harm. That is all that I have to say to you."

But if it was Confucius who was older than Lao-tzu, then he could have passed on to his younger countryman these three great thoughts. The first: "How can you know how to serve gods if you do not know how to serve people?" The second: "Why do you pay back evil with good? How then will you pay back good?" And third: "Till you know about the living, how are you to know about the dead?"

The philosophies of Confucius and of Lao-tzu (if indeed he existed) arose in the twilight of the Chou dynasty, at around the Epoch of the Warring Kingdoms, when China was torn asunder, divided into numerous states waging fierce, population-decimating war with one another. A man who managed momentarily to escape the carnage is still haunted by uncertainty and fear of tomorrow, and perforce asks himself: How does one survive? This is the question that Chinese thought attempts to answer. It is perhaps the most practical philosophy the world has ever known. In contrast to Hindu thought, it rarely ventures into the realms of transcendence, and tries instead to offer the ordinary man advice on enduring the situation in which he finds himself for the simple reason that, without either his will or consent, he was born into this cruel world of ours.

It is at this point that the paths of Confucius and Lao-tzu (if he existed) diverge, or, more precisely, it is to the most fundamental of worldly questions—"How do I survive?"—that each gives a different answer. Confucius holds that man, being born into society, has certain obligations. The most important are those of carrying out the commands of the authorities and submissiveness to one's parents. Also—respect for ancestors and tradition; the strict observance of the rules of etiquette; fealty to the existing order; and resistance to change. The Confucian man is loyal and docile vis-à-vis those in power. If you obediently and conscientiously hew to their dictates, says the master, you will survive.

Lao-tzu (if he existed) recommends a different stance. The

creator of Taoism advises keeping oneself at a remove from everything. Nothing lasts, says the master. So do not become attached to anything. All that exists will perish; therefore rise above it, maintain your distance, do not try to become somebody, do not try to pursue or possess something. Act through inaction: your strength is weakness and helplessness; your wisdom, naïveté and ignorance. If you want to survive, become useless, unnecessary to everyone. Live far from others, become a hermit, be satisfied with a bowl of rice, a sip of water. And most important—observe the Tao. But what is Tao? It's impossible to say, because the essence of Tao is its vagueness and inexpressibleness: "If Tao lets itself be defined as Tao, then it is not genuine Tao," says the master. Tao is a path, not a heading, and to observe Tao is to keep to that path and walk straight ahead.

Confucianism is the philosophy of power, of bureaucrats, of structure, order, and of standing at attention; Taoism is the wisdom of renouncing the game, of contenting oneself with being only an insignificant particle of indifferent nature.

In their message to the simple man, however, Confucianism and Taoism have a common denominator: the recommendation of humility. It is interesting that at approximately the same time, and also in Asia, arise two other intellectual disciplines, Buddhism and Ionian philosophy, which offer lesser mortals the identical advice: be humble.

The paintings of Confucian artists depict court scenes—a seated emperor surrounded by stiff standing bureaucrats, chiefs of palace protocol, pompous generals, meekly bowing servants. In Taoist paintings we see distant pastel landscapes, barely discernible mountain chains, luminous mists, mulberry trees, and in the foreground a slender, delicate leaf of a bamboo bush, swaying in the invisible breeze.

Strolling with Comrade Li along the streets of Shanghai and observing the passersby, I now ask myself whether each is a Confucian, a Taoist, or a Buddhist.

But this is a pointlessly inquisitive stance. For the great strength of Chinese philosophy is its flexible and unifying syncretism, the way varied trends, views, and positions merge into a single whole while in no way jeopardizing the core integrity of each separate school of thought. In the course of thousands of years of Chinese history, many and different philosophies (it is difficult to call them religions in the European sense of that word, since they do not include the concept of God) held sway—Confucianism prevailed, or Taoism, or Buddhism, to name the most prominent; now and then a conflict or tension would arise among them; occasionally an emperor would throw his support behind one or another of the spiritual trends, at times fostering their coexistence, at other times inciting competition and strife among them. But sooner or later there would be compromise, interpenetration, accord of one kind or another. So much fell into the immense chasm of this civilization's history, was absorbed by it, subsequently to emerge with an unmistakably Chinese shape and character.

This synthetic transformative process could also occur in the soul of the individual Chinese. Depending on the situation, the context, and the circumstances, the Confucian element might take the upper hand in him, or the Taoist, because nothing in his world was determined once and for all, signed and sealed, written in stone. To survive, he would be an obedient executor. Humble and meek on the outside, he would as well be on the inside aloof, unreachable, independent.

We returned to Peking and our hotel. I went back to my books. I began studying the life of the great ninth century poet, Han Yü. At one point Han Yü, a follower of Confucius, begins to combat the influences of Buddhism in China, on the grounds of its being a foreign Hindu ideology. He pens critical essays, fiery pamphlets. The great poet's chauvinism so angered the ruling emperor, an adherent of Buddhism, that he condemned Han Yü to death and then, propitiated by his courtiers, changed the sentence to exile in what is today the province of Kwangtung, a place infested with crocodiles.

Before I was able to find out what happened next, someone arrived from the editorial offices of *Chungkuo* bringing with him a gentleman from the headquarters of international trade, who in turn handed me a letter from my colleagues at *Sztandar Młodych* in Warsaw. Because our team had spoken out against the closing of "*Po prostu*," they wrote, the newspaper's entire editorial board had been removed by the Central Committee and the paper was now under the direction of three specially appointed commissioners. Some of the journalists had resigned in protest, while others were hesitating, waiting it out. What was I going to do, my friends wanted to know.

The gentleman from the international trade department left, and without giving it a second's thought I informed Comrade Li that I had received urgent orders to return home. I would start packing right away. Comrade Li's face didn't so much as twitch. We looked at each other for a moment, then went downstairs to the dining room, where dinner awaited us.

I was leaving China, as I had India, with a feeling of loss, even of sorrow; but at the same time there was something purposeful about my flight. I had to escape, because a new, hitherto unfamiliar world was pulling me into its orbit, completely absorbing me, obsessing and overwhelming me. I was seized at once with a profound fascination, a burning thirst to learn, to immerse myself totally, to melt away, to become as one with this foreign universe. To know it as if I had been born and raised there, begun life there. I wanted to learn the language, I wanted to read the books, I wanted to penetrate every nook and cranny.

It was a kind of malady, a dangerous weakness, because I also realized that these civilizations are so enormous, so rich, complex, and varied, that getting to know even a fragment of one of them, a mere scrap, would require devoting one's whole life to the enterprise. Cultures are edifices with countless rooms, corridors, balconies, and attics, all arranged, furthermore, into such twisting, turning labyrinths, that if you enter one of them, there is no exit, no retreat, no turning back. To become a Hindu scholar, a Sinologist, an Arabist, or a Hebraist is a lofty, all-consuming pursuit, leaving no space or time for anything else.

Whereas I had the urge to submit to such seductions, I also remained attracted to what lay beyond the confines of their respective worlds—I was tempted by people still unmet, roads yet untraveled, skies yet unseen. The desire to *cross the border*, to look at what is beyond it, stirred in me still.

I returned to Warsaw. The reasons for my bizarre situation in China, my lack of real purpose, my senseless suspension in a vacuum, quickly became clear. The idea of sending me to China arose in the aftermath of two thaws: that of October 1956 in Poland, and in China, that of Chairman Mao's One Hundred Flowers. Even before I arrived in China, an upheaval was under way in Warsaw and in Peking. The head of the Polish Communist Party, Władysław Gomułka, initiated a campaign against the liberals, and Mao Tse-tung was launching the draconian politics of the Great Leap Forward.

Practically speaking, I should have left Peking the day after I arrived. But my newspaper was mum—fearful and fighting for its survival, it had forgotten about me. Or perhaps the editors had my interests in mind—perhaps they reckoned that away in China I would somehow be safe? In any event, I now think that the editors of *Chungkuo* were being informed by the Chinese embassy in Warsaw that the correspondent of *Sztandar Młodych* is the envoy of a newspaper hanging by a thread and it is only a matter of time before it goes under the ax. I think, too, that it was traditional Chinese principles of hospitality, the importance the Chinese ascribe to saving face, as well as their highly cultivated politeness, that kept me from being summarily expelled. Instead, they created conditions which they assumed would lead me to guess that the models of cooperation that had been agreed to earlier no longer obtained. And that I would say of my own accord: I am leaving.

MEMORY ALONG THE ROADWAYS
OF THE WORLD

Immediately upon returning home I left the newspaper and got a job at the Polish Press Agency. Because I had arrived from China, my new boss, Michał Hofman, concluded my expertise must lie in matters of the Far East and decided that this would now be my beat—specifically, the part of Asia to the east of India and extending to the innumerable islands of the Pacific.

We all know a little about everything, but I knew nothing about the countries I had been assigned, and so I burned the midnight oil studying up on guerrilla warfare in the jungles of Burma and Malaysia, the revolts in Sumatra and Sulawesi, the rebellions of the Moro tribe in the Philippines. The world once again presented itself to me as something impossible to even begin to comprehend, let alone master. And all the more so because, given my work, I had so little time to devote to it. All day long, dispatches arrived in my office from various countries, which I had to read, translate, condense, edit, and send on to newspapers and radio stations.

In this manner, because news reached me daily from places like Rangoon or Singapore, Hanoi, Manila, or Bandung, my travels through the countries of Asia—commenced in India and Afghanistan, continued in Japan and China—went on uninterrupted. On my desk, under glass, I had a prewar map of the Asian continent, over which I often wandered with my finger, searching for Phnom Penh or Surabaya, the Solomon Islands or the difficult-to-locate Laoag, places where there had just been a coup attempt against Someone Important, or where the workers at a rubber plantation had just gone on strike. I transported myself in my thoughts now here, now there, trying to imagine those locales and events.

Sometimes, when the offices emptied in the evening and the hallways grew quiet, and I wanted a respite from telegrams about the strikes and armed conflicts, the coups and explosions convulsing countries I did not know, I reached for *The Histories* of Herodotus, lying in my drawer.

Herodotus begins his book with a statement explaining why he set out to write it in the first place:

Here are presented the results of the enquiry carried out by Herodotus of Halicarnassus. The purpose is to prevent the traces of human events from being erased by time, and to preserve the fame of the important and remarkable achievements produced by both Greeks and non-Greeks; among the matters covered is, in particular, the cause of the hostilities between Greeks and non-Greeks.

This passage is the key to the entire book.

First of all, Herodotus informs us therein that he carried out some sort of "enquiry" (I would prefer to use the term "investigation"). Today we know that he devoted his entire life to this—and it was, for its time, a long life indeed. Why did he do it? Why, still in his youth, did he make such a decision? Did someone encourage him to conduct these investigations? Commission him to undertake them? Or did Herodotus enter the service of some potentate, or of a council of elders, or of an oracle? Who needed this intelligence? And what for?

Or maybe he did everything on his own initiative, possessed by a passion for knowledge, driven by a restless and unfocused compulsion? Perhaps he had a naturally inquiring mind, a mind that continuously generated a thousand questions giving him no peace, keeping him up at nights? And if he was gripped by such an absolute private mania—which after all has been known to happen—how did he find the time to satisfy it, year after year after year?

Herodotus admits that he was obsessed with memory, fearful on its behalf. He felt that memory is something defective, fragile, impermanent—illusory, even. That whatever it contains, whatever it is storing, can evaporate, simply vanish without a trace. His whole generation, everyone living on earth at that time, was possessed by that same fear. Without memory one cannot live, for it is what elevates man above beasts, determines the contours of the human soul; and yet it is at the same time so unreliable, elusive, treacherous. It is precisely what makes man so unsure of himself. Wait, wasn't that...? Come on, you can remember, when was that...? Wasn't it the one that...? Try to remember, how was it...? We do not know, and stretching beyond that "we do not know" is the vast realm of ignorance; in other words—of nonexistence.

Man does not obsess about memory today as he once did because he lives surrounded by stockpiles of it. Everything is at his fingertips—encyclopedias, textbooks, dictionaries, compendia, search engines. Libraries and museums, antiquarian bookshops and archives. Audio and video recordings. Infinite supplies of preserved words, sounds, images—in apartments, in warehouses, in basements, in attics. If he is a child, his teacher will tell him everything he needs to know; if he is a university student, he will be informed by his professors.

Of course none, or almost none, of these institutions, devices, or techniques existed in Herodotus's time. Man knew as much, and only as much, as his mind managed to preserve. A few privileged individuals started to learn to write on rolls of papyrus and on clay tablets. But the rest? Culture was always an aristocratic enterprise. And wherever it departs from this principle, it perishes as such.

In the world of Herodotus, the only real repository of memory is the individual. In order to find out that which has been remembered, one must reach this person. If he lives far away, one has to go to him, to set out on a journey. And after finally encountering him, one must sit down and listen to what he has to say—to listen, remember, perhaps write it down. That is how reportage begins; of such circumstances it is born.

So Herodotus wanders the world, meets people, listens to what they tell him. They speak of who they are, they recount their history. But how do they know who they are, and where they came from? Ah, they answer, they have it on the word of others—first and foremost, from their ancestors. It is they who transmitted their knowledge to this generation, just as this one is now transmitting it to others. The knowledge takes the form of various tales. People sit around the fire and tell stories. Later, these will be called legends and myths, but in the instant when they are first being related and heard, the tellers and the listeners believe in them as the holiest of truths, absolute reality.

They listen, the fire burns, someone adds more wood, the flames' renewed warmth quickens thought, awakens the imagination. The spinning of tales is almost unimaginable without a fire crackling somewhere nearby, or without the darkness of a house illuminated by an oil lamp or a candle. The fire's light attracts, unites, galvanizes attentions. The flame and community. The flame and history. The flame and memory. Heraclitus, who lived before Herodotus, considered fire to be the origin of all matter, the primordial substance. Like fire, he said, everything is in eternal motion, everything is extinguished only to flare up again. Everything flows, but in flowing, it undergoes transformation. So it is with memory. Some of its images die out, but new ones appear in their place. The new ones are not identical to those that came before—they are different. Just as one cannot step twice into the same river, so it is impossible for a new image to be exactly like an earlier one.

It is this principle of an irreversible passing away that Herodotus understands perfectly, and he wants to set himself in opposition to its destructive power: *to prevent the traces of human events from being erased by time.*

Still, what boldness, what a sense of self-importance and mission: presuming to *prevent the traces of human events from being erased by time.* Human events! But how did he know that any such thing as "human events" even exists? His predecessor, Homer, described the history of a single, specific war, the one with Troy, and then the adventures of a solitary wanderer, Odysseus. But human events? That term in itself represents a new way of thinking, a new concept, a new horizon. With that sentence, Herodotus reveals himself to us as anything but a provincial scribe, a narrow-minded lover of his own little polis, mere patriot of one of the dozens of city-states of which Greece was then composed. No! From the very outset, the author of *The Histories* enters the stage as a visionary on a world scale, an imagination capable of encompassing planetary dimensions—in short, as the first globalist.

Of course, the map of the world which Herodotus has before him, or which he imagines, differs from the one confronting us today. His world is much smaller than ours. Its center consists of the mountainous and (at the time) forested lands around the

Aegean Sea. Those lying on the western shore constitute Greece; those on the eastern, Persia. And so right away we hit upon the heart of the matter—Herodotus is born, grows up, and just as he starts to figure out everything around him, one of his very first observations is that the world is sundered, split into East and West, and that these halves are in a state of dissension, conflict, war.

The question that immediately suggests itself to him, as well as to any thinking human being, is "Why should this be so?" And it is this very question that informs the foreword of Herodotus's masterpiece: *Here are presented the results of the enquiry carried out by Herodotus of Halicarnassus. . . . in particular, the cause of the hostilities . . .*

Precisely. We can see that this question, oft repeated since the dawn of history, has vexed humankind for thousands of years now: Why do peoples wage war against one another? What are the origins of wars? What do people hope to accomplish when they start a war? What drives them? What do they think? What is their goal? An unending litany of questions! Herodotus dedicates his life, diligently, tirelessly, to finding the answers. But from among the many issues, some quite general and abstract, he selects the most concrete to investigate, the events that took place before his very eyes or of which memories were still fresh and alive or, even if slightly faded, still very much available. In other words, he concentrates his attention and his inquiries on the following subject: Why does Greece (that is, Europe) wage war with Persia (that is, with Asia)? Why do those two worlds—the West (Europe) and the East (Asia)—fight against each other, and do so to the death? Was it always thus? Will it always be thus?

He is profoundly intrigued by this subject; indeed he is preoccupied, absorbed, insatiable. We can imagine a man like him possessed by an idea that gives him no peace. Activated, unable to sit still, moving constantly from one place to another. Wherever he appears there is an atmosphere of agitation and anxiety. People who dislike budging from their homes or walking beyond their own backyards—and they are always and everywhere in the majority—treat Herodotus's sort, fundamentally unconnected to anyone or anything, as freaks, fanatics, lunatics even.

Could it be that Herodotus is regarded in just this way by his contemporaries? He says nothing about this himself. Did he even pay attention to such things? He was occupied with his travels, with the preparations for them and then with the selection and organization of the materials he brought home. A journey, after all, neither begins in the instant we set out, nor ends when we have reached our doorstep once again. It starts much earlier and is really never over, because the film of memory continues running on inside of us long after we have come to a physical standstill. Indeed, there exists something like a contagion of travel, and the disease is essentially incurable.

We do not know in what guise Herodotus traveled. As a merchant (the proverbial occupation of people of the Levant)? Probably not, since he had no interest in prices, goods, markets. As a diplomat? That profession did not exist yet. As a spy? But for which state? As a tourist? No, tourists travel to rest, whereas Herodotus works hard on the road—he is a reporter, an anthropologist, an ethnographer, a historian. And he is at the same time a typical wanderer, or, as others like him will later be called in medieval Europe, a pilgrim. But this wandering of his is no picaresque, carefree passage from one place to another. Herodotus's journeys are purposeful—they are the means by which he hopes to learn about the world and its inhabitants, to gather the knowledge he will feel compelled, later, to describe. Above all, what he hopes to describe are *the important and remarkable achievements produced by both Greeks and non-Greeks.*

That is his original intent. But with each new expedition the world expands on him, multiplies, assumes enormous proportions. It turns out that beyond Egypt there is still Libya, and beyond that the land of the Ethiopians, in other words, Africa; that to the East, after traversing the expanses of Persia (which requires more than three months of rapid walking), one arrives at the towering and inaccessible Babylon, and beyond that at the homeland of the Indians, the outer boundaries of which lie who knows where; that to the West the Mediterranean Sea stretches far indeed, to Abyla and the Pillars of Herakles, and beyond that, they say, there is still another sea; and there are also seas and steppes to the north, and forests inhabited by countless Scythian peoples.

Anaximander of Miletus (a beautiful city in Asia Minor), who predated Herodotus, created the first map of the world. According to him, the earth is shaped like a cylinder. People live on its upper surface. It is surrounded by the heavens and floats suspended in the air, at an equal distance from all the heavenly bodies. Various other maps come into being in that epoch. Most frequently, the earth is represented as a flat, oval shield surrounded on all sides by the waters of the great river Oceanus. Oceanus not only bounds all the world, but also feeds all the earth's other rivers.

The center of this world was the Aegean Sea, its shores and islands. Herodotus organizes his expeditions from there. The further he moves toward the ends of the earth, the more frequently he encounters something new. He is the first to discover the world's multicultural nature. The first to argue that each culture requires acceptance and understanding, and that to understand it, one must first come to know it. How do cultures differ from one another? Above all in their customs. Tell me how you dress, how you act, what are your habits, which gods you honor—and I will tell you who you are. Man not only creates culture, inhabits it, he carries it around within him—man is culture.

· · ·

Herodotus, who knows a lot about the world, nevertheless does not know everything about it. He never heard of China or Japan, did not know of Australia or Oceania, had no inkling of the existence, much less of the great flowering, of the Americas. If truth be told, he knew little of note about western and northern Europe. Herodotus's world is Mediterranean–Near Eastern; it is a sunny world of seas and lakes, tall mountains and green valleys, olives and wine, lambs and fields of grain—a bright Arcadia which every few years overflows with blood.

THE HAPPINESS AND
UNHAPPINESS OF CROESUS

Seeking an answer to the question most important to him, namely, where did the conflict between East and West originate, and why does this hostility exist, Herodotus proceeds with great caution. He does not lay claim to understanding. On the contrary, he keeps to the shadows and has others do the talking. The others are, in this case, *the learned Persians*. These learned Persians, Herodotus says, maintain that the instigators of the worldwide East-West conflict are neither the Greeks nor the Persians, but a third people, the Phoenicians, peripatetic merchants. It was they who first began the business of kidnapping women, which in turn triggered this global storm.

Indeed, the Phoenicians kidnap in the Greek port of Argos a king's daughter called Io and take her by ship to Egypt. Later, several Greeks land in the Phoenician city of Tyre and abduct Europa, the daughter of its king. Still other Greeks kidnap from the king of Colchis his daughter, Medea. Paris of Troy, in turn, seizes Helen, wife of the Greek king Menelaus, and carries her off to Troy. In revenge, the Greeks invade Troy. A great war breaks out, whose history is immortalized by Homer.

Herodotus paraphrases the commentary of Persian wise men:

Although the Persians regard the abduction of women as a criminal act, they also claim that it is stupid to get worked up about it and to seek revenge for the women once they have been abducted; the sensible course, they say, is to pay no attention to it, because it is obvious that the women must have been willing participants in their own abduction, or else it could never have happened. And as proof he cites the case of the Greek princess Io, as the Phoenicians present it: *The Phoenicians say that they did not have to resort to kidnapping to take her to Egypt. According to them, she slept with the ship's captain in Argos, and when she discovered that she was pregnant, she could not face her parents, and therefore sailed away willingly with the Phoenicians, to avoid being found out.*

Why does Herodotus begin his great description of the world with what is, according to the Persian sages, a trivial matter of tit-for-tat kidnappings of young women? Because he respects the laws of the narrative marketplace: to sell well, a story must be interesting, must contain of bit of spice, something sensational, something to send a shiver up one's spine. Accounts of the abductions of women satisfy these requirements.

Herodotus lived at the juncture of two epochs: although the era of written history was beginning, the oral tradition still predominated. It is possible, therefore, that the rhythm of Herodotus's life and work was as follows: he made a long journey, and upon his return traveled to various Greek cities and organized something akin to literary evenings, in the course of which he recounted the experiences, impressions, and observations he had gathered during his peregrinations. It is entirely likely that he made his living from such gatherings, and that he also financed his subsequent trips in this way, and so it was important to him to have the largest auditorium possible, to draw a crowd. It would be to his advantage, therefore, to begin with something that would rivet attention, arouse curiosity—something a tad sensational. Story plots meant to move, amaze, astonish pop up throughout his entire opus; without such stimuli, his audience would have dispersed early, bored, leaving him with an empty purse.

But the accounts of the abductions of women weren't merely

cheap sensationalism, provocative and piquant story lines. Here already, at the very start of his investigations, Herodotus tries to formulate his first law of history. His ambition here stems from his having gathered on his journeys an abundance of material from various epochs and places and wanting to determine and define some principle of order to impose upon this seemingly chaotic and unsorted collection of facts. Is it even possible to arrive at such a principle? Yes, Herodotus replied. That principle is the answer to the question *"who . . . first undertook criminal acts of aggression."* Having this question as to precedence in mind makes it easier to negotiate the tangled and intricate twists and turns of history, to explain to ourselves what forces and events set it in motion.

The defining of this principle, the awareness of it, is hugely significant, because in Herodotus's world (as well as in various societies today), the eternal law of revenge, the law of reprisal, of an eye for an eye, was (and remains) alive and well. Revenge is not only a right—it is a most sacred obligation. Whoever does not fulfill this charge will be cursed by his family, his clan, his society. The necessity of seeking retribution weighs not only on me, the member of the wronged tribe. The gods, too, must submit to its imperatives, and so too must even impersonal and timeless Fate.

What function does vengeance serve? Fear of it, dread in the face of its inescapability, should be enough to stop anyone from committing a dishonorable act that is damaging to another. It should function as a brake, a restraining voice of reason. If, however, it turns out to be an ineffectual deterrent, and someone commits an offense, the perpetrator will be seen to have set into motion a chain of retribution that can stretch for generations, for centuries even.

There is a kind of dreary fatalism in the mechanism of revenge. Something inevitable and irreversible. Misfortune suddenly befalls you and you cannot fathom why. What happened? Simply this: that you have been revenged upon for crimes perpetrated ten generations ago by a forefather whose existence you weren't even aware of.

The second law of Herodotus, pertaining not only to history but also to human life, is that *human happiness never remains long in the same place.* And our Greek proves this theorem by describing the dramatic, affecting fortunes of the king of the Lydians, Croesus, whose story resembles that of the biblical Job, for whom Croesus was perhaps the prototype.

Lydia, his kingdom, was a powerful Asiatic state situated between Greece and Persia. Croesus accumulated great riches in his palaces, entire mountains of gold and silver for which he was renowned in the world and which he willingly displayed to visitors. This show took place in the middle of the sixth century B.C.E., several decades before the birth of Herodotus.

The capital of Lydia, Sardis, *was visited on occasion by every learned Greek who was alive at the time, including Solon of Athens* (he was a poet, a creator of Athenian democracy, and famed for his wisdom). Croesus personally received Solon and ordered his servants to show him his treasures, and, certain that the sight of them astonished his guest, he queried him: "*So I really want to ask you whether you have ever come across anyone who is happier than everyone else?*"

In asking this question, he was expecting to be named as the happiest of all men.

But Solon did not flatter him in the least and instead cited as the happiest of men several heroically fallen Athenians, adding: "*Croesus, when you asked me about men and their affairs, you were putting your question to someone who is well aware of how utterly jealous the divine is, and how it is likely to confound us. Anyone who lives for a long time is bound to see and endure many things he would rather avoid. I place the limit of a man's life at seventy years. Seventy years makes 25,200 days ... No two days bring events which are exactly the same. It follows, Croesus, that human life is entirely a matter of chance....*

"Now, I can see that you are extremely rich and that you rule over large numbers of people, but I won't be in a position to say what you're asking me to say about you until I find out that you died well.... Until [a man] is dead, you had better refrain from calling him happy, and just call him fortunate.

"... It is necessary to consider the end of anything ... and to see how it will turn out, because the god often offers prosperity to men, but then destroys them utterly and completely."

And in fact, after Solon's departure, the punishment of the gods descended brutally upon Croesus, in all likelihood precisely because he thought himself the happiest man on earth. Croesus had two sons—the strapping Atys and another, who was deaf and dumb. Atys was the apple of his father's eye, protected and watched over. And yet, despite this, not on purpose but purely by accident, a guest of Croesus, one Adrastus, killed him during a hunt. When Adrastus realized what he had done, he broke down. During Atys's funeral, he waited until everyone had left and it grew quiet around the tomb, *and then, realizing that there was no one in his experience who bore a heavier burden of misfortune than himself, he took his own life at the graveside.*

After his son's death, Croesus lives for two years in profound grief. During this time, the great Cyrus comes to power in neighboring Persia, and under him the might of the Persians increases rapidly. Croesus is worried that if Cyrus's nation continues to gather strength it could one day threaten Lydia, and so he hatches a plan for a preemptive strike.

It is the custom at the time for the wealthy and powerful to consult an oracle before making important decisions. Greece abounds in these oracles, but the most important resides in a temple on a towering mountainside—in Delphi. In order to obtain a favorable prophecy from the oracle, one must propitiate the Delphic deity with gifts. Croesus, therefore, orders a gigantic collection of offerings. Three thousand cattle are to be killed, heavy bars of gold melted, countless objects forged out of silver. He commands that a huge fire be lit, on which he burns in sacrifice gold and silver couches, purple cloaks and tunics. *He also told all the Lydians that every one of them was to sacrifice whatever he could.* We can imagine the numerous and humbly obedient Lydian people as they make their way along the roads to where the great pyre is burning and throw into the flames what until now was most precious to them—gold jewelry, all manner of sacral and domestic vessels, holiday vestments, even favorite everyday attire.

The opinions which the oracle delivers are typically pronouncements of cautious ambiguity and intentional murkiness. They are texts so composed as to allow the oracle, in the event that things turned out otherwise (which occurred often), to retreat adroitly from the whole affair and save face. And yet so undiminished and indestructible is the force of the desire to have the veil lifted on tomorrow that people, with a stubbornness lasting thousands of years already, still listen greedily and with flushed cheeks to the utterances of soothsayers. Croesus, as one can see, was also in that desire's thrall. Impatiently he awaited the return of the envoys he had sent to the various Greek oracles. The answer of the Delphic oracle was: If you set out against the Persians, you will destroy a great state. And Croesus, who desired this war, blinded by the lust of aggression, interpreted the prediction to mean: If you set out against Persia, you will destroy it. Persia, after all—and in this Croesus was correct—was truly a great state.

So he attacked, but he lost the war, and as a result—and in accordance with the prophecy—annihilated his own great state and was himself enslaved. *The Persians took their prisoner to Cyrus, who built a huge funeral pyre and made Croesus (who was tied up) and fourteen Lydian boys climb up to the top. Perhaps he intended them to be a victory-offering for some god or other, or perhaps he wanted to fulfil a vow he had made, or perhaps he had heard that Croesus was a god-fearing man and he made him get up on to the pyre because he wanted to see if any immortal would rescue him from being burnt alive. . . . Although Croesus's situation up on top of the pyre was desperate, his mind turned to Solon's saying that no one who is still alive is happy, and it occurred to him how divinely inspired Solon had been to say that. This thought made him sigh and groan, and he broke a long silence by repeating the name "Solon" three times.*

Now, at the request of Cyrus, who is standing near the pyre, the interpreters ask Croesus whom he is calling and what does it mean. Croesus answers, but as he is telling the story, the pyre, which has already been lit, starts to burn in earnest at its farthest edges. Cyrus, moved by pity but also fearing retribution, reverses his decision and orders the fire extinguished as quickly as possible and Croesus and the boys accompanying him brought down. But all attempts to control the blaze fail.

Croesus realized that Cyrus had changed his mind. When he saw that it was too late for them to control the fire, despite everyone's efforts to quench it, he called on Apollo. . . . Weeping, he called on the god, and suddenly the clear, calm weather was replaced by gathering clouds; a storm broke, rain lashed down, and the pyre was extinguished.

. . . Once [Cyrus] had got Croesus down from the pyre he asked him who had persuaded him to invade his country and be his enemy rather than his friend. "My lord," Croesus replied, "it was my doing. You have gained and I have lost from it. But responsibility lies with the god of the Greeks who encouraged me to make war on you. After all, no one is stupid enough to prefer war to peace; in peace sons bury their fathers and in war fathers bury their sons. However, I suppose the god must have wanted this to happen." . . .

Cyrus untied him and had him seated near by. He was very impressed with him, and he and his whole entourage admired the man's demeanour. But Croesus was silent, deep in thought.

And so two of Asia's then mightiest rulers—the defeated Croesus and the victorious Cyrus—sit side by side, looking at the remnants of the pyre upon which just a while ago one of them was going to immolate the other. We can imagine that Croesus, who only one hour earlier was awaiting death in dreadful torment, is still in shock, and when Cyrus asks him what he could do for him, he starts to rail against the gods: "Master," Croesus replies, "nothing would give me more pleasure than to be allowed to send these shackles of mine to the god of the Greeks, whom I revered more than any other god, and to ask him if it is his normal practice to trick his benefactors."

What sacrilege! What is more, Croesus, having received Cyrus's permission, sent a delegation of Lydians to Delphi. He told them to lay the shackles on the threshold of the temple and ask the god if he was not ashamed to have used his oracles to encourage Croesus to march against the Persians ... And they were also to ask whether Greek gods were normally so ungrateful.

To which the Delphic Pythia was said to reply with the sentence that will constitute the third law of Herodotus:

"Not even a god can escape his ordained fate. Croesus has paid for the crime of his ancestor four generations ago, who, though a member of the personal guard of the Heraclidae, gave in to a woman's guile, killed his master, and assumed a station which was not rightfully his at all. In fact, Apollo wanted the fall of Sardis to happen in the time of Croesus' sons rather than of Croesus himself, but it was not possible to divert the Fates. . . ."

This was the Pythia's response to the Lydians. They ... relayed the statement to Croesus. When he heard it he realized that the fault was his and not the god's.

THE BATTLE'S END

I thought that I had heard all I was going to hear regarding Croesus, who had actually come to seem quite sympathetically human to me—at first in his naïve and unconcealed pride in the treasures that the whole world admired (all those tons of gold and silver filling his vaults), and then, as well, in his unwavering faith in the prophecies of the Delphic oracle; in his bottomless despair over the death of his son, to which he had indirectly contributed; in his breakdown after the bitter loss of his nation; in his apathetic acquiescence to a martyr's death upon the pyre; in his sacrilegious repudiation of divine verdicts; and then, finally, in the necessity of his costly atonement for the sin of an ancestor he did not even know. Yes, I thought that I had once and for all said goodbye to this punished, humiliated man, when suddenly he appeared again in the pages of Herodotus, once more in the company of King Cyrus, who, at the head of the Persian army, has set out to conquer the Massagetae, a wild and warlike people living deep in central Asia, all the way on the banks of the Amu Darya.

It is the sixth century B.C.E. and the Persians are aggressively on the move—they are conquering the world. Years, centuries later, one superpower after another will make the same attempt, but the ambitious striving of the Persians, back in that dim and distant epoch, remains arguably unrivaled in its boldness and scope.

They had already conquered the Ionians and the Aeolians; captured Miletus, Halicarnassus, and many other Greek colonies in western Asia; grabbed the Medes and Babylon—in short, everything that could be seized in the near and distant vicinity came under Persian rule. And now Cyrus sets off to subjugate a tribe somewhere at the very ends of what was then the known and imagined world. Perhaps he believes that if he crushes the Massagetae, takes over their lands and herds, he will come yet another inch closer to the moment when he can triumphantly proclaim: "The world is mine!"

But this need to possess everything, which earlier had led to Croesus's downfall, will now in turn bring about Cyrus's defeat. The punishment for man's unrestrained rapaciousness befalls him always at the very moment—and here lies the particularly cruel and destructive irony—when he appears to be but a step away from attaining his dreams. The comeuppance is therefore accompanied by a savage disappointment in the world, a profound resentment toward a vengeful fate, and a depressing sense of humiliation and powerlessness.

For now, however, Cyrus sets off for the depths of Asia, for the north—to conquer the Massagetae. The expedition did not surprise his contemporaries, because everyone *noticed how he attacked every race indiscriminately.... There were a number of significant factors tempting and inducing him to undertake this campaign. The main two were the apparently miraculous nature of his birth, and the good fortune that attended him in war, in the sense that any race which Cyrus sent his troops after found it impossible to escape.*

What is known about the Massagetae is that they live on the great flat steppes of central Asia, as well as on islands in the Amu Darya, which call Araxes, where in the summer they dig up various roots to eat, storing the ripened fruit they find in the trees for subsequent winter consumption. We learn that the Massagetae used something akin to narcotics, and were therefore the forerunners of today's addicts and junkies: *They have also discovered a kind of plant whose fruit they use when they meet in groups. They light a bonfire, sit around it, throw this fruit on the fire, and sniff the smoke rising from the burning fruit they have thrown on to the fire. The fruit is the equivalent there to wine in Greece: they get intoxicated from the smoke, and then they throw more fruit on to the fire and get even more intoxicated, until they eventually stand up and dance, and burst into song.*

In those days the queen of the Massagetae is a woman called Tomyris. A deadly, bloody drama will be enacted between her and Cyrus, one in which Croesus will also play a part. Cyrus starts with a subterfuge: he pretends that it is Tomyris's hand that he is after. But the queen of the Massagetae quickly senses that the Persian king's designs are not on her but on her kingdom. Cyrus, seeing that he will not attain his goal in the way he had hoped, decides to wage open war against the Massagetae on the other side of the Amu Darya, the river whose shores his forces have just reached.

From the Persian capital of Susa to the shores of the Amu Darya the road is long—or, more accurately, there is no road. One must cross mountain passes, traverse the burning desert of Kara-Kum, and then wander the endless steppes.

One is reminded of Napoleon's mad campaign for Moscow. The Persian and the Frenchman are in the grips of an identical passion: to seize, conquer, possess. Both will suffer defeat on account of having transgressed a fundamental Greek principle, the law of moderation: never to want too much, not to desire everything. But as they are launching their ventures, they are too blind to see this; the lust for conquest has dimmed their judgment, has deprived them of reason. On the other hand, if reason ruled the world, would history even exist?

For now, though, Cyrus's expeditionary force is still on the march. It must be an interminable column of men, horses, and matériel. Tired soldiers keep falling off mountain cliffs, later many perish of thirst in the desert, later still some units are lost in the roadless expanses of the steppes. There were no maps in those days, after all, no compasses, no binoculars, no road signs. They must reconnoiter with the help of tribes they encounter along the way, ask around, find guides, perhaps even consult fortune-tellers. Whatever the case may be, the great army advances—laboriously, indefatigably, and at times surely, as was wont to happen with the Persians, under the lash.

Only Cyrus enjoys all possible comforts along this road of suffering. *Now, the Great King goes on his military expeditions well equipped with food and livestock from home, and he also brings water from the River Choäspes (on whose banks the city of Susa is situated), because water from no other river except the Choäspes is allowed to pass the king's lips. This Choäspes water is boiled, and wherever the king might be campaigning on any given occasion, he is accompanied by a large number of four-wheeled wagons, drawn by mules, which carry the water in silver containers.*

I am fascinated by this water. Water that has been boiled ahead of time. Stored in silver vessels to keep it cool. One has to cross the desert freighted with those vessels.

We know that the water is transported on numerous four-wheeled wagons drawn by mules. What connection between the water wagons and the soldiers dropping of thirst along the way? There is none: the soldiers die, and the wagons keep rolling. They do not stop, because the water they carry is not for the soldiers; it is water that has been boiled expressly for Cyrus. The king, after all, drinks no other, so if it ran out, he would die of thirst. How could one even contemplate such an eventuality?

Another thing interests me as well. There are de facto two kings in this procession—the great, reigning Cyrus and the dethroned Croesus, who only yesterday just barely escaped death on a burning pyre, a fate that the first king had been preparing for him. What are relations between them like now? Herodotus maintains that they are cordial. But he did not take part in this expedition—he wasn't even born yet. Do Cyrus and Croesus ride in the same equipage, no doubt adorned with gold-plated wheels, gold-plated stanchions, and a gold-plated shaft? Does Croesus sigh wistfully at the sight? Do the two gentlemen converse? If they do, it must be through an interpreter, because they share no language. And what is there to talk about, anyway? They ride thus for days, then weeks; sooner or later, they will have exhausted all possible subjects of conversation. And what if, moreover, one of them—or both—is the quiet sort, with a secretive and introverted personality?

I wonder what happens when Cyrus wants a drink of water. He calls to the servants. These water bearers must be retainers of exceptional trustworthiness, who have taken an inviolable oath; otherwise, what would prevent their taking sips of the priceless liquid on the sly? And so, at the command, they fetch a silver pitcher. Does Cyrus now drink alone, or does he say, "Care for some, Croesus?" Herodotus is silent on this subject, but it is an important moment to consider—one cannot live in the desert without water; deprived of it, a human being succumbs quickly to dehydration.

But perhaps the two kings do not ride together—in which case the problem does not arise. Or maybe Croesus has his own barrel of water, ordinary water, not necessarily from that special river, Choäspes. But all this is mere speculation, because Herodotus makes no further mention of Croesus until the expedition reaches the broad and calm Amu Darya.

Cyrus, who failed at possessing Tomyris, declared war on her. His first step was to order the construction of pontoon bridges on the river, to give his army passage to the other side. While this work is in progress, a messenger arrives from the queen, who sends Cyrus commonsensical words full of wise caution: *"Abandon your zeal for this enterprise. . . . Stop and rule your own people, and put up with the sight of my ruling mine. But no: you are hardly going to take this advice, since peace is the last thing you desire. If you really are committed to a trial of strength with the Massagetae, you need not bother with all the hard work of bridging the river; we will pull back three days' journey away from the river and then you can cross over into our land. Or if you would rather meet us in your own land, you withdraw the same distance."*

Upon hearing this, Cyrus convenes a meeting of elders and asks for their views. All of them, unanimously, advise a retreat, proposing that the engagement with Tomyris's forces take place on their own, Persian side of the river. But there is one dissenting voice— that of Croesus. He begins philosophically: *"The first thing you should appreciate,"* he tells Cyrus, *"is that human affairs are on a wheel, and that as the wheel turns around it does not permit the same people always to prosper."*

In short, Croesus warns Cyrus point-blank that good fortune might desert him and that things could then go very badly indeed. He counsels crossing to the other side of the river and there—because he has heard that the Massagetae are unaccustomed to riches such as the Persians have and have experienced few pleasures—to slaughter herds of sheep, set out fine wine and tempting dishes, and organize a great feast for them. The Massagetae will eat and drink, fall into a drunken sleep, whereupon they can be taken prisoner. Cyrus accepts Croesus's plan, Tomyris retreats from the river, and the Persian troops cross into the lands of the Massagetae.

Tensions soon arise, as is typical before a great confrontation. After Croesus's earlier words sink in, those about fortune turning like a wheel, Cyrus, who is an experienced ruler, having now reigned over Persia for twenty-nine years, starts to grasp the seriousness of what is about to transpire. He is no longer sure of himself, no longer, as before, arrogant and self-satisfied. He has a nightmare, and when daylight comes, concerned for the life of his son, Cambyses, sends him back to Persia accompanied by Croesus. In addition, plots and conspiracies against him proliferate.

But he is the commander of an army and must issue orders; everyone is waiting to hear what he will say, where he will lead them. And what Cyrus does is execute, point by point, Croesus's advice, unaware that he is thereby proceeding step by step toward his own destruction. (Did Croesus consciously mislead Cyrus? Did he set a trap for him in order to avenge the defeat he endured and the humiliation he suffered? We do not know—about this Herodotus is silent.)

Cyrus sends in first the part of his army most unfit for battle—various camp hangers-on, vagabonds, the weak and the sick, all sorts of, as one used to say in the gulags, *dokhodiagi* (goners). He is in effect condemning these people to death, which is precisely what happens, because in the encounter with the elite of the Massagetae forces, they are cut down to a man. Now the Massagetae, having slaughtered the Persian rear guard, *noticed the feast, which had been laid out, and they reclined and ate it. When they had eaten and drunk their fill, they fell asleep—and then the Persians fell on them. Many of the Massagetae were killed, but even more were taken prisoner, including Queen Tomyris' son, who was the commander of the army and whose name was Spargapises.*

At the news of her son's and her army's fate, Tomyris sends Cyrus a messenger with the following words: *"Give me back my son, and then you can leave this country without paying for the brutality with which you treated a third of the Massagetan army. But if you do not, I swear by the sun who is the lord of the Massagetae that for all your insatiability I will quench your thirst for blood."*

These are strong, sinister words, of which Cyrus nevertheless takes not the slightest notice. He is intoxicated by his victory, pleased that he has led Tomyris up the garden path and succeeded in revenging himself upon one who rejected his advances. At this moment the queen is still unaware of the depth of her own misfortune, namely: *When Spargapises, the son of Queen Tomyris, recovered from the wine and saw the trouble he was in, he begged Cyrus to release him from his chains. Cyrus granted his request, but as soon as Spargapises was free and had regained control of his hands, he killed himself.*

An orgy of death and blood begins.

Tomyris, seeing that Cyrus had not heeded her counsel, gathered her forces and engaged him in battle. Herodotus: *I consider this to be the fiercest battle between non-Greeks there has ever been . . .* Initially, both armies rain arrows down upon each other. When there are no arrows left, they fight with lances and daggers. And finally, they resort to barehanded wrestling. Although they are equally matched at the start, gradually the Massagetae gain the upper hand. Most of the Persian army perishes. Cyrus, too, is among the dead.

What ensues now is a scene from a Greek tragedy. The plain is strewn with the corpses of soldiers from both armies. Onto this battlefield steps Tomyris, carrying an empty wineskin. She walks from one slaughtered soldier to the next and collects blood from the still fresh wounds, enough to fill the wineskin. The queen must be drenched with human blood, she must be positively dripping with it. It is hot, so she surely wipes her face with her bloodied hands. Her face is smeared with blood. She looks around, searching for Cyrus's corpse. *When she found it, she shoved his head into the wineskin, and in her rage addressed his body as follows: "Although I have come through the battle alive and victorious, you have destroyed me by capturing my son with a trick. But I warned you that I would quench your thirst for blood, and so I shall."*

That is how the battle ends.

That is how Cyrus dies.

The stage empties, and the only one left standing is the despairing, hate-filled Tomyris.

Herodotus offers no commentary, adding only, with a reporter's sense of duty, several pieces of information about Massagetan customs, which were, after all, unfamiliar to the Greeks: *If a Massagetan desires a woman, he hangs his quiver outside her wagon and has sex with her, with no fear of reprisal. The only imposed limit on life there is as follows. When a person becomes very old, all his relatives come together and sacrificially kill him and some livestock along with him; then they stew the meat and eat it. They believe that there is no more fortunate way to die, whereas anyone who dies after an illness is buried in the ground rather than eaten, and they regard it as a calamity that he did not get to be sacrificed.*

ON THE ORIGIN OF THE GODS

I put Herodotus away into the drawer of my office desk, leaving Tomyris on the corpse-strewn battlefield, in defeated victory, despairing but also triumphant—the indomitable and incandescent Antigone of the Asiatic steppes—and I start to leaf through the latest batch of telegrams sent by the correspondents for Reuters and Agence France-Presse in China, Indonesia, Singapore, and Vietnam. They report that Vietnamese guerrillas near Bing Long have engaged in yet another skirmish with the troops of Ngo Dinh Diem (the result of the clash and the number of casualties—unknown). That Mao Tse-tung has proclaimed another campaign: Dead is the politics of One Hundred Flowers; now the task is the reeducation of the intelligentsia—whoever knows how to read and write (these skills have suddenly metamorphosed into liabilities) will be forcibly deported to the countryside, where, pulling a plow or digging irrigation canals, coming to know real proletarian peasant life, he or she will be rid of liberal, One Hundred Flower–like chimera. That the president of Indonesia, Sukarno, one of the ideologues of the new politics of Pancasila power, has ordered the Dutch to leave his country, their former colony. One can learn little from these brief dispatches; they lack context and what one might call local color. I can perhaps imagine most easily the professors of Peking University, see them riding in a truck, hunched over from the chill, not even knowing where they're headed because their eyeglasses are fogging over in the cold.

Yes, much is happening in Asia, and the lady who distributes the dispatches around the various offices keeps placing fresh piles of them on my desk. But with time I notice that another continent starts to draw my attention: Africa. As in Asia, there is turmoil in Africa: tempests and revolts, coups and riots. But because Africa lies closer to Europe (only a single body of water, the Mediterranean Sea, separates them) one hears the rumblings of this continent with more immediacy, as though they were coming from just next door.

Africa's contribution to world history has been immense—nothing less than a transformation of a centuries-old global hierarchy. By furnishing the New World its labor force, it enabled it to amass enough wealth and power to surpass the Old World. Later, having given over many generations of its best, strongest, and most resilient people, the depopulated and exhausted continent fell easy prey to European colonizers. Now, however, it was awakening from its lethargy, gathering its strength for independence.

I began to incline toward Africa also because, from the very outset, Asia had greatly intimidated me. The civilizations of India, China, and the great steppes were for me colossi, and even to imagine drawing near to any one of them required a lifetime of study—one could scarcely hope to know them all well. Africa, on the other hand, struck me as more fragmentary, differentiated, miniaturized by its multiplicity, and thus more graspable, approachable.

For centuries people have been attracted by a certain aura of mystery surrounding this continent—a sense that there must be something unique in Africa, something hidden, some glistening oxidizing point in the darkness which it is difficult or well nigh impossible to reach. And many had the ambition to test their mettle here, to discover and uncover its bewildering, confounding core.

Herodotus was so intrigued. He writes that people from Cyrene, who had visited the oracle of Ammon, told him of a conversation they'd had with the king of the Ammonians, Etearchus (the Ammonians lived in the oasis of Siwa, in the Libyan desert). *Etearchus told them about a visit he had once had from some Nasamones, a Libyan tribe who live around the Gulf of Syrtis and the land a little way east of the Syrtis. During the course of their visit, the Nasamones were asked whether they could add to what was known about the uninhabited desert parts of Libya. In response, they told how some high-spirited chiefs' sons of their tribe, once they had reached adulthood, concocted a number of extraordinary schemes, including casting lots to choose five of their number to go and explore the Libyan desert, to find out if they could see more than had ever been seen before. Libyans—many tribes of them— have spread out along the whole of the Libyan coastline of the northern sea ... Then there is the part of Libya which is inland from the sea and from the people who occupy the seaboard: this is the part of Libya which is infested by wild animals. Further inland from the part full of animals Libya is sandy desert, totally waterless, and completely uninhabited by anyone or anything. So when the young men left their friends, the story goes, they were well equipped with food and water; they first passed through the inhabited region and then reached the part which is infested by wild animals. Next they started to travel in a westerly direction through the desert. After they had crossed a great deal of sandy country, surrounded by nothing but desert, they at last, after many days, saw trees growing on a plain. They approached the trees and tried to pick the fruit that was growing on them, but as they were doing so they were set upon by small men of less than normal human stature, who captured them and took them away. The two groups—the Nasamones and their guides—could not understand each other's language at all. They were taken through vast swamps and on the other side of these swamps they came to a town where everyone was the same size as their guides and had black skin. The town was on a sizeable river, which was flowing from west to east, and in it they could see crocodiles.*

This is a fragment from Book Two of Herodotus—the account of his trip into Egypt. In this passage, running several dozen pages, we can clearly observe the Greek's technique.

How does Herodotus work?

He is a consummate reporter: he wanders, looks, talks, listens, in order that he can later note down what he learned and saw, or simply to remember better.

How does he travel? If by land, then he goes on horseback, donkey, mule, or, most frequently, on foot.

Is he alone, or accompanied by a slave? We do not know for certain, but in those days, whoever had the means took a slave along on journeys. The slave carried the luggage, the gourd with water, the food, the writing implements—a roll of papyrus, clay tablets, brushes, gravers, ink. Because the hardships of the road leveled class differences, the slave was more of a traveling companion: he sustained one's spirits, afforded protection, asked for directions, reconnoitered. We can imagine how the relations between Herodotus—an inquisitive romantic desirous of knowledge for knowledge's sake, a diligent student of the impractical and the largely useless—and his slave, who on the road had to take care of things mundane, pedestrian, everyday, resembled those between Don Quixote and Sancho Panza. They were the ancient Greek progenitors of that later Castilian pair.

In addition to one's slave, a traveler also hired a guide and an interpreter. Herodotus's team might therefore have numbered—not counting himself—at least three people. But often wanderers headed in the same direction eventually joined up.

In the hot Egyptian climate, one makes best progress in the

morning. Travelers therefore rise at dawn, eat breakfast (wheat cakes, figs, sheep cheese, diluted wine—it's still permissible to drink, Islam will not seize control here for another thousand years), and then set out.

The goal of Herodotus's journeys? To collect new information about a country, its people, and their customs, or to test the reliability of data already gathered. Herodotus is not content with what someone else has told him—he tries to verify each thing, to compare and contrast the various versions he has heard, and then to formulate his own.

When he arrives in Egypt, its king, Psammetichus, has already been dead for one hundred and fifty years. Herodotus discovers (perhaps having been told this while still in Greece) that Psammetichus had been especially preoccupied with the question of *which was the oldest race on earth*. The Egyptians believed that they were, but Psammetichus, although their king, nevertheless had his doubts. He ordered a shepherd to raise two infants in uninhabited mountains. The language in which they spoke their first word would be proof that the people who speak that language are the oldest on earth. When the children were two years old and were hungry, they cried, "*Bekos!*," which meant "bread" in the Phrygian language. Psammetichus therefore proclaimed that the first people on earth were the Phrygians and that the Egyptians came only later, and with this clarification he earned his place in history. Psammetichus's inquiries interest Herodotus because they prove that the Egyptian ruler understood that unalterable law of history according to which whoever elevates himself will be humbled: Be not voracious, do not jostle your way to the fore, maintain moderation and humility; otherwise the chastising hand of Fate, which beheads braggarts and all who presume to lord it over others, will descend upon you. Psammetichus wanted to spare

Egyptians this misfortune and so moved them from history's front row to the second: the Phrygians were first, and you only came after.

This is what I heard . . . in Memphis during my conversations with the priests of Hephaestus. The information I gained there led me to travel to Thebes and to Heliopolis, to try to find out whether their accounts would agree with what I had heard in Memphis. Herodotus travels, therefore, to check, to compare, to clarify. He listens to the priests' descriptions of Egypt, its dimensions and geography, and comments: *My view is that they are right in saying this about the country.* He has his own opinion about everything and searches for confirmation in the stories of others.

Herodotus is especially fascinated by the Nile, this powerful and mysterious river. Where are its sources? Where do its waters come from? Whence comes the silt it carries, with which it fertilizes the rich delta of this immense nation? *As for the question where the Nile rises, no Egyptian or Libyan or Greek I have spoken to claimed to have a definite answer . . .* So he decides to search for the river's sources himself, venturing as far as he can into Upper Egypt. *I myself travelled as far as Elephantine and saw things with my very own eyes, and subsequently made enquiries of others . . .*

After Elephantine the land rises steeply, so that from then on one has to have a rope running from the boat to both banks, as one harnesses an ox, and to proceed like that. If the rope were to break, the boat would be carried downstream by the force of the current. This kind of terrain lasts for four days' travelling, and the Nile here twists and turns as much as the Meander. Another two months of traveling and sailing up the Nile *will bring you to a big city called Meroë. . . . But from then there is no reliable information to be had about it: the land is uninhabited because of the heat.*

He abandons the Nile, the mystery of its sources, the enigma of the seasonal rising and falling of its waters, and begins to observe closely the Egyptians, their way of being, their habits, their customs. He states that *almost all Egyptian customs and practices are the opposite of those of everywhere else.*

And he carefully, scrupulously records:

For instance, women go out to the town square and retail goods, while men stay at home and do the weaving ... Or again, men carry loads on their heads, while women do so on their shoulders. Women urinate standing up, while men do so squatting. They relieve themselves indoors, but eat outside on the streets; the reason for this, they say, is that things that are embarrassing but unavoidable should be done in private, while things which are not embarrassing should be done out in the open. There are no female priestesses of any god or goddess; all their gods, and goddesses too, are served in this capacity by men. Sons do not have to look after their parents if they do not want to, but daughters must even if they are reluctant.

Everywhere else in the world, priests have long hair, but in Egypt they shave their heads. . . . Everywhere else in the world people live separately from their animals, but animals and humans live together in Egypt. . . . They knead dough with their feet and clay with their hands ... Other people, unless they have been influenced by the Egyptians, leave their genitals in their natural state, but the Egyptians practise circumcision.

And on and on like this stretches the long list of Egyptian customs and behaviors, which surprise and astonish the newcomer with their otherness, distinctness, uniqueness. Herodotus is saying: Look, these Egyptians are so different from us Greeks, and yet we coexist so well together (there are many Greek colonies in Egypt at this time, whose inhabitants live on friendly terms with the local population). Yes, Herodotus is never shocked at difference, never condemns it; rather, he tries to learn about it, to understand and describe it. Difference? It serves by some paradox only to emphasize a greater oneness, speaking to its vitality and richness.

All the while he returns to his great passion, his obsession almost: reproaching his kinsmen for their pride, their conceitedness, their belief in their own superiority (it is from the Greek that the word "barbarian" comes, from the word "*barbaros,*" signifying someone who does not speak Greek but rather something garbled, incomprehensible, and who by the same token is a lower, inferior being). It was the Greeks who later instilled in other Europeans this tendency to turn up one's nose, and Herodotus fights the impulse every step of the way. And he does so when juxtaposing Greeks and Egyptians—as if purposely traveling to Egypt to gather there material and proof for his philosophy of moderation, modesty, and common sense.

He begins with a fundamental, transcendent matter: Where did the Greeks get their gods? Where do they come from? What do you mean, where do they come from? the Greeks respond. They are our gods! Oh, no, blasphemes Herodotus, we got our gods from the Egyptians!

How fortunate for him that he proclaimed this in a world in which mass communication did not yet exist and only a handful of people heard or read him. If his views had been disseminated widely, our Greek would have been instantly stoned, or burned on the pyre! But because Herodotus lived in a pre-media epoch, he could safely say that *the Egyptians were the first people in the world to hold general festive assemblies, and religious processions and parades, and the Greeks learnt from the Egyptians.* And what of the great Greek hero Heracles? . . . *The Greeks got the name of Heracles from Egypt, rather than the other way round . . . I have a great deal of evidence pointing in this direction. Here is just one item: both parents of the Greek Heracles, Amphitryon and Alcmene, trace their lineage back to Egypt. . . . In fact Heracles is a very ancient Egyptian god; as they themselves say, it was seventeen thousand years before the reign of King Amasis when the Twelve Gods descended from the Eight Gods, and they regard Heracles as one of the Twelve.*

I wanted to understand these matters as clearly as I could, so I also sailed to Tyre in Phoenicia, since I had heard that there was a sanctuary sacred to Heracles there, and I found that the sanctuary there was very lavishly appointed with a large number of dedicatory offerings. . . . I talked to the priests of the god there and asked them how long ago the sanctuary was founded, and I discovered that they too disagreed with the Greek account . . .

What is striking in these investigations is their secularism; in fact, the total absence in them of the sacred and the sublime, of the solemn language that typically attends such discourse. In this history the gods are not something unattainable, absolute, superworldly; the discussion is matter-of-fact and revolves around the simple question of who invented them—the Greeks or the Egyptians?

THE VIEW FROM THE MINARET

Herodotus's dispute with his countrymen is not over the existence of gods (our Greek would not conceive of the world without Higher Beings), but over who borrowed from whom their names and concepts.

To shore up his position that the entire Greek pantheon, or at least a significant portion of it, was derived from that of the Egyptians, he reached for what to him was an irrefutable argument—that of time, of precedence, of age. Which culture, he asks, is older, the Greek or the Egyptian? And he immediately answers as follows: *Some time ago the writer Hecataeus was in Thebes. He had studied his own lineage and had traced his family history back to a divine ancestor in the sixteenth generation. So the priests of Zeus there did to him what they did to me too (not that I had looked into my family history): they took me into the temple, showed me the wooden figures there, and counted them for me, up to the number I have mentioned [341].* (Clarification: Hecataeus is a Greek, and the colossi are Egyptian, and each one of them symbolizes one generation.) Observe, you Greeks, Herodotus seems to be saying, our genealogy goes back barely fifteen generations, whereas that of the Egyptians runs as much as 341. So exactly who borrowed gods from whom, if not we from the Egyptians, who are so much older than we are? And in order all the more emphatically to impress upon his compatriots the chasm of historic time separating the two nations, he elaborates: *Now, three hundred human generations make 10,000 years, because there are three generations in a hundred years.* And he quotes the opinion of Egyptian priests, that during this period *no god ever appeared in human form.* And so, Herodotus seems to be concluding, the gods that we deem to be our very own, Greek gods, already existed in Egypt for more than ten thousand years!

If one accepts that Herodotus is correct and that not only the gods, but culture in its entirety arrived in Greece (i.e., in Europe) from Egypt (i.e., from Africa), then one could argue for the non-European origins of European culture. A debate about this, brimming with ideology and emotion, has been raging for some two and a half thousand years already, and instead of stepping now onto such a dangerous minefield, let's note one thing: In Herodotus's world, one in which many cultures and civilizations existed side by side, relations between them were quite varied and fluid; we know of instances in which one civilization was in conflict with another, but there were others which maintained relations of exchange and mutual indebtedness, enriching one another politically. Moreover, there were civilizations that had once fought but subsequently cooperated, only later to find themselves once again at war. In short, for Herodotus, the world's multiculturalism was a living, pulsating tissue in which nothing was permanently set or defined, but which continually transformed itself, mutated, gave rise to new relationships and contexts.

I first see the Nile in 1960. My initial glimpse is in the evening, as my airplane approaches Cairo. From up high, the river at this time of day resembles a black, glistening trunk, forking and branching, surrounded by garlands of streetlights and bright rosettes defining the squares of this immense and bustling city.

Cairo at this moment in history is the hub of Third World

liberation movements. Many who live here will tomorrow become the presidents of new states, and various anticolonial African and Asian political parties have their seats in the city.

Cairo is also the capital of the United Arab Republic, which came into being two years earlier with the union of Egypt and Syria and whose president is the forty-two-year-old Egyptian Gamal Abdel Nasser—a tall, massive, commanding, and charismatic figure. In 1952, Nasser, then thirty-four, led the military coup that overthrew King Farouk; he became president four years later. For a long time he faced strong internal opposition: on the one hand Communists fought him, and on the other the Muslim Brotherhood, a conspiratorial organization of fundamentalists and Islamic terrorists. To combat them both Nasser maintained numerous police units of all sorts.

I rose early to go into the center of the city, which was a ways off. I was staying in a hotel in Zamalek, a rather wealthy residential neighborhood on an island in the Nile once largely the precinct of foreigners but by now also already inhabited by well-to-do Egyptians. Knowing that my suitcase would be searched as soon as I left the hotel, I thought it wise to remove an empty bottle of Czech pilsner beer I had stashed there and dispose of it along the way (in those days Nasser, a zealous Muslim, was conducting an anti-alcohol campaign). I concealed the bottle in a gray paper bag and walked out with it into the street. It was morning still, but already sultry and hot.

I looked around for a garbage can. But as I was doing so, I encountered the gaze of a guard sitting on a stool in the entryway from which I had just emerged. He was observing me. Eh, I thought, I won't throw out the bottle in front of him, because later he will rifle through the garbage can, find it, and report me to the hotel police. I walked on a bit and spotted an empty chest. I was on the verge of throwing in my bottle when I noticed two people in long white djellabas. They were standing and conversing, but at the same time watching me. No, I couldn't dispose of the bottle here: they would surely see it, and, moreover, the chest was not meant for refuse. I kept walking until I noticed another garbage can—and sitting nearby, at the entrance of a building, an Arab gazing at me attentively. No, no, I said to myself, you cannot risk it, he is looking at you very suspiciously. So, bag and bottle firmly in my hand, I nonchalantly strolled on.

Further on lay an intersection, in the middle of which stood a policeman with a club and a whistle—and on one of the corners sat a man on a stool, watching me. I noticed that he had only one eye, but this eye stared at me so insistently, so importunately, that I started to feel uncomfortable, even afraid that he would order me to show him what it was exactly that I was carrying. I quickened my pace to remove myself from his field of vision, and did so with all the more alacrity because I saw, flickering like a mirage in the distance ahead of me, a garbage can. Unfortunately, not far from it, in the shade of a small, scrawny tree, was an elderly man—seated and staring at me.

The street now turned, but beyond the turn everything was exactly as before. I couldn't throw the bottle out anywhere, because no matter where I tried, I encountered someone's gaze turned in my direction. Cars drove along the streets, donkeys pulled carts loaded with goods, a small herd of camels passed by stiffly, as if on stilts, but all this seemed to be taking place in the background, on some plane other than the one on which I was walking, caught in the sightlines of perfect strangers, who stood, strolled, talked, most frequently sat, and all the while stared at what I was doing. I grew increasingly nervous, and as I started to sweat profusely, the paper bag in my hand was getting soggy. I was afraid that the bottle would slip out of it and shatter on the sidewalk, further arousing the street's interest. I was truly at a loss as to what my next move should be, so I returned to the hotel and stuffed the bottle back into my suitcase.

It wasn't until nighttime that I walked out with it again. It was easier at night. I dropped the bottle into a garbage can, turned back, and with relief lay down to sleep.

Now, walking around the city, I began surveying the streets more closely. They all had eyes and ears. Here a building janitor, there a guard, over there a motionless figure in a beach chair, a bit farther on someone standing idly, just looking. Many of these people were not doing anything in particular, yet taken together their multiple lines of vision created a crisscrossing, coherent, panoptic observation network, covering the entire space of the street, on which nothing could occur without it being noticed. Noticed and reported.

It is an interesting subject: superfluous people in the service of brute power. A developed, stable, organized society is a community of clearly delineated and defined roles, something that cannot be said of the majority of Third World cities. Their neighborhoods are populated in large part by an unformed, fluid element, lacking precise classification, without position, place, or purpose. At any moment and for whatever reason, these people, to whom no one pays attention, whom no one needs, can form into a crowd, a throng, a mob, which has an opinion about everything, has time for everything, and would like to participate in something, mean something.

All dictatorships take advantage of this idle magma. They don't even need to maintain an expensive army of full-time policemen.

It suffices to reach out to these people searching for some significance in life. Give them the sense that they can be of use, that someone is counting on them for something, that they have been noticed, that they have a purpose.

The benefits of this relationship are mutual. The man of the street, serving the dictatorship, starts to feel at one with the authorities, to feel important and meaningful, and furthermore, because he usually has some petty thefts, fights, and swindles on his conscience, he now acquires the comforting sense of immunity. The dictatorial powers, meantime, have in him an inexpensive—free, actually—yet zealous and omnipresent agent-tentacle. Sometimes it is difficult even to call this man an agent; he is merely someone who wants to be recognized, who strives to be visible, seeking to remind the authorities of his existence, who remains always eager to render a service.

Once, as I was leaving the hotel, one of these people stopped me and asked that I follow him—he would show me an old mosque (I surmised that the man was one of them, as he always stood in the same spot, surveying what was probably his beat). I am by nature quite credulous, to the point even of regarding suspicion not as a manifestation of reason but as a character flaw; now the fact that an undercover agent proposed a visit to a mosque instead of ordering me to report to a police station brought me such relief—joy, even—that I agreed without a moment's hesitation. He was polite, wore a tidy suit, and spoke passable English. He told me that his name was Ahmed. "And mine is Ryszard," I replied, "but call me Richard, that will be easier for you." First, we walk. Then we ride for a long time on a bus. We get off in an old neighborhood—narrow little streets, winding alleyways, cramped passages, small palaces, dead ends, crooked, grayish-brown clay walls, corrugated tin roofs. Whoever walks in here without a guide will not walk out. An occasional door here and there, but all of them shut, bolted fast. It's deserted. Sometimes a woman hurries past like a shadow, sometimes a group of children appear, but the little ones quickly vanish again, frightened by Ahmed's shouts.

We arrive at a pair of massive metal doors, on which Ahmed taps out a code. There's a shuffling of sandals within, then the loud scraping of a key in the lock. A guard of indeterminate age and appearance opens the door and exchanges a few words with Ahmed. He leads us across a small enclosed courtyard to the doors of the minaret, its threshold slightly sunken into the ground. The doors are open, and both men gesture to me that I should enter. A dense twilight prevails within, but I can just make out the outlines of a winding staircase running along the minaret's interior wall, which in its shape resembles a large factory chimney. Somewhere way up high gleams a point of light, which from where we are standing looks like a pale and distant star—it is the sky.

"We go!" declares Ahmed, in a half-cajoling, half-commanding voice, having earlier told me that from the minaret's summit one can see all of Cairo. "Great view!" he assured me. We set off. From the start things don't look good. The stairs are not only extremely narrow, but slippery, covered in sand and loose plaster. But the worst thing is that they have no handrail, no handles, no ropes—nothing to grab on to.

Oh, well—we're off. We climb and we climb.

The most important thing is to not look down. Neither down nor up, but only at the closest point straight ahead, the steps directly in front at eye level. To turn off one's imagination, because the imagination only frightens. Some sort of yoga would be useful, some sort of nirvana and tantra, karman or mokosh, something that would allow one not to think, not to feel, or be.

Oh, well. Off again.

It is dark and cramped. Steep and twisting. From up there, from the top of the minaret, if the mosque is in use, a muezzin calls the faithful to prayer five times a day. These are drawn-out calls, uttered in singsong, sometimes very beautiful—solemn, moving, romantic. But nothing about this minaret suggested that it had been used by anyone in years. It was an abandoned place, smelling of dankness and old dust.

I don't know if it was from the effort, or from a still vague yet growing anxiety, but I started to feel fatigued and must have slowed down noticeably, because Ahmed began urging me on.

"Up! Up!" And because he walked behind me, he blocked all possibility of my turning around, retreating, escaping. I could not double back and pass him—the abyss was right there, to the side. Well, that's that, I said to myself, there's nothing to do but keep climbing.

We climb and we climb.

We had already ascended so far along this dangerous stairway with no railing or handholds that any sudden motion either of us might make would cause us both to tumble down several stories. We were united by a paradoxical embrace of untouchability—whoever would so much as touch the other would surely fall after him.

That symmetry would soon change to my disadvantage. At the end of the stairs, at the very top, was a small, narrow exterior terrace that encircled the minaret—the muezzin's perch. Normally, it would be surrounded by a brick or metal barrier. Here it appeared that the barrier had been metal, but after many centuries it had rusted and fallen away; the outcropping in the wall had no protection. Ahmed gently pushed me outside and, still standing on the stairs himself, leaning safely against the opening in the wall, said:

"Give me your money."

I had my money in my pants pocket, and was afraid that even as insignificant a gesture as reaching into it would cause me to plunge to the ground. Ahmed noticed my hesitation and repeated, this time in a sharper tone of voice:

"Give me your money!"

Looking up into the sky, anything just to not look down, carefully, cautiously, I slid my hand inside my pocket, and then just as slowly, very slowly, pulled out my wallet. He took it without a word, turned around, and started climbing down.

Now the most difficult thing was the route back from the exposed terrace to the first step of the stairs—a distance of less than one meter, which I crossed centimeter by painful centimeter. And then the torment of the descent, which I managed seemingly not on my own legs, but on oddly heavy, almost paralytic limbs that felt as though they had been nailed to the wall.

The guard opened the gates for me, and some children—the best guides in such back alleys—led me to a taxi.

I lived for several more days in Zamalek. I walked to downtown Cairo along the same street as before. I encountered Ahmed every day. He always stood in the same spot, covering his beat.

He looked at me with no expression on his face, as if we had never met.

And I looked at him, I believe, also without expression, as if we had never met.

ARMSTRONG'S CONCERT

Emerging from the airport in Khartoum, I told the taxi driver: Hotel Victoria. But without a word, with no explanation or justification, he took me to the Grand.

"It's always like this," explained a Libyan I met here later. "If a white man arrives in the Sudan, they think he must be an Englishman, and if he is an Englishman, then naturally he must be staying at the Grand. It's a good meeting place. Everybody comes here in the evening."

The driver, lifting my suitcase out of the trunk with one hand, inscribed a semicircle in the air with the other, indicating the kind of view I would have, and said with pride: "Blue Nile!" I looked at the river flowing below us—it had a grayish-emerald hue, was very wide, and flowed swiftly. The terrace of the hotel, long and shady, gave onto the river and was separated from it by a wide boulevard lined with old, branching fig trees.

A ceiling fan whirred in the room to which the porter led me, but its blades did not cool, merely churned the hot air about. It's a furnace in here, I thought, and decided to go into town. I had no idea what I was doing: I had walked barely several hundred meters when I realized that I had fallen into a trap. The heat emanating from the sky above ground me against the asphalt. My head was

117

pounding and I was short of breath. I felt unable to walk further, yet I also realized that I lacked the strength to turn back. I started to panic: if I didn't find some shade soon, the sun, I was certain, would kill me. I began to look about frantically, but saw that in the entire neighborhood I was the only moving thing. Everything around me was lifeless, shuttered, still. No people, not a single animal. My god, what was I to do? The sun was beating like a blacksmith's hammer on my head; I could feel its blows. It was too far to the hotel, and there was no building nearby, no entryway, no awning—no shelter. Finally, I spotted a mango tree. It was the closest thing in sight, and I dragged myself to it.

I reached the trunk and slid onto the ground, into the shade. Shade in such moments is something utterly tangible, and the body receives it as greedily as parched lips imbibe water.

In the afternoon the shadows lengthen, start to overlap, then darken and finally turn to black—it is evening. People come alive then, their will to live returns; they greet one another, converse, clearly happy that they have somehow managed to endure the quotidian cataclysm, to survive yet another day from hell. The city starts to bustle, cars appear in the streets, shops and bars fill with people.

I am in Khartoum awaiting two Czech journalists, with whom I am to travel to the Congo. The country is ablaze, consumed by the fires of civil war. I am growing agitated, because there is still no sign of my companions, who were supposed to fly in from Cairo. It is impossible to walk around the city by day, but it's also too hot in the room. And I can't stand it any longer on the terrace, because every few moments someone walks up to me and asks, Who are you? Where are you from? What is your name? Why did you come here? Do you want to start a business? Buy a plantation? If not, then where will you go next? Are you alone? Do you have a family? How many children do you have? What do you do? Have you been in the Sudan before? How do you like Khartoum? And the Nile? And your hotel? And your room?

The questions have no end. For the first few days I politely answer them. For what if they're being asked out of friendly curiosity, in accordance with local custom? On the other hand, it could be that those who are asking are from the police—better not to irritate them.

The questioners usually appear just once, replaced the following day by a fresh contingent; I am being passed along like a baton in a relay race, it seems.

Then two of them—always together—started to appear more repeatedly. They were extremely friendly. Students, I guess, with a lot of time on their hands these days, since the chief of the ruling junta, General Abboud, had shut down the university, as a breeding ground of discontent and rebellion.

One day, looking warily around them, they ask sotto voce if I would give them several pounds—they will buy some hashish, we will go out of the city, into the desert. What to do in the face of such an offer? I have never smoked hashish and am curious about how it makes one feel. On the other hand, what if these two are from the police, and trying to set me up, perhaps to extort money from me or else have me deported? And this at the very start of a journey that is promising to be so fascinating. I'm nervous, but choose the hashish and give them the money.

They pull up in the early evening in a beat-up, open Land Rover. It has only one headlight, but it is as strong as an antiaircraft reflector. Its beam parts the tropical darkness, a seemingly impenetrable black wall, opening it for a moment to allow the car through before it immediately closes in again. So dense is the dark that one would have the impression—were it not for the brutal potholes—that the vehicle is actually standing still.

We drive for maybe an hour, at first on blacktop, thin and crumbling along the edges, which soon peters out into a desert road along which lie occasional immense boulders, as if cast in bronze. At one of them we make a sharp turn and drive on for a moment longer, then come to a sudden halt. We are at the top of an escarpment, and the Nile glimmers silver below, illuminated by the moon. The landscape is reduced to a minimalist ideal—desert, river, moon—which at this moment is world enough.

One of the Sudanese removes from his bag a small and already opened bottle of White Horse, enough for a couple of swallows for each of us. Then he carefully twists together two thick joints, handing one to his friend and one to me. In the light of the match I suddenly see, emerging from the night, his dark face and shining eyes, with which he looks at me as if he is considering something. Perhaps he has given me poison, I think, but I don't know if I actually thought that, or if I thought about anything at all because I am already in another world, one in which I have become weightless, in which everything is incorporeal and everything is in motion. This movement is gentle, soft, wavy. It is a tender swaying. Nothing barrels ahead, nothing explodes. All is calm and quiet. A pleasant touch. A dream.

But the most extraordinary thing is the state of weightlessness. Not that awkward, ungainly weightlessness we have seen with astronauts, but a nimble, adroit, controlled one.

I do not remember how precisely I rose up off the ground, but I do distinctly remember floating through the skies, which were dark but of a darkness that was bright, even luminous, soaring amidst multicolored circles which parted, revolved, filled the space all around, and which resembled the light twirling of hula hoops.

Sailing along this way, I feel immense joy at being liberated from the burden of my own body, from the resistance it presents at every step, from its stubborn, relentless opposition. Who would have thought, but it turns out that your body need not be your enemy but rather can, if only for a moment, if only under such extraordinary circumstances, be your friend.

I can see in front of me the hood of the Land Rover, and out of the corner of my eye the shattered side-view mirror. The horizon is intensely pink, and the sand of the desert a graphite gray. The Nile in this predawn moment is a light navy. I am sitting in the open car and trembling from the cold. At this time of day the desert is as cold as Siberia; the chill pierces you to the bone.

But by the time we are once again entering the city, the sun has risen and it is instantly hot again. A terrible headache. The only thing I want is to sleep. Just to sleep. To not move, to not be, to not live.

Two days later, the Sudanese came to the hotel to ask how I was feeling. How am I feeling? Oh, my friends, you want to know how I feel? Yes, how do you feel, because Louis Armstrong is coming, there's a concert tomorrow in the stadium.

I am instantly better.

The stadium was quite a distance outside the city, small, shallow, with a capacity of at most five thousand spectators. Even so, only half the seats were occupied. In the center of the field stood a podium, weakly illuminated, but we were sitting near the front and could see Armstrong and his small orchestra well. The evening was hot and airless, and when Armstrong walked out, attired moreover in a jacket and bow tie, he was already soaked with perspiration. He greeted everyone, raising into the air the hand holding his golden trumpet, and said into the cheap, crackling microphone that he was pleased to be playing in Khartoum, and not only pleased, but downright delighted, after which he broke into his full, loose, infectious laugh. It was laughter that invited others to laugh along, but the audience remained aloofly silent, not quite certain how to behave. The drums and the bass resounded and Armstrong launched into a song appropriate enough to the time and place—"Sleepy Time Down South." It is actually difficult to say when one first heard Armstrong's voice; there is something in it that makes one feel one has known it forever, and when he starts to sing, everyone, with the most sincere conviction of his or her connoisseurship, proclaims: Why yes, that's him, that's Satchmo!

Yes, that was him—Satchmo. He sang "Hello Dolly, this is Louis, Dolly," he sang "What a Wonderful World" and "Moon River," he sang "I touch your lips and all at once the sparks go flying, those devil lips." But the spectators continued to sit silently. There was no applause. Did they not understand the words? Was there too much openly expressed eroticism in all this for Muslim tastes?

After each number, and even during the playing and singing, Armstrong wiped his face with a large white handkerchief. These handkerchiefs were constantly changed for him by a man whose sole purpose in accompanying Armstrong around Africa seemed to have been this. I saw later that he had an entire bag of them, dozens and dozens probably.

After the concert people dispersed quickly, vanishing into the night. I was shocked. I had heard that Armstrong's concerts elicited great enthusiasm, frenzy, ecstasy. There was no trace of these raptures in the stadium in Khartoum, despite the fact that Satchmo played many songs from the American South, from Alabama and Louisiana, where he himself came from—songs that had originated with African slaves. But by then their Africa and this one here belonged to different worlds, lacking a common language, unable to communicate much less partake of an emotional oneness.

The Sudanese drove me back to the hotel. We sat down on the terrace for some lemonade. Moments later a car brought Armstrong. He sat down with relief at a table, or, more precisely, he collapsed into the chair. He was a stout, thickset man with wide, drooping shoulders. The waiter brought him an orange juice. He downed it in a single gulp, and then another glass, and another. He was depleted, sitting with his head bowed, silent. He was sixty years old at the time and—something I didn't then know—already suffering from heart disease. Armstrong during the concert and Armstrong immediately after it were two entirely different people: the first was merry, cheerful, animated, with a powerful voice, able to coax an astonishing range of tones from his trumpet; the second was heavy, exhausted, weak, his face covered in wrinkles, extinguished.

Whoever leaves the safe walls of Khartoum and sets off into the desert must remember that danger and traps lie in wait. Sandstorms constantly change the configuration of the landscape, moving the orientation points about, and if as a result of these relentless natural caprices the traveler should lose his way, he will surely perish. The desert is mysterious and can arouse fear. No one goes off into it alone, largely because no one can carry enough water to conquer the distance separating one well from the next.

During his trip through Egypt, Herodotus, knowing that the Sahara was all around, wisely kept to the river, staying always close to the Nile. The desert is a sunny fire, and fire is a wild beast, which can devour everything: *the Egyptians regard fire as a living creature (one which consumes everything it takes hold of until at last, when it is sated, it dies along with the object it has been devouring)* ... And he offers as an example what happened when the king of the Persians, Cambyses, having set off to conquer Egypt and then Ethiopia, dispatched part of his army against the Ammonians, a people inhabiting the oases of the Sahara. These troops, departing from Thebes, arrived after seven days of marching through the desert in a city called Oäsis, at which point all trace of them disappeared: ... *after that the only information available comes directly or indirectly from the Ammonians themselves; no one else can say what happened to them, because they did not reach the Ammonians and they did not come back either. The Ammonians, however, add an explanation for their disappearance. They say that after the army had left Oäsis and was making its way across the desert towards them—in other words, somewhere between Oäsis and their lands—an extraordinarily strong south wind, carrying along with it heaps of sand, fell on them while they were taking their midday meal and buried them.*

The Czechs arrived, Dushan and Jarda, and we set off immediately for the Congo. The first settlement on the Congolese side was a roadside hamlet—Aba. It nestled in the shade of an enormous green wall, the jungle, which began here abruptly, rearing up like a steep mountain from the plain.

There was a gas station in Aba, as well as several shops. These were shaded by decaying wooden arcades, beneath which lounged several idle, motionless men. They sprang to life when we stopped to ask about what awaited us deeper inside the country, and where we could change some pounds into local francs.

They were Greeks, and formed a colony similar to the hundreds that were already scattered around the world in Herodotus's time.

That type of settlement had clearly survived among them to this day.

I had my copy of Herodotus in my bag, and when we were leaving I showed it to one of the Greeks as he was saying goodbye. He saw the name on the cover and smiled, but in such a way that I couldn't tell if he was expressing pride, or else embarrassment at having no idea who this was.

THE FACE OF ZOPYRUS

We have come to a standstill on the outskirts of the little town of Paulis (Congo, Eastern Province). We have run out of gas, and live in hope that someone will pass this way one day and agree to give us some, if only a jerry can full. Until then, we wait in the only place possible—a school run by Belgian missionaries, whose prior is the delicate, emaciated, and seriously ailing Abbé Pierre. Because the country is in the grips of civil war, the missionaries instruct their charges in military drills. The children march around in fours, holding long thick sticks against their shoulders, singing and shouting out. How stern their facial expressions are, how vigorous their gestures, how at once solemn and exciting is this game of soldier!

I have a cot in an empty classroom at the end of the school barracks. It is quiet here, and the sounds of the battle drills barely reach me. Out front is a flower bed full of blooms—lush, tropically overgrown dahlias and gladioli, centauries, and still other beauties, which I am seeing for the first time and whose names I do not know.

I too am infected with the contagion of war—not the local one, but another, distant in place and time, which the king of the Persians, Darius, is waging against rebellious Babylon, and which Herodotus describes. I am sitting in the shade on the verandah, swiping at flies and mosquitoes and reading his book.

Darius is a young, twenty-something-year-old man, who has just become the king of what was then the world's most powerful empire. In this multinational realm, one people or another are constantly lifting up their heads, rebelling, and battling for liberty. All such uprisings and revolts the Persians quash with ruthless ease. But this time a great threat has arisen, a genuine danger that could severely affect Persia's destiny: Babylon, the capital of the Babylonian empire that had been incorporated by King Cyrus into the Persian empire nineteen years earlier, in 538 B.C.E., is in mutiny.

That Babylon desires independence is hardly surprising. Situated at the intersection of trade routes connecting the East with the West and the North with the South, it is the largest and most dynamic city on earth. It is the center of world culture and learning, renowned especially for mathematics and astronomy, geometry and architecture. A century will pass before Greek Athens is able to rival it.

For the time being, the Babylonians are preparing an anti-Persian uprising and a declaration of sovereignty. Their timing is good. They know that the Persian court has just come through a long period of anarchy, during which power had been held by the priestly caste of the Magi. They were recently overthrown in a palace coup staged by a group of Persian elites, who had only just selected from among themselves a new king—Darius. Herodotus notes that the Babylonians *were very well prepared.* Clearly, he writes, *they had spent the whole troubled period of the Magus' rule ... getting ready for a siege, and somehow nobody had noticed that they were doing so.*

The following passage now appears in Herodotus's text: *Once their rebellion was out in the open, this is what they did. The Babylonian men gathered together all the women of the city—with the exception of their mothers and of a single woman chosen by each man from his own household—and strangled them. The single woman was kept on as a cook, while all the others were strangled to conserve supplies.*

I do not know if Herodotus realized what he was writing. Did he think about those words? Because at that time, in the sixth century, Babylon had at least two to three hundred thousand inhabitants. It follows, then, that tens of thousands of women were condemned to strangulation—wives, daughters, sisters, grandmothers, cousins, lovers.

Our Greek says nothing more about this mass execution. Whose decision was it? That of the Popular Assembly? Of the Municipal Government? Of the Committee for the Defense of Babylon? Was there some discussion of the matter? Did anyone protest? Who decided on the method of execution—that these women would be strangled? Were there other suggestions? That they be pierced by spears, for example? Or cut down with swords? Or burned on pyres? Or thrown into the Euphrates, which coursed through the city?

There are more questions still. Could the women, who had been waiting in their homes for the men to return from the meeting during which sentence was pronounced upon them, discern something in their men's faces? Indecision? Shame? Pain? Madness? The little girls of course suspected nothing. But the older ones? Wouldn't instinct tell them something? Did all the men observe the agreed silence? Didn't conscience strike any of them? Did none of them experience an attack of hysteria? Run screaming through the streets?

And later? Later, they gathered them all together and strangled them. There must have been a meeting place, where everyone had to report and where the selection took place. Those who were to live to one side. And the others? Were there municipal guards of some sort who strangled one by one the girls and women brought to them? Or did the husbands and fathers have to strangle them themselves, in the presence of judges appointed to supervise the executions? Was there silence? Or were there moans, and pleading for the lives of infants, daughters, sisters? How were the bodies disposed of, the tens of thousands of them? Because a decent burial of the dead is a condition for the continued peace of the living; without it, the spirit of the departed returns by night and torments the survivors. Did Babylon's nights terrify its men from that moment onward? Did they wake in panic? Did nightmares haunt them? Were they unable to fall asleep? Did they feel demons seizing them by the throat?

To conserve supplies. Yes, because the Babylonians were preparing for a long siege. They understood the value of Babylon, a rich and flowering metropolis, a city of hanging gardens and gilded temples, and knew that Darius would not readily retreat but would do his utmost to continue their subjugation, if not by the sword, then by siege of hunger.

The king of the Persians did not waste a moment. As soon as news of the rebellion reached him, *he mustered his army in full strength and marched against them. Once he reached Babylon he began to besiege the city, but the inhabitants were not in the slightest bit concerned. They used to climb up to the bastions of the city wall and strut about there, taunting Darius and his army. Once one of them called out, "What are you doing sitting there, men of Persia? Why don't you just go away? Babylon will fall into your hands only when mules start bearing young."* (And mules, as we are meant to know, are usually infertile.)

They jeered at Darius and his army.

Let us imagine this scene. The world's largest army has arrived at the gates of Babylon. It has made camp around the city, which is encircled by massive walls of clay brick. The city wall is several meters high and so wide that a wagon drawn by four horses all in a row can be driven along its top. There are eight great gates, and the whole thing is additionally protected by a deep moat. In the face of this monumental fortification, Darius's army is helpless. It will be twelve hundred more years before gunpowder makes its appearance in this part of the world. Firearms won't be invented for another two thousand years. There aren't even any siege machines—the Persians do not possess battering rams, catapults. So the Babylonians feel invincible, able to behave with impunity—nothing can happen to them. It is no wonder, therefore, that standing atop their wall, they *were taunting Darius and his army.* Taunting the greatest army in the world!

The distance between both sides is so small that the besieged and the besiegers can converse, the former cursing the latter's names. If Darius happens to ride close to the walls, he can hear the worst invectives and terms of abuse hurled his way. It is quite humiliating, all the more so because the siege has lasted so long already: *A year and seven months passed, and Darius and his men were getting frustrated with their inability to overcome the Babylonians.*

And then something changes. *In the twentieth month a remarkable thing happened to Zopyrus . . . : one of his packmules gave birth.*

Young Zopyrus is the son of the Persian noble Megabyzus and belongs to the small elite of the Persian empire. He is excited by the news that his mule has produced offspring. He sees a sign from the gods in this, their signal that Babylon can indeed be conquered. He goes to Darius, recounts everything, and asks how important the capture of Babylon is to him.

Very, Darius replies. But the Persians have been laying siege to the city for almost two years, they have already tried countless methods, stratagems, and subterfuges, none of which have made even the slightest dent in the walls of Babylon. Darius is discouraged and doesn't know what to do: to withdraw covered in shame, and, moreover, losing the empire's most important satrapy; to press on, the prospects for conquering the city looking impossibly slim.

Doubts, dilemmas, hesitations. Seeing the king so dejected, Zopyrus tried *to find a way whereby he could be the one to bring about the fall of Babylon, as his own achievement.* After giving it some thought, he takes up an iron or brass knife, cuts off his own nose and ears, shaves his head (as criminals are shorn), and has himself flogged. Thus mutilated, wounded, streaming with blood, he presents himself to Darius. At the sight of Zopyrus's injuries, Darius goes into shock. *He jumped up from his throne with a cry and asked who it was who had disfigured him and why.*

The wound where his nose had been, the damaged bone, must have been horribly painful, and the upper lip, cheeks, and the rest of his face were surely grotesquely swollen, his eyes bloodied, and yet Zopyrus manages to answer:

"No one did it to me, my lord; after all, you are the only person who could. I did it to myself, because I think it's dreadful to have Assyrians mocking Persians."

To which Darius replies:

"No, that won't do at all. To claim that you have given yourself these permanent injuries as a way of doing something about the people we are besieging is to gloss over the utter vileness of your deed. It's just stupid to think that your injuries might hasten our opponents' surrender. You must be out of your mind to have disfigured yourself like this."

In Zopyrus's preceding statement Herodotus presents to us a mind-set that had manifested itself in this culture thousands of years before—namely, that a man whose dignity was undermined, who felt himself humiliated, could free himself from the burning sensation of shame and disgrace only by an act of self-destruction. I feel that I have been scarred, and being thus scarred, I cannot live. Death is preferable to a life with the mark of shame burning into my face. Zopyrus wants to liberate himself from just such a feeling. And he does this by altering his face, changing that ignominious Persian physiognomy which the Babylonians mocked into a more dreadful and terrifying version of itself.

It is noteworthy that Zopyrus does not consider the Babylonians' affront as an individual act of injustice, directed against him alone. He does not say, They insulted me; he says, They insulted us—all us Persians. Yet he does not see exhorting all Persians to war as the way out of this degrading predicament and chooses instead a singular, individual act of self-destruction (or self-mutilation), which for him is a liberation.

It is true that Darius condemns Zopyrus's action as irresponsible and reckless, but he will soon take advantage of it, seizing upon it as a last resort, a way to save the nation, the empire, the majesty of monarchical power from disgrace.

He accepts Zopyrus's plan, which is as follows: Zopyrus will go to the Babylonians, pretending that he is fleeing from persecutions and tortures inflicted upon him by Darius. And what better proof of this than his wounds! He is certain that he will convince the Babylonians, that he will gain their confidence, and that they will give him command of the army. And then he will let the Persians into Babylon.

One day, from atop their wall, the Babylonians notice a bloodied human figure dressed in rags dragging itself toward their city-fortress. The wretch keeps looking over his shoulder, checking to be sure he is not being pursued. *The look-outs posted on the towers spotted him, ran down, opened one of the gates a crack, and asked him who he was and what he had come for. He answered that he was Zopyrus and that he was deserting to their side. At this, the gatekeepers took him to the Babylonian council, where he stood forth and complained to them about his sufferings. He blamed Darius for his self-inflicted injuries ... He said, "... He will certainly not get away with mutilating me like this."*

The council believes these words and gives him an army, so that he can exact his vengeance. That is precisely what Zopyrus was waiting for. As prearranged, on the tenth day after Zopyrus's pretend flight to Babylon, Darius sends one thousand of his weakest troops toward one of the besieged city's gates. The Babylonians burst out from the gate and cut down the Persians to the last man. Seven days later, once again as Darius and Zopyrus have prearranged, the Persian king sends another contingent of inferior soldiers to Babylon's gate, two thousand of them this time, and the Babylonians, under Zopyrus's command, decimate these as well. Zopyrus's fame among the Babylonians grows: they consider him a hero and a savior. Twenty days pass and in accordance with the plan Darius sends out another four thousand soldiers. The Babylonians annihilate them, too, and then gratefully appoint Zopyrus their commander in chief and defender of the city.

Zopyrus is now in possession of the keys to all the gates. On the appointed day, Darius storms Babylon from all sides, and Zopyrus opens the gates. The city is conquered. *Now that the Babylonians were in his power, Darius demolished the city wall and tore down all its gates . . . and he also had about three thousand of the most prominent men impaled on stakes.*

Once again Herodotus treats these catastrophic events in a most offhanded fashion. Let's skip the demolishing of the walls—although this must have been a gargantuan undertaking. But impaling three thousand men on the stake? How was this done? Was one stake set, as the men of Babylon stood in a line, awaiting their turn? Did each look on as the man in front of him was impaled? Were they bound to prevent their escape? Or were they simply paralyzed with fear? Babylon was the center of world learning, a city of the world's preeminent mathematicians and astronomers. Were they also impaled? If so, then for how many generations, centuries even, did this retribution stunt the growth of human knowledge?

But at the same time Darius was thinking about the future of that metropolis and its inhabitants. *He returned the city to the remaining Babylonians and let them live there. As was explained earlier, the Babylonians had strangled their wives to ensure that they had enough to eat; so in order to make sure that they would have enough women to have offspring, Darius ordered all the nearby peoples to send women to Babylon, and gave each a quota, which resulted in a grand total of fifty thousand women congregating there. Today's Babylonians are descended from these women.*

As a reward, he gave Zopyrus command over Babylon for the rest of his life. But *it is said that Darius often expressed the opinion that he would prefer to see Zopyrus without his injuries than gain twenty more Babylons.*

THE HARE

Whose arrows are sharp
and all their bows bent
their horses' hoofs shall be counted like flint
and their wheels like a whirlwind.

—ISAIAH 5:28

The king of Persia concludes one conquest and immediately embarks on another: *After the capture of Babylon, the next military expedition commanded by Darius in person was against the Scythians.*

Consider where Babylon lay in relation to Scythian territories. To get from one to the other, one had to traverse easily half of the known world in Herodotus's time. The march must have lasted months. It took a month in those days for an army to cover five or six hundred kilometers, and here we are proposing a distance several times greater.

This enterprise surely took its toll even on hardy Darius. Yes, he rode in a royal carriage, but one can easily imagine that in those days even such a conveyance must have lurched and rattled horribly. Springs and suspensions were unknown, as were tires or even rubber rings. Furthermore, over long stretches of the journey there would have been no roads at all.

The ambition must therefore have been powerful enough to overrule all feelings of discomfort, fatigue, physical pain. In Darius's case it was to expand his empire, and by doing so to increase his sway over the world. It is interesting to ponder what people in those times understood by "the world." There were still no adequate maps, atlases, or globes. Ptolemy would not be born for another four centuries, Mercator not for another two millennia. It was impossible to gaze down on our planet taking a bird's-eye view (could there even have been such a concept?). One acquired geographical knowledge by becoming aware of a neighbor not of one's own people, and one passed on that knowledge orally:

We are called the Giligamae. Our neighbors are the Asbystae. And you, Asbystae, whom do you share a border with? We Giligamae? We share one with the Auschisae. And the Auschisae with the Nasamones. And you, Nasamones? To the south, with the Garamantes, and to the west, with the Macae. And these Macae—whom do they adjoin? The Macae abut the Gindanes. And you? We share a border with the Lotus-eaters. And they? With the Ausees. And who lives beyond that, truly far, far away? The Ammonians. And beyond them? The Atlantes. And beyond the Atlantes? No one knows, and no one even attempts to imagine.

So there was no glancing at a map (which didn't exist, after all) to ascertain, as is taught in schools (which didn't yet exist, either), that Russia neighbors China. To determine that fact, one had to question dozens of Siberian tribes (having first elected to travel in an easterly direction), until one finally encountered those that shared a border with the Chinese ones. But when Darius set out against the Scythians, he already possessed some knowledge about them and knew—more or less—where to look for them.

The Great Ruler, occupied with the conquest of the world, goes about it somewhat like an avid but still methodical collector. He says to himself: I already have the Ionians, I have the Carians and the Lydians. Who's missing? I lack the Trachinians, I lack the Getae, I lack the Scythians. And instantly the desire to possess those still beyond his grasp begins to burn in his heart. Whereas they, still free and independent, do not yet comprehend that by attracting the attention of the Great Ruler, they have caused a sentence to be passed upon themselves. Nor that the rest is merely a matter of time. Because rarely is such a sentence carried out with reckless and irresponsible impetuosity. Usually in these situations, the King of Kings resembles a skulking predator, who already has his prey in his ken and waits patiently for the propitious moment.

In the realm of human affairs, admittedly, one also needs a pretext. It is important to give it the rank of a universal imperative or of a divine commandment. The range of choices is not great: either it is that we must defend ourselves, or that we have an obligation to help others, or that we are fulfilling heaven's will. The optimal pretext would link all three of these motives. The attackers should appear in the glory of the anointed, in the role of those who have found favor in his chosen god's eye.

Darius's pretext?

Centuries ago, the Scythians invaded the territory of the Medes (another Iranian people, like the Persians) and ruled over them for twenty-eight years. Darius decides that he will avenge this now-forgotten episode. We have here another example of Herodotus's law: the one who started something is always responsible, and because he did some evil, he must be punished, however many years after the fact. Darius launches a campaign against the Scythians.

It is difficult to define the Scythians.

They appeared seemingly out of nowhere, existed for a thousand years, and then vanished, leaving behind beautiful metal artifacts and the mounds in which they buried their dead. They organized themselves into groups, later even a confederation of tribes that inhabited the expanses of eastern Europe and the Asiatic steppe. Their elite and vanguard were the Royal Scythians—mounted warriors, restless and rapacious, whose home base was the lands to the north of the Black Sea, between the Danube and the Volga.

The Scythians were also a terrifying myth. Their name was synonymous with foreign and mysterious peoples, savage and cruel, who swoop down out of nowhere, attack, loot, slash, kidnap.

It is difficult to see the Scythian lands, their homes and their herds, at close range, because all is obscured by a snow-white veil: *Beyond the territory of their neighbours to the north there are such piles of feathers, according to the Scythians, that nothing can be seen and the land cannot be traversed either. They say that there are too many feathers filling the land and the air to enable sight to function.* Which Herodotus comments upon this way: *What about the feathers with which, according to the Scythians, the air is filled, and which stop them either seeing or travelling over more of the continent? My view is that it is constantly snowing north of the region in question (less in summer than in winter, of course), and that it is the harshness of the winter that makes the northern part of the continent uninhabitable. Now, snow does look like feathers, as anyone who has ever seen snow falling thickly from close up can confirm; so I think that the Scythians and their neighbours are describing the snow metaphorically as feathers.*

As Napoleon will do twenty-four centuries later, Darius now sets forth for these lands. He is counseled against it: *Artabanus the son of Hystaspes asked him to cancel his expedition against the Scythians and cited the difficulty of getting at them as the reason for his request.* But Darius does not listen, and after massive preparations departs at the head of a great army comprising *all the tribes and peoples . . . he ruled.* Herodotus cites what was then an astronomical figure: *The total number of men—*

including cavalry contingents, but excluding the fleet—was 700,000, and then there were six hundred ships assembled there too.

He orders a bridge built over the Bosporus. Sitting on this throne, he observes his army crossing it. The next bridge he constructs is over the Danube. Once his army has made its way across, he orders the bridge dismantled. But one of his commanders, a certain Coës, pleads with him not to do so:

"My lord," he said, "you are about to invade a land where agriculture is completely unknown and there are no settlements. I would suggest that you leave this bridge in place . . . Then, if we find the Scythians and do what we came for, we have a way out of the country afterwards; alternatively, if we fail to locate them, our return, at least, is ensured. I'm confident that the Scythians will never defeat us in battle, but I still worry in case something untoward happens to us as we roam here and there trying and failing to locate them."

This Coës will turn out to be a prophet.

Darius agrees to leave the bridge intact and continues on his way.

Meantime, the Scythians learn that a great army is advancing against them, and sending word to the kings of the neighboring nations for a meeting, they find a conference already in progress. Among those in attendance is the king of the Budinians—*a large and populous tribe, with piercing grey eyes and bright red hair.* There is the king of the Agathyrsians, among whom *any woman is available to any man for sex, to ensure that the men are all brothers and that they are on amicable and good terms with one another* . . . There is the king of the Taurians—if they *capture their enemies, each of them cuts off a head and takes it back to his house, where he sticks it on the end of a long pole and sets it up to tower high above his house, usually over the chimney. It is their belief that these heads, hanging there, protect the whole household.*

The Scythian delegates address the various assembled kings and, informing them of the approaching Persian avalanche, make an appeal: *"You absolutely must not stand idly by and watch us being destroyed.*

We should form a common plan and resist the invasion together." And to per-suade them to join forces and cooperate, the Scythians say that the Persians aim to conquer not only the Scythians, but all peoples. *No sooner has [the Persian] entered this continent of ours than he sets about subjugating everyone in his path.*

As Herodotus tells it, the kings listened to the Scythian argu-ment but were divided in their views. Some believed that they should indeed help the Scythians unconditionally and support them in their hour of need, but others preferred to remain on the sidelines for the time being, and believed that in point of fact the Persians, wishing only to revenge themselves upon the Scythians, would leave the others alone.

In the face of this disunity, the Scythians, knowing their oppo-nent to be very powerful, *decided against straight fighting and open warfare, and in favour of retreat. The plan was that as they rode back in retreat they would fill in any wells and springs they passed, and destroy any vegetation they found growing in the ground.* Furthermore, they would divide into two groups and, keeping themselves always at a distance of one day's march from the Persians, always retreating, would disorient them with constant change of direction, all the while drawing them ever deeper into the interior of the country.

What they decided upon they now set about implementing.

But first *the wagons in which all their women and children lived were sent off with orders to keep heading north, and all their livestock was sent with the wagons . . .* North, where the cold and the snow would offer them protection from the people of the hot south, the Persians.

When Darius's army finally enters, the Scythians do not wage open warfare against it. Their tactic, their weapon, is deceit, eva-sion, ambush. Where are they? Cunning, fast, elusive as the hare, they appear suddenly on the steppe and vanish just as rapidly.

Darius sees their cavalry over here, over there, spots their swift vanguard only for it to disappear moments later beyond the horizon. He receives reports of their being observed somewhere in the north. He steers his army there, but when it arrives, everyone realizes that they have entered into a wasteland. *This seven-day stretch of empty land, completely uninhabited by human beings, lies to the north of the Budinian territory*, etc., etc. Herodotus writes at length about this: The Scythians, in order to force their recalcitrant neighbors into battle, weave about in such a way as to propel Darius's pursuing troops onto the lands of the tribes that had refused to commit themselves to battle. Now, finding themselves invaded by the Persians, they must fight against Darius alongside the Scythians.

The king of the Persians feels increasingly helpless, and finally sends a messenger to the Scythian king demanding that his troops either stand and fight or else recognize his dominion over them. To which the king of the Scythians replies: They are not in flight but having neither cities nor farmland they have nothing to defend. Therefore he sees no reason to fight. But as for the Persians claiming to be their master, and demanding acknowledgment of same—the Scythian promises Darius will pay dearly.

The mention of slavery made the Scythian kings furious. They loved liberty. They loved the steppe. They loved boundless space. Outraged by how Darius was treating them, his shaming insult, they now adjust their tactics. They decide not only to bob and weave, making zigzags and loops, but also to attack the Persians wherever they forage to feed themselves and their horses.

Darius's army finds itself in an increasingly difficult predicament. Here, on the great steppe, we can observe the collision of two military styles, two structures: the tight, rigid, monolithic organization of the regular army and the loose, mobile, ever-shifting configurations of small tactical cells. The latter is also an army, but an amorphous army of shadows, of phantoms, of thin air.

"Show yourselves!" cries Darius into the emptiness. But the only answer is the silence of an alien, unattainable, immeasurable land, upon which his mighty army stands—useless, impotent, and feckless, for only an opponent could actualize it, and he does not wish to appear.

The Scythians, seeing that Darius understands his predicament, send a herald with gifts for him—a bird, a mouse, a frog, and five arrows.

Every human being has his own particular web of associations for identifying and interpreting reality, which, most often instinctively and unthinkingly, he superimposes upon every set of circumstances. Frequently, however, those external circumstances do not conform with, or fit, the structure of our webs, and then we can misread the unfamiliar reality, and interpret its elements incorrectly. On such occasions, we move about in an unreal world, a landscape of dead ends and misleading signs.

It is now thus for the Persians.

Having received the gifts, *the Persians talked the matter over among themselves. Darius' opinion was that the Scythians were giving him earth and water and tokens of their surrender. His reasoning was as follows: a mouse is born in the ground and eats the same food as human beings, a frog lives in water, a bird closely resembles a horse, and they gave arrows as symbols of their own military might. This was the view that Darius expressed, but Gobryas ... challenged this view of Darius' and came up with an alternative. This is how he explained the message of the gifts: "Listen, men of Persia: if you don't become birds and fly up into the sky, or mice and burrow into the ground, or frogs and jump into the lakes, you'll never return home, because you'll be shot down by these arrows." So the Persians were trying to work out what the gifts meant.*

Meantime, *the Scythians ... drew up their infantry and cavalry and prepared to attack the Persians.* They must have been an awesome sight. Excavations of Scythian burial mounds—and they interred their dead fully dressed, together with their horses, weapons, tools, and jewelry—indicate their clothing was covered in gold and copper, that their horses wore harnesses studded and clasped with sculpted metal, that they wielded swords and axes, and carried carefully chiseled and richly decorated bows and quivers.

Two armies face each other. One the Persian, the largest in the world, and the second the Scythian, small, standing in defense of a land whose interior is hidden from Darius by a white curtain of snow.

It must be a moment brimming with tension, I think to myself—and just then a boy arrives to say that Abbé Pierre is inviting me to the other end of the courtyard, where a meal has been set out on a table in the shade of a spreading mango tree.

"In a moment! Just one second!" I call out. I wipe my forehead, damp from the excitement, and keep reading:

They were ready and waiting in their ranks when a hare ran across the open space between the two sides, and one after another all the Scythians spotted it and gave chase. Seeing the Scythians in disarray and hearing their cries, Darius asked why his opponents were in such a state of commotion. When he heard that they were chasing a hare, he told his confidants, "These Scythians certainly hold us in contempt. I now think that Gobryas' interpretation of their gifts was right, and what we need is a good plan for getting safely back home."

The historic role of a hare? Scholars agree that it was the Scythians who stopped Darius's march on Europe. If this hadn't happened, the fate of the world might have been quite otherwise. And what decided Darius's final retreat was that the Scythians, lightheartedly pursuing a hare in plain view of the Persian army, demonstrated that they were ignoring it, thumbing their nose at it, holding it in contempt. And this disdain, this humiliation, was a more dreadful blow for the king of the Persians than losing a great battle.

Night falls.

Darius orders the campfires lit, as is customary at this time of day. The soldiers who no longer have the strength to march—the camp hangers-on, the vagabonds, the sick—are to remain by the fires. He commands that the donkeys be tethered, so that they will bray, creating the impression that life as usual continues in the Persian camp. And he himself, at the head of his army, begins the retreat under the cover of darkness.

AMONG DEAD KINGS
AND FORGOTTEN GODS

Wishing to stay awhile longer with Darius, I break the sequential order of my travels and leap now from Congo in 1960 to Iran in 1979—the country of a raging Islamic revolution at whose head stands a hoary, sullen, and unbowed old man, Ayatollah Khomeini.

Slaves and victims as we are of time's implacable progression, we find it tempting now and then to jump this way from epoch to epoch, and thereby, if only for a moment, if only illusorily, to stand above time and juxtapose at will, assemble or separate, its different points, stages, periods.

So why is Darius so compelling? Reading what Herodotus writes on eastern rulers, we can see that although all of them perform cruel deeds, there are occasionally those capable of more, and that this "more" can be something useful and even good. It was thus with Darius. On the one hand, he was a murderer. Here he is setting off with his army against the Scythians: *At this point a Persian called Oeobazus, all three of whose sons were in the army, asked Darius whether one of them could be left behind. Darius replied in a friendly fashion, as if the request were reasonable, and said that he would leave all three behind. Oeobazus was overjoyed at the prospect of his sons being released from military service, but Darius ordered those responsible for such things to kill all three of them. So he did leave them there in Susa—with their throats cut.*

On the other hand, however, Darius was a good administrator, took care of the roads and the mail, minted money, and supported trade. And first and foremost, almost from the moment when he donned the royal diadem, he began to erect a magnificent city, Persepolis, whose importance and luster we would compare to that of Mecca and Jerusalem.

I am witness in Tehran to the last weeks of the shah's regime. The gigantic, even normally chaotic city scattered over a large swath of sandy terrain is now in a state of total disarray. Traffic is paralyzed by endless daily demonstrations. Men, invariably black-haired, and women, invariably in hijabs, walk in kilometer- and even several-kilometer-long columns, chanting, shouting, rhythmically shaking their raised fists. Every now and then armored trucks drive into the streets and squares and fire at the demonstrators. They fire for real, and as the dead and wounded fall, the panicked crowds disperse, or hide in the entryways of buildings.

Snipers fire from the rooftops. Someone hit by a bullet makes a gesture as if he had tripped and was falling forward, but he is instantly caught by those walking beside him, who carry him to the edge of the sidewalk while the procession continues on, fists rising rhythmically. Sometimes, white-clad girls and boys march at the front of the columns, their foreheads encircled by white headbands. They are martyrs—ready to meet their deaths. It is so written on their headbands. On occasion, before the procession starts to move, I walk up to them, trying to understand what their faces express. Nothing—in any event, nothing that I would know how to describe, for which I could find the appropriate words.

In the afternoon the demonstrations ceased, merchants opened their shops, secondhand-book sellers, of whom there were many here, spread out their collections in the streets. I purchased two albums from them about Persepolis. The shah was proud of this city. He held great ceremonies and festivals there, to which he invited guests from around the world. As for me, I wanted to go there at all costs because it was Darius who had begun its construction.

Luckily Ramadan arrived, and Tehran grew calm. I located the bus terminal and bought a ticket to Shiraz, which is close to Persepolis. I had no trouble getting the ticket, although later the bus turned out to be full. It was a luxurious, air-conditioned Mercedes and it glided soundlessly over the excellent highway. We passed large stretches of dark beige, rocky desert, occasional poor, mud-house villages devoid of any trace of green, groups of children playing, herds of goats and sheep.

At the rest stops one always gets the same thing: a plate of buck-wheat grits, a hot lamb shish kebab, a glass of water, and, for dessert, a cup of tea. I can't converse because I don't know Farsi, but the atmosphere is pleasant; the men are friendly, they smile. The women, on the other hand, gaze the other way. I know that I must not look at them, that it is forbidden, and yet when one spends some time in their proximity, now and then one of them will adjust her chador in such a way that for a moment an eye can be seen peering out from under it—invariably black, large, shining, framed by long lashes.

I have a window seat on the bus, but after several hours the view is still the same, so I take Herodotus out of my bag and read about the Scythians.

Here is how they conduct themselves in war. When a Scythian kills his first man, he drinks some of his blood. He presents the king with the heads of those he kills in battle, because his reward for doing so is a share of the spoils they have taken in the battle, but no head means no spoils. The way a Scythian skins a head is as follows:

he makes a circular cut around the head at the level of the ears and then he picks it up and shakes the scalp off the skull; next he scrapes the skin with a cow's rib, and then, having kneaded the skin with his hands, he has a kind of rag, which he proudly fastens to the bridle of the horse he is riding. The reason for his pride is that the more of these skin rags a man has, the braver he is counted. Many of them make coats to wear by sewing the scalps together into a patchwork leather garment like leather coats.... Human skin, apparently, is thick and shiny-white—shinier, in fact, than any other kind of skin. I read no further, because suddenly palm groves appear outside the window, broad green fields, buildings, and further on streets and streetlights. Above the rooftops glisten the cupolas of mosques. We are in Shiraz, city of gardens and carpets.

I am informed at the hotel reception desk that the only way to get to Persepolis is by taxi and that it is best to set out before dawn, because that way one will see how the sun rises and illuminates the royal ruins with its first beams.

It was dark still when I found the driver waiting for me in front of the hotel, and we set off at once. The moon was full, so I could see that we were on a plain as flat as the bottom of a dried-up lake. After a half hour along the empty road, Jafar—that was the driver's name—stopped and took a bottle of water out of the trunk. It was so cold at this early hour that the water was icy, and I myself was shaking so much that he took pity on me and covered me with a blanket.

We communicated solely via sign language. He showed me that I was supposed to wash my face. I did so, but when I wanted to dry it, he made a gesture forbidding it: one cannot wipe one's face— the sun must dry off the moisture. I understood this to be a ritual, and stood patiently waiting.

Sunrise in the desert is invariably a luminous, and in moments a mystical spectacle, during which the world that sailed away from us in the evening and vanished into the night suddenly returns. The sky reappears, the earth and people reappear. It all exists once again, we can see it all again. Should there be an oasis somewhere close by, we will see it; if a well, we will see it, too. In this affecting moment, Muslims fall to their knees and say their first prayer of the day—the *salat as-subh*. But their rapture communicates itself also to unbelievers. Everyone in the desert experiences the return of the sun to the earth in the same way; it elicits perhaps the only truly ecumenical emotion.

Bright daylight arrives and then Persepolis reveals itself in all of its royal glory. It is a great stone city of temples and palaces situated on a vast, broad terrace carved into the slopes of mountains which rise abruptly, without any intermediate stages, in the place where the plain on which we are now standing ends. The sun dries my face, and the point of this ritual is as follows: The sun, much like man, needs water in order to live; if, upon awaking, it sees that it can drink a few drops from a man's face, it will be kinder to him in the hour when it becomes cruel—at noon. And it will manifest its kindness by providing him with shade. It does not give shade directly, but by the agency of various other things—a tree, a roof, a cave. We know full well that without the sun, in and of themselves those things would have no shade. And so the sun, smiting us, also supplies us with a defensive shield.

It was a dawn exactly like the one now when, two centuries after Darius began to build Persepolis, at the end of January of 330 B.C.E., Alexander the Great approaches the city at the head of his armies. He doesn't yet see the buildings, but he has heard about their magnificence, and that they conceal countless treasures. On this very plain on which Jafar and I are standing, he encounters a strange group: "They encountered the first delegation immediately beyond the river. But these ragged figures differed greatly from the elegant opportunists and collaborators with whom Alexander hitherto had dealings. Their cries of greeting, as well as the branches of supplicants they carried in their hands, signified that they were Greeks: people either middle-aged or elderly, perhaps former mercenaries who had fought on the wrong side against the cruel monarch Artaxerxes Ochos. They were a pitiful, downright ghastly sight, because each of them was horribly disfigured. In accordance with the typical Persian method, they had all had their ears and noses cut off. Some were missing hands, others feet. All had a disfiguring brand on their foreheads. 'These were people,' says Diodor, 'who were skilled in the arts and in various crafts, and did good work; they had their appendages cut off in such a way as to leave only those necessary for performing their profession.'"

These unfortunates nevertheless ask Alexander that he not order them to return to Greece, but rather leave them here, in Persepolis, which they are building: in Greece, with their appearance, "each one of them would feel isolated, would be an object of pity, a social outcast."

We arrive in Persepolis. A long, wide staircase leads to the city, flanked on one side by a tall bas-relief carved in dark gray, well-polished marble and representing vassals walking to the king in order to pay him homage, proffer their loyalty and subservience. There is one vassal for every step, and there are several dozen steps. When you place your feet upon one step, you are accompanied by its appointed vassal, who, when you walk a step higher, will hand you over to the next vassal while he himself remains where he was, guarding his own step. It is astonishing that the figures of the vassals are identical to one another down to the most minute details of their appearance, proportions, and shape. They all have rich, floor-length gowns, creased head coverings, long spears which they hold before them with both hands, and decorated quivers slung over their shoulders. Their facial expression is serious, and despite the fact that an act of servility awaits them, they walk erect, their posture full of dignity.

The sameness of appearance of the vassals accompanying your ascent up the stairs creates a paradoxical impression of motion within immobility: you climb the stairs, but because you always see the same vassal, you simultaneously have the impression of standing still, as if you were trapped in invisible trick mirrors. When you have reached the top, you turn and look back. The view is magnificent: below you stretches a boundless plain, at this hour already bathed in blinding sunlight, and traversed by only one road—the one leading to Persepolis.

This scenery creates two entirely different, even opposite psychological situations:

—From the king's point of view: The king stands at the top of the stairs and looks down at the plain. At its other end, meaning very far, far away, he sees that some specks have appeared, some motes of dust, grains, particles barely visible and difficult to identify. The king watches, wonders—what could this be? After a while the motes and kernels of grain draw nearer, grow larger, and slowly crystallize. Those are probably vassals, he thinks, but because the first impression is always the most important, and in this case it was "motes and kernels of grain," such will always remain the king's view of his liege men. A certain amount of time passes: he can already see figures, the outlines of people. Well, I wasn't mistaken, the king says to the courtiers surrounding him, those are vassals; I must hurry to the Audience Hall, so that I can sit down on the throne before they arrive (the king does not speak with subordinates other than while sitting on the throne).

—And now from the opposite point of view, that of the vassals and of everyone else: They appear on the stage from the opposite side, facing Persepolis. They see its magical, astounding constructions, its gilding and glazing. Speechless, they fall to their knees (although they do so, they are not yet Muslims; it will be another one thousand years before Islam arrives here). Having recovered their composure, they rise and shake the dust from their garments. That is what the king sees as being the movement of specks and particles. As they draw nearer to Persepolis, their rapture increases, but so does their humility, their awareness of their own wretchedness, baseness, worthlessness. Yes, we are nothing, the king can do with us as he pleases; even if he condemns us to death, we will accept the sentence without a word. But if they succeed in leaving here in one piece, what a distinguished rank they will acquire among their people! He is the one who visited the king, others will say. And later—he is the son of the one who visited the king, the grandson, the great-grandson, etc. One secures in this way one's family's standing for generations to come.

It is possible to walk endlessly around Persepolis. The complex is deserted and quiet. No guides, guards, hawkers, touts. Jafar stayed below, and I am alone on the great burial ground of stones. Stones shaped into columns and pillars, sculpted into bas-reliefs and portals. No stone here has a natural shape, none is as it would be in the ground, or as it would appear lying on a mountainside. Each is carefully cut, fitted, worked over. How much exacting labor went into all this over the years, how much toil and drudgery on the part of thousands upon thousands of people? How many of them died, hoisting these gigantic boulders? How many dropped from exhaustion and thirst?

When we look at lifeless temples, palaces, and cities, we can't help but wonder about the fate of their builders. Their pain, their broken backs, their eyes gouged out by errant splinters of stone, their rheumatism. About their unfortunate lives, their suffering. But the very next question that invariably arises is: Could these wonders have come into being without that suffering? Without the overseer's whip, the slave's fear, the ruler's vanity? In short, was not the monumentality of past epochs created by that which is negative and evil in man? And yet, does not that monumentality owe its existence to some conviction that what is negative and weak in man can be vanquished only by beauty, only through the effort and will of his creation? And that the only thing that never changes is beauty itself, and the need for it that dwells within us?

I walk through the propylaeum, through the Hall of the Hundred Columns, through Darius's Palace, the Harem of Xerxes, the Treasury. It is terribly hot and I don't have strength left for Artaxerxes' Palace, or for the Council Hall, or for the dozens of other buildings and ruins making up this city of dead kings and forgotten gods. I descend the great staircase, passing once again the procession of vassals emerging from the stone, on their way to pay homage to the king.

Jafar and I drive back to Shiraz.

I look over my shoulder—Persepolis grows smaller and smaller, the dust rising in the car's wake increasingly obscures the rear view, until finally, as we are entering the city, it disappears altogether behind the first turn.

I return to Tehran. To demonstrating crowds, to chants and shouts, to the crack of small-arms fire and the stench of gases, to snipers and secondhand-book sellers.

I have with me Herodotus, who recounts how, on Darius's order, one of the commanders he had left behind in Europe, Megabazus, conquers Thrace. There is among the Thracians, writes Herodotus, a tribe called the Trausians. *Trausian customs are basically identical with those found elsewhere in Thrace, except for what they do at birth and death. Whenever a baby is born, its relatives gather around and grieve for the troubles it is going to have to endure now that it has been born, and they recount all the sufferings of human life. When anyone dies, however, they bury him in high spirits and with jubilation, on the grounds that he has been released from so many ills and is now in a perfectly happy state.*

HONORS FOR THE HEAD
OF HISTIAEUS

I left Persepolis and now I am leaving Tehran, going back twenty years and returning once more to Africa. But along the way I must stop—in my thoughts, that is—in the Greco-Persian world of Herodotus, for dark clouds are beginning to gather over it.

Darius does not succeed in conquering the Scythians; they have stopped the Asian at the gates of Europe. He sees that he cannot prevail against them. Moreover, he is suddenly afraid that they will now attack and destroy him. And so under cover of night he begins his escape-retreat, desiring one thing only: to get out of Scythia and return as quickly as possible to Persia. As his enormous army withdraws, the Scythians immediately set off in pursuit.

Darius has only one path of retreat: over the bridge on the Danube which he himself built at the start of the invasion. It is being guarded for him by the Ionians (Greeks inhabiting Asia Minor, which in Herodotus's time was under Persian rule).

How the world's fortunes turn. The Scythians, knowing the shortest routes and mounted on swift horses, reach the bridge ahead of the Persian forces and try to head off their retreat. They appeal to the Ionians to destroy the bridge, which would allow the Scythians to finish off Darius and by the same token would give the Ionians their freedom.

It would seem that from the Ionians' perspective the proposal is indeed an excellent one, and so when they gather a council to discuss it, the first to speak, Miltiades, says: Great, let's tear down the bridge! And everyone else seems to concur (it is not the Ionian people who participate in the council, but the tyrants, whom, as de facto lieutenants, Darius has installed over the population). The next one to speak is Histiaeus of Miletus: *[He] took the opposite line; he argued that every one of them owed his position as tyrant of his community to Darius, and that if Darius were to fall, he would not be able to rule Miletus and none of them would remain in power either, because there was not one of their communities which would not prefer democracy to tyranny. Histiaeus' argument immediately won everyone at the meeting over to his point of view, although they had previously been in favor of Miltiades' proposal.*

This change of mind is of course understandable: the tyrants realized that if Darius loses his throne (and probably his head), tomorrow they will lose their positions (and probably their heads) as well. Though they tell the Scythians that they will dismantle the bridge, in reality they continue to protect it and permit Darius safe passage back to Persia.

Darius, appreciating the historic role Histiaeus has played in this decisive moment, rewards him richly according to the latter's desires. But he does not allow him to return to his seat as tyrant of Miletus, taking him instead to Susa, the Persian capital, as an adviser. Histiaeus is ambitious and cynical, and it is best to keep a close eye on his kind, all the more so now that he has risen to the status of savior of the empire, which without his voice, there by the bridge over the Danube, might have ceased to exist.

But all is not lost for Histiaeus. The tyranny of Miletus, the principal city of Ionia, is now assumed by his faithful son-in-law, Aristagoras. He, too, is ambitious and hungry for power. All this is happening at a time when discontent with, even resistance to, the

Persian domination is growing among the subjugated Ionians. The father and the son-in-law intuit that the time is ripe to take advantage of the prevailing mood.

But how are they to communicate, how to agree on a plan of action? It would take a messenger three months at a brisk pace to traverse the distance between Susa (where Histiaeus dwells) and Miletus (where Aristagoras rules)—and there are both deserts and mountains along the way. Histiaeus has no choice route: It ... so happened, in fact, that a man with a tattooed head arrived from Histiaeus in Susa with a message telling Aristagoras to rebel against the king. Histiaeus could find no other safe way to communicate to Aristagoras the message he wanted to get through to him, because the roads were guarded, so he shaved the head of his most trustworthy slave, tattooed the message on his scalp, and then waited for his hair to grow back. As soon as it had, he sent him to Miletus with just the one task—to tell Aristagoras, when he got to Miletus, to shave his hair off and examine his scalp. And as I have already said, the tattooed message was that Aristagoras should revolt. The reason Histiaeus took this step was because he hated being kept in Susa.

Aristagoras presents Histiaeus's appeal to his supporters. They listen and vote unanimously for the uprising. Aristagoras now sets off beyond the sea in search of allies, because Persia is many times stronger than Ionia. First, he sails to Sparta. Its king, Cleomenes, is thought, Herodotus notes, not to be in full possession of his faculties—practically insane, in fact—but he manages to display a great deal of sagacity and common sense. Upon hearing that the matter at hand was war against a king who ruled over all of Asia and resided in a capital city called Susa, he sensibly asked how far it was to this Susa. At that point Aristagoras, who up till then had been so clever and had been successfully taking Cleomenes in, made a mistake. In pursuit of his aim of seducing the Spartiates to Asia, he should not have told the truth, but he did: he told him that the journey inland would take three months. He was going on to say more about the journey, but Cleomenes interrupted him. "Sir," *he said, "I order you to leave Sparta before sunset. You are not saying anything attractive to the Lacedaemonians, if you want them to travel three months' journey away from the sea."*

So dispatched, Aristagoras traveled to Athens—the most powerful city in Greece. Here he changed tactics: instead of speaking with the ruler, he addressed the crowd (in accordance with another of Herodotus's rules, that *it seems to be easier to fool a crowd than a single person*) and appealed directly to the Athenians to help the Ionians. *So now that they had been won over, the Athenians voted to send a fleet of twenty ships to help the Ionians ... These twenty ships proved to be the beginning of misfortune for Greeks and non-Greeks alike*—meaning, they were the germ of the great Greco-Persian war.

Before it comes to that, however, there are some smaller incidents. To begin with, there is the Ionian uprising against the Persians, which will last several years before it is bloodily suppressed. Several scenes:

Scene 1: The Ionians, supported by the Athenians, occupy and burn Sardis (the second largest Persian city after Susa).

Scene 2 (a famous one): After a certain time, that is, after two or three months, news of this reaches the Persian king, Darius. *It is said, however, that his first reaction to the news was to discount the Ionians, because he was confident of punishing them for their rebellion, and to ask who the Athenians were. On hearing the answer, he is said to have asked for his bow; he took hold of it, notched an arrow, and shot it up towards the sky. And as he fired it into the air, he said, "Lord Zeus, make it possible for me to punish the Athenians." Then he ordered one of his attendants to repeat to him three times, every time a meal was being served, "Master, remember the Athenians."*

Scene 3: Darius summons Histiaeus, whom he begins to suspect of something, because it was after all his son-in-law, Aristagoras, who fomented the Ionian uprising. Histiaeus denies everything and lies to the king's face: "*My lord ... how could I be involved in planning anything that would cause you even the slightest amount of distress? What possible motive could I have for doing so?*" And he blames the king for having brought him to Susa, because if he, Histiaeus, were in Ionia, no one would have mutinied against Darius. *So now let me go as quickly as possible to Ionia, so that I can restore order out of all the chaos in your affairs there and deliver into your hands this man I left in charge of Miletus, who is responsible for all this.* Darius lets himself be persuaded, allows Histiaeus to go, and commands him to return to Susa once he has accomplished the promised mission.

Scene 4: Meantime, battles between the Ionians and the Persians unfold with varying and inconclusive results. In time, however, the Persians, more numerous and powerful, gradually gain an edge. Histiaeus's son-in-law, Aristagoras, notices this and decides to withdraw from the uprising, even to leave Ionia. Herodotus writes about this decision with contempt: *Aristagoras of Miletus proved himself to be somewhat of a coward. He had caused all the commotion in Ionia and had stirred up a great deal of trouble, but seeing the current situation, and because he now despaired of ever defeating King Darius, he began to contemplate flight. He therefore convened a meeting of his supporters ... claiming that they should have a bolt-hole available in case they were ever thrown out of Miletus ... He ... recruited a band of volunteers, and set sail for Thrace. There he gained control of the land he had set out for and made it his military headquarters. However ... the Thracians destroyed his army, and Aristagoras himself was one of the casualties.*

Scene 5: Histiaeus, released by Darius, reaches Sardis and calls on the satrap Artaphrenes, Darius's nephew. They converse. What do you think, the satrap asks him, why did the Ionians revolt? I have no idea, Histiaeus replied, feigning ignorance. But Artaphrenes knows what he knows: "*I'll tell you what actually happened, Histiaeus: it was you who stitched the shoe, while Aristagoras merely put it on.*"

Scene 6: Histiaeus realizes that the satrap has seen through him and that calling on Darius for help is futile: It would take three months for a messenger to get to Susa, and the return trip under safe-conduct from Darius another three to six months altogether, during which time Artaphrenes could have him beheaded a hundred times. Therefore he flees from Sardis by night heading west, toward the sea. It takes several days to reach the shore, and it is easy to imagine Histiaeus pushing ahead with his heart in his mouth, constantly looking behind him to look for Artaphrenes' myrmidons in pursuit. Where does he sleep? What does he eat? We do not know. One thing is certain: he wants to assume leadership over the Ionians in the war against Darius. Histiaeus therefore proves a traitor twice over: first, he betrayed the cause of the Ionians in order to save Darius; and now he betrays Darius by inciting the Ionians against him.

Scene 7: Histiaeus makes his way to the island of Chios, inhabited by Ionians. (This is a beautiful island. I could gaze forever at its bay and the navy blue mountains visible on the horizon. In general, the drama is set amidst such magnificent landscapes.) But he has barely made landfall when the Ionians arrest him and throw him into prison. They suspect him of serving Darius. Histiaeus swears that this is not so, that he wants to command an anti-Persian uprising. They believe him in the end and set him free, but are not inclined to offer him support. He feels isolated, and his plans for a great war against Darius appear increasingly delusional. Yet his ambition still burns. Despite everything, he does not lose hope, continues to lust for power; the desire to command leaves him not a moment's peace. He asks the locals for help sailing back to the mainland, to Miletus, where he was once tyrant. *The Milesians, however, were glad to have got rid of Aristagoras, and, now that they had tasted independence, they were in no great hurry to welcome another tyrant into their land. In fact, when Histiaeus tried to bring about his restoration by force and under cover of darkness, he was wounded in the thigh by one of the Milesians. Banished from his native city, he returned to Chios. He tried to persuade the Chians to give him a fleet, but they refused, so he went over to Mytilene, where he persuaded the Lesbians to give him some ships.* Great Histiaeus, once the plenipotentiary of the famous city of Miletus, having sat so recently at the side of Darius, king of kings, now roams from island to island, searching for a place to call his own, for a sympathetic ear, for support. But invariably he either has to flee, or is thrown into dungeons, or is shoved away from the city gates, beaten and wounded.

Scene 8: But Histiaeus does not give up; still he struggles to keep his head above water. It could be that he continues to fantasize about the scepter, visited by dreams of absolute might. He manages to make a good enough impression for the inhabitants of Lesbos to offer him eight ships. He sails at the head of this fleet to Byzantium, *where they set up a base and proceeded to seize all ships sailing out of the Euxine Sea, unless the crews promised to recognize Histiaeus as their leader.* Thus his degradation continues. Little by little, he turns into a pirate.

Scene 9: News reaches Histiaeus that Miletus, vanguard of the Ionian uprising, has been conquered by the Persians. *After their naval victory over the Ionians, the Persians blockaded Miletus by land and sea. They used all kinds of stratagems, such as undermining the walls, until the city fell into their hands, acropolis and all, in the sixth year after Aristagoras' revolt. They reduced the city to slavery ...*

(For the Athenians, the defeat of Miletus was a terrible blow. When the playwright *Phrynichus composed and produced a play called* The Fall of Miletus, *the audience burst into tears.* The Athenian authorities imposed a draconian fine of a thousand drachmas on the play's author and banned any future productions of it in their city. A play was meant to raise one's spirits, not reopen wounds.)

At the news of Miletus's fall, Histiaeus reacts bizarrely. He stops plundering ships and sails with the Lesbians to Chios. Does he want to be closer to Miletus? To run further away? But where? For the time being, he organizes a slaughter on Chios: *a garrison of islanders ... refused to let him pass; battle was joined and a great many of the Chians died. Then, with the help of his Lesbians, he gained control of the rest of the island ...*

But this carnage does not solve anything. It is a gesture of despair, rage, madness. He abandons the lifeless land and sails to Thasos—an island of gold mines situated near Thrace. He lays siege to Thasos, but is not wanted there, and the island does not submit. Abandoning hope for gold, he sails for Lesbos—he had enjoyed the best reception there. But there is hunger on Lesbos now, and because he has an army to feed, he makes his way to Asia, to the country of Mysia, where he hopes to harvest some crops, find something, anything, to eat. The noose is tightening; he really has nowhere to go. He is trapped, he is at the bottom. There is no limit to man's smallness. A small man immersing himself in smallness is only engulfed by it, until finally he perishes.

Scene 10: *A Persian, Harpagus, happened to be in that part of the country* which Histiaeus reached, *with a sizeable army under his command. He engaged Histiaeus just as he disembarked, captured him alive, and wiped out most of his troops.* But before this happened, Histiaeus, upon disembarking, tried to escape: *As he was running away from the battlefield, a Persian soldier caught up with him and was just about to stab him to death when Histiaeus spoke in Persian to him and let him know that he was Histiaeus of Miletus.*

Scene 11: Histiaeus is brought to Sardis. Here Artaphrenes and Harpagos order that he be publicly impaled. They cut off his head, have it embalmed, and send it to King Darius in Susa. (To Susa! After three months on the road, what must that head, even embalmed, have looked like!)

Scene 12: On learning about all that has happened Darius rebukes Artaphrenes and Harpagos for not sending him Histiaeus alive. He orders the scrap he received washed, appropriately dressed, and buried with honors.

He wants, if only in this way, to pay homage to the head in which, several years earlier, near the bridge over the Danube, arose the idea that saved Persia and Asia, as well as Darius's kingdom and his life.

AT DOCTOR RANKE'S

The events described by Herodotus so absorbed me while I was in the Congo that at times I experienced the dread of the approaching war between the Greeks and the Persians more vividly than I did the events of the current Congolese conflict, which I was assigned to cover. And the country of *The Heart of Darkness* was also taking its toll on me, of course, what with the frequent eruption of gunfights, the constant danger of arrest, beatings, and death, and the pervasive climate of uncertainty, ambiguity, and unpredictability. The absolute worst could happen here at any moment and in any place. There was no government, no rule of law and order. The colonial system was collapsing, Belgian administrators were fleeing to Europe, and in their place was emerging a dark, deranged power, which most frequently assumed the guise of drunken Congolese military police.

One could see clearly how dangerous freedom is in the absence of hierarchy and order—or, rather, anarchy in the absence of ethics. Under such circumstances, the forces of evil aggression—all manner of villainy, brutishness, and bestiality—instantly gain the upper hand. And so it was in the Congo, which fell under the rule of these gendarmes. An encounter with any one of them could be deadly.

Here I am walking down the street in the small town of Lisali.

It is sunny, empty, and quiet.

Suddenly, I spot two policemen approaching from the opposite direction. I freeze. But running away makes no sense—there is no place to run to, and, furthermore, it is dreadfully hot and I can barely drag one foot after the other. The gendarmes are in fatigues, with deep helmets which cover half their faces, and bristling with armaments, each carrying an automatic rifle, grenades, knife, flare pistol, truncheon, and a metal implement combining spoon and fork—a portable arsenal. Why do they need it all? I wonder. And there is more. Their imposing silhouettes are also encircled with all kinds of belts and detachable linings, to which are sewn garlands of metal circles, pins, hooks, buckles.

Dressed in shorts and shirts, perhaps they would have seemed pleasant young men, the sort who would greet you politely and pleasantly offer directions if asked. But the uniform and the weaponry altered their nature and stance, and also performed yet another function: rendering difficult, even impossible, any normal human contact. The men walking toward me were not ordinary people to be casually encountered, but dehumanized creatures, extraterrestrials. A new species.

They were drawing nearer and I was dripping with sweat, my legs leaden and getting heavier by the second. The key to the entire situation was that they knew as well as I did that to whatever sentence they might impose there was no appeal. No higher authority, no tribunal. If they wanted to beat me, they would beat me; if they wanted to kill me, they would kill me. I have only ever felt true loneliness in circumstances such as these—when I have stood alone face-to-face with absolute violent power. The world grows empty, silent, depopulated, and finally recedes.

Furthermore, it is not merely two gendarmes and a reporter who are participating in this street scene in a small Congolese town. Also present is a huge swath of world history, which already set us against one another many centuries ago. Here between us stand generations of slave traders; the myrmidons of King Leopold, who cut off the hands and ears of the grandfathers of these policemen; the overseers of cotton and sugar plantations, whips in their hands. The memory of those torments was passed down for years in tribal stories, and the men whom I am about to encounter would have been reared on those tales, on legends ending with a promise of a day of retribution. And today is that day—both they and I know it.

What will happen? We are close already, and getting closer and closer. Finally, they stop. I too stop. And then, from under that mountain of gear and scrap iron, emerges a voice that I will never forget, its tone humble, even pleading:

"*Monsieur, avez-vous une cigarette, s'il vous plaît?*"

What a sight it must have been, the zeal and the haste, the politeness, the servility even, with which I reached into my pocket for a pack of cigarettes, my last, but what does it matter, take it, my dear boys, take them all, sit and smoke the entire pack, right away, until not a puff of smoke is left!

Doctor Otto Ranke is pleased at my good fortune. These encounters often end very badly. The gendarmes have killed many people already. White and black both come to see Doctor Ranke about their injuries; the badly tortured must be carried in by others. The policemen spare no race, and massacre their own as readily as, even more frequently than, they do the Europeans. In this way they are occupiers of their own country, men who observe no moderation and no boundaries. "If they do not touch me," says the doctor, "it's only because they need me. When they are drunk and have no civilian handy upon whom to discharge their rage, they fight amongst themselves, and then they are brought here, for me to sew up their heads and set their bones." Dostoevsky, Ranke says, described the phenomenon of pointless cruelty. So it is with these gendarmes, he says; they are cruel without reason or necessity.

Doctor Ranke is an Austrian and has been living in Lisali since the end of World War II. Slight, fragile-looking, yet still lively and indefatigable approaching his eightieth year. He owes his relative good health, he says, to his taking each day in the morning, when the sun is still gentle, a walk out into the green and flowering courtyard, where seated on a stool, he has a servant wash his back with a sponge and a brush so vigorously as to produce from the doctor actual little moans of both satisfaction and pain. These moans, snorts, and the laughter of overjoyed children who have gathered around the doctor to watch the rubdown, awaken me, because the windows of my room are nearby.

The doctor has a little private hospital—a white-painted barrack standing near the villa where he lives. He did not flee with the Belgians, he says, because he is old already and has no family anywhere. Here people know him and he hopes that they will protect him. He took me in, he says, for safekeeping. As a correspondent, I have nothing to do, because there are no means of communication with Poland. Not a single newspaper is being published in this part of the country, there is no functioning radio station, no government. I am trying to get out of here—but how? The closest airport—in Stanleyville—is closed, the roads (now in the rainy season) are swamped, the ship that once plied the river Congo has long ceased to do so. I do not know what it is exactly that I am counting on. A little bit of luck, I suppose, and the goodwill of the people around me. Most of all I am hoping that the world will change for the better, a chimerical idea to be sure, but I must believe in something. Still it does not keep me from walking around tense and nervous. I feel anger and helplessness—by turns familiar states of mind in this line of work, in which so much time is given over to fruitless waiting for a way to communicate with one's country and with the world.

If one happens to hear that there are no gendarmes in town, one can venture an expedition into the jungle. It is all around, rearing up in every direction, screening out the world. One can enter the forest only along the laterite road that has been cut through it. There is no entrance to this otherwise impregnable fortress, a green mass of branches, vines, and leaves; legs sink into slimy, foul-smelling bogs, as all sorts of spiders, beetles, and worms begin to rain down upon one's head. The inexperienced in any event do not dare plunge into the virgin forest, and the idea of hacking one's way through it is unthinkable to the locals. The jungle no less than the ocean, or a range of high mountains, is a closed, discrete, independent entity, not to be idly entered into. It always fills me with fear—that from its thickets a predator will suddenly pounce, that a poisonous snake will with invisible speed strike me, or that I will hear too late the swish of an approaching arrow.

Usually a group of children catches up with me just as I'm setting out toward the green colossus—they want to accompany me. At the outset they are in high spirits, laughing and frolicking about. But when the road enters the forest, they grow silent, serious. Perhaps they imagine that somewhere, in the darkness of the jungle, lurk phantoms, wraiths, and witches that kidnap disobedient children. It is well to be mindful of what even children understand, to be quiet and pay attention.

Sometimes we stop along the road, right near the edge of the jungle. It resembles twilight here, and the air is thick with aromas.

There are no animals on the road, but you can hear the birds. And the sound of drops falling on leaves. Unaccountable rustlings. The children like to come here, they feel at home and know everything. Which plant one can pick and bite into, and which one cannot so much as touch. Which fruit is comestible, and which poisonous. They know that spiders are very dangerous, and lizards not at all. And they know that one must look up at the branches, because a snake might be lurking there. The girls are more serious and more careful than the boys, and so I observe their actions and order the boys to follow suit. All of us are subject to the same sensation, that which reminds me of entering a great, lofty cathedral, in which a human being feels minuscule and conscious of how much larger than himself everything else is.

Doctor Ranke's villa stands beside a wide road that cuts through northern Congo and, running close to the equator, leads through Bangui to Douala on the Gulf of Guinea, where it ends roughly at the height of Fernando Po. But that is far from here, more than two thousand kilometers away. A portion of this road had been paved, but only shapeless scraps of asphalt remain today. When I have to walk here on a moonless night (and tropical darkness is thick, impenetrable), I advance slowly, dragging my feet along the ground, to feel, testing the way as best I can—*shur-shur, shur-shur*—vigilantly, carefully, because there are so many invisible holes, pits, depressions. When columns of fugitives pass this way at night, one sometimes hears a sudden cry—of someone having fallen into a deep hole and probably broken a leg.

Fugitives. Suddenly, everyone has become a fugitive. The Congo's independence in the summer of 1960 was accompanied by the eruption of tribal strife, and eventually warfare, and ever since the roads have been filled with fugitives. Gendarmes, soldiers, and ad hoc tribal militias engage in the actual fighting, whereas civilians, which usually means women and children, flee. The routes of these flights are often difficult to re-create. Generally, the goal is to get as far away as possible from the battle, though not so far as to lose one's way and later be unable to return. Another important consideration is whether or not one will be able to find something to eat along a particular escape route. These are poor people, and they have but a few belongings: the women, a percale dress; the men, a shirt and a pair of pants. Other than that, perhaps a piece of cloth for cover at night, a pot, a cup, a plastic plate, and a basin in which to carry everything.

But the single most important factor in choosing a route is tribal relationships: whether a given road goes through friendly territory or, God forbid, leads straight into enemy lands. The relations among the various clans and tribes inhabiting the roadside villages and jungle clearings constitute a difficult and complex body of knowledge, which everyone begins to absorb in childhood. It is what enables people to live in relative safety, avoiding avoidable conflicts. Dozens of tribes inhabit just the one region where I happen to be right now. They are grouped in a variety of associations and confederations whose customs and regulations are known only to themselves. As a foreigner, I have no way of mentally navigating, organizing, deciphering, understanding even a fraction of this knowledge. What possible guide could I have to the state of relations between Mwaka and Panda, or between Banda and Baya?

But the locals know the state well; their lives depend upon it.

They know who places poisoned thorns on which path, where a hatchet lies buried.

Why so many tribes? Just one hundred and fifty years ago there were still ten thousand of them in Africa. Even today, all you have to do is walk down the road a ways: in one village, the Tulama tribe; in the very next one, the Arusi; on one side of the river, the Murle; on the other bank, the Topota. On the summit of the mountain lives one tribe; at its foot, an entirely different one.

Each has its own language, its own rituals, its own gods.

How did it come to this? Whence this fantastic diversity, this improbable richness of variation? How did it all begin? When? In what place? Anthropologists tell us it started with a small group. Perhaps with several. Each had to number approximately thirty to fifty. If smaller, men could not defend themselves; bigger ones could not find enough to eat. Even in my time I managed to encounter in East Africa two tribes neither of which numbered more than one hundred people.

All right, then—let's say, thirty to fifty individuals. Such is the nucleus of a tribe. But why does such a nucleus necessarily come to need its own language? How could the human mind even invent such an astonishing array of forms of speech, each one with its own vocabulary, grammar, inflections, and so on? A great, million-strong nation creating a language for itself through a prolonged communal effort—that one can grasp. But here in the African bush it is a matter of small tribes barely eking out a living, walking barefoot and eternally hungry; and yet they had the will and the capacity to devise languages for themselves—distinct, proprietary, theirs alone.

And not just languages. Because simultaneously, since their very origins, they invent gods. Each tribe has its own unique deities. And why should they not have started with one god, but right away with several? Why does humanity endure for thousands and thousands of years before developing the idea of a single deity? Reason might suggest such a concept would first arise.

And so to resume, science has determined that in the beginning there was only one group—in any event not more than a few. With time, others developed. Curious, that a new group, arriving on the scene, as it were, would not first survey the terrain, size up the situation, listen to the prevailing parlance. No—it emerges with its own language, its own pantheon of gods, its own universe of traditions. With relative immediacy it demonstratively underscores its own otherness.

Over years, over centuries, there are more and more of these tribal nuclei. It starts to get crowded on this continent of many people, many languages, and many gods.

Herodotus, wherever he was, always tried to note the names of tribes, their location and customs. Where someone lives. Who are his neighbors. This because knowledge of the world—whether back then in Libya and Scythia or today here in the northern Congo—accrues not vertically but horizontally, synthetically from a bird's-eye view. I know my nearest neighbors, and that is all; they know theirs; and those know others still. In this way we will arrive at the ends of the earth. And who is to gather up all these bits and arrange them?

No one.

They cannot be arranged.

When one reads in Herodotus those lists of tribes and their customs, which stretch for pages on end, it seems as if neighbors select one another based on differences. That is why there is so much enmity between them, so much fighting. It is thus in Doctor Ranke's hospital as well. Night and day families at the patients' bedside, individual clans and tribes, occupy separate rooms. The goal is to have everyone feel at home, and to prevent one side from casting spells on the other.

Discreetly, I try to infer the differences. I walk around the little hospital, look into the rooms—not a difficult thing to do, because in this hot and humid climate everything is wide open. But the people all seem alike, invariably poor and listless, and only if one listens carefully does one notice that they speak different languages. If one smiles at them, they will respond in kind, but a smile such as theirs will take a long time forming and will remain upon the face for only a moment.

THE GREEK'S TECHNIQUE

I'm leaving Lisali because I have managed to hitch a ride. Hitching a ride—that is how one travels here these days. All of a sudden, a car appears on a road that has been deserted for days. At the mere sight our hearts start to beat faster. We flag it down as it draws near. *"Bonjour, monsieur,"* we say ingratiatingly to the driver, and then, hopefully, *"avez-vous une place, s'il vous plaît?"* Of course he doesn't—the cars are always full. But everyone inside, already squeezed together, now, instinctively and without prodding or persuasion, squeezes together even more, and somehow, all of us jammed into the most back-bending positions, now set off. It is only when the car is once again on its way that we ask those sitting closest to us if by any chance they know where we are going. There really isn't a clear answer to this question, because no one actually knows our destination. We are simply driving where we can.

One quickly gets the impression that everyone would like to journey as far as possible. The war surprised people in the farthest corners of the Congo—an enormous country with no public transportation system—and now those who were far away from their homes, either looking for work or visiting their families, would like to return but have no means of doing so. Their only hope is to hitch rides going in more or less the desired direction—simply to drive.

There are people who have already been on the road for weeks, months. They have no maps, but even if they should happen on one, it is doubtful that they would find upon it the name of the village or town to which they wish to return. Even if it were there, it would be of little use to them—they are largely illiterate. What is astounding about these wanderers is their acquiescence to everything they encounter. If there is an opportunity to get a ride, they take it. If there isn't, they squat down on a roadside rock and wait. I was most fascinated by those who, having lost any sense of direction and unable to associate the names of locales they came across with any familiar to them, ended up someplace far from home in every sense. Now what? How exactly would they reorient themselves? Where they now found themselves, the names of their home villages meant nothing to anyone.

When drifting and straying in this way, it is best to stay together, to travel in a larger, tribal group. Of course, one cannot then count on getting a ride, and one has to walk—for days, weeks. Just walk. One encounters such wandering clans and tribes often. Sometimes they form long, staggered columns, carrying all their possessions on their heads—in bundles, basins, buckets. The hands are always kept free, which is necessary for maintaining one's balance and useful for chasing away flies and mosquitoes as well as wiping the sweat off one's face.

One can stop at the edge of the road and strike up a conversation with these wayfarers. If they know how to reply, they answer one's questions willingly. Asked "Where are you going?" they respond, to Kindu, to Kongolo, to Lusambo. Asked "Where is that?" they are embarrassed; how does one explain to a stranger where Kindu is? But on occasion some of them indicate a direction with their hand—to the south. Asked "Is it far?" they are even more embarrassed, because, if truth be told, they don't know. Asked

"Who are you?" they answer that they are called Yeke, or Tabwa, or Lunda. "Are there many of you?" This again they do not know. If one queries the young, they will suggest that one go and speak to the elderly. If one asks the elderly, they will begin to argue among themselves.

From the map which I'm carrying ("Afrique. Carte Generale," published in Bern by Kummerly + Frey, undated), it appears that I am somewhere between Stanleyville and Irunu. I am trying to get to Kampala, in then still peaceful Uganda, from where I hope to be able to communicate with London and with their assistance to start sending dispatches to Warsaw. In this profession, the pleasure of traveling and the fascination with what one sees is inevitably subordinate to the imperative of maintaining one's ties with headquarters and of transmitting to them what is current and important. That is why we are sent out into the world—and there are no other self-justifications. If I can just reach Kampala, I think to myself, then I'll be able to get to Nairobi, from there to Dar es-Salaam and Lusaka, then on to Brazzaville, Bangui, Fort Lamy, and beyond. Plans, intentions, dreams, drawn with a finger on a map while sitting on the wide verandah of a charming villa drowning in bougainvillea, sage, and climbing geraniums, which has been abandoned by a Belgian, the owner of a now-shuttered sawmill. Children standing around the villa observe the white man attentively, in silence. Strange things are happening in the world—not long ago, adults were telling them that the whites had gone, and now it seems that they are back again.

The African journey goes on and on, and with the passage of time places and dates become tangled—there is so much of everything here: the sheer number of events—that my impressions of the continent swell uncontrollably. I travel and write, the whole while feeling that all around me important and unique things are occurring to which I must also bear witness, however fragmentarily.

Despite this, however, I still try, in my spare moments and if I have strength enough, to read: the 1899 *West African Studies*, by the Englishwoman Mary Kingsley, who was penetrating in her observations and courageous in her compass; *Bantu Philosophy*, by the priest Placide Tempels, published in 1945; or the profound, thoughtful *Afrique ambiguë*, by French anthropologist Georges Balandier (Paris, 1957). And in addition, of course, Herodotus.

But during this period, I abandoned momentarily the fortunes of the people and wars he wrote about and concentrated instead on his technique. How did he work, i.e., what interested him, how did he approach his sources, what did he ask them, what did they say in reply? I was quite consciously trying to learn the art of reportage and Herodotus struck me as a valuable teacher. I was intrigued by his encounters, precisely because so much of what we write about derives from our relation to other people—I-he, I-they. That relation's quality and temperature, as it were, have their direct bearing on the final text. We depend on others; reportage is perhaps the form of writing most reliant on the collective.

I noticed also from reading books about Herodotus that no authorities concerned themselves exclusively with the Greek's text itself, with its accuracy and reliability, generally paying no heed to how he gathered his raw material and then wove from it his immense and rich tapestry. It is precisely that aspect that seemed to me worth delving into.

And there was more to the idiosyncrasy of my engagement. As time went by and I kept returning to *The Histories*, I began to feel something akin to warmth, even friendship, toward Herodotus. I actually became attached not so much to the book, as to its voice, the persona of its author. A complicated feeling, which I couldn't describe fully. It was an affinity with a human being whom I did not know personally, yet who charmed me by the manner of his relationships with others, by his way of being, by how, wherever he appeared, he instantly became the nucleus, or the mortar, of human community, putting it together, bringing it into being.

Herodotus was a child of his culture and of the climate—so favorable to humans—within which it developed. It was a culture of long and hospitable tables, at which one sat in large groups of a warm evening to eat cheese and olives, drink cool wine, converse. Open space unrestricted by walls, either at the seashore or on a mountainside, liberated the human imagination. The conviviality afforded confabulators the chance to shine, to engage in spontaneous tournaments during which those who recounted the most beguiling tale, retold the most extraordinary events, would reap regard. Facts mixed here with fantasy, times and places were misstated, legends were born, myths arose.

Reading Herodotus, we have the impression that he eagerly participated in such banquets as an attentive and self-applied listener. He must have had a phenomenal memory. We modern folk, spoiled by the power of technology, are cripples when it comes to recollection, panicking whenever we do not have a book or computer at hand. Yet even today there are societies to be found that demonstrate how prodigiously capacious human memory can be. And it is precisely in such a world of seemingly total recall that Herodotus lived. The book was a great rarity, inscriptions on stones and walls an even greater one.

The stuff of community was made up of two essential elements: first, individuals, and second, that which they transmitted to one another through immediate, personal contact. Man, in order to exist, had to communicate, and in order to communicate, had to feel beside him the presence of another, had to see him and hear him—there was no other form of communication, and so no other way of life. The culture of oral transmission drew them closer; one knew one's fellow not only as one who would help them gather food and defend against the enemy, but also as someone unique and irreplaceable, one who could interpret the world and guide his fellows through it.

And how much richer is this primeval, antique language of direct contact and Socratic give-and-take! Because it is not only words that matter in it. What is important, and frequently paramount, is what is communicated wordlessly, by facial expression, hand gesture, body movement. Herodotus understands this, and like every reporter or ethnologist he tries to be in the most direct contact with his interlocutors, not only listening to what they say, but also watching how they say it, how they act as they speak.

His task is complex: on the one hand, he knows that the most precious and almost the only source of knowledge is the memory of those he meets; on the other hand, he is aware that this memory is a fragile thing, volatile and evanescent—that memory has a vanishing point. That is why he is in a hurry—people forget, or else move away somewhere and one cannot find them again, and eventually they die. And Herodotus is out to collect as many reasonably credible facts as possible.

Knowing that he is on such untrustworthy and unstable ground, he is very careful in his accounts, constantly issuing warnings, emphasizing his distance from the material he presents:

• *As far as we know, Gyges was the first non-Greek to dedicate offerings at Delphi ...*
• *He wished, so they say, to reach Ithaca ...*

- *As far as I know, the following customs exist among the Persians ...*
- *And thus, so I assume, drawing conclusions from the known about the unknown ...*
- *And as I learned from what they say ...*
- *This is my account of what is said about the most distant countries ...*
- *If this is true, I don't know. I write only that which is said ...*
- *I cannot accurately state which of the Ionians proved to be cowards in this battle, and which courageous, because they all accuse one another ...*

Herodotus understands that he is in a world of uncertain things and imperfect knowledge, which is why he frequently makes excuses for his shortcomings, explains and justifies himself:

- *It is impossible to argue against the person who spoke about the Ocean, because the tale is based on something which is obscure and dubious. I do not know of the existence of any River Ocean, and I think that Homer or one of the other poets from past times invented the name and introduced it into his poetry.*
- *Clearly no one knows about Europe, neither about the parts lying to the East nor to the North, and whether it is surrounded by the sea ...*
- *What lies beyond this land ... no one knows precisely; I can find out nothing from anyone who can say that he saw it with his own eyes ...*
- *I was unable to determine precisely how numerous were the Scythians, and heard quite contradictory things about this ...*

But to the extent that it is possible to do so—and, given the epoch, this speaks to a tremendous expenditure of effort and to great personal determination—he tries to check everything, to get to the sources, to establish the facts:

- *Although I tried very hard, I was unable to learn from any eyewitness if a sea exists north of Europe ...*

- *This temple, as I discovered through research, is the oldest of all the temples to Aphrodite ...*
- *Wanting to obtain reliable information from people who would be able to impart it to me, I even sailed to Tyre in Phoenicia, because I had heard that there was a temple to Heracles there ... and I engaged in a conversation with the priests of the god and asked them ... But I saw that their answer does not agree with what the Greeks say ...*
- *There is a place in Arabia where I went myself to gather information about winged snakes. Upon arrival there, I saw the snakes' bones and backbones in quantities impossible to describe ...*
- (about the island Chemmis) ... *it is said by the Egyptians to be a floating island. I myself never saw it floating or moving, and ...*
- But these stories are in my opinion nonsense ... *because I saw myself that ...*

And if he knows something, how does he know it? Because he heard, he saw:

- *I say only that which the Libyans themselves recount ...*
- *Whether this is true or not, I do not know. I write only that which is told ...*
- *According to the stories of the Trachis, the left bank of the Ister is populated by bees ...*
- *Until now my accounts were driven by my own observations, judgments, and investigations: from now on, however, I intend to speak of Egyptian history according to what I have heard about it; this will also be accompanied from time to time by what I myself saw ...*
- *Anyone who finds such things credible can make of these Egyptian stories what he wishes. My job, throughout this account, is simply to record whatever I am told by each of my sources.*
- *When I queried the priests as to whether the story told by the Greeks is sheer blather or not, they declared that they know about it from an interview conducted with Menelaus himself ...*
- (about the Colchians) *I first came to realize myself, and then heard from*

others later, that the Colchians are obviously Egyptian.... I myself had guessed their Egyptian origin not only because the Colchians are dark-skinned and curly-haired ... but more importantly because Colchians, Egyptians, and Ethiopians are the only peoples in the world who practice circumcision and have always done so.

· *And I will write as some Persians, who do not want to beautify the history of Cyrus but to present the actual truth, say ...*

Herodotus is by turns surprised, astounded, delighted, terrified by things. To some he simply gives no credence, knowing how easily people can be carried away by fantasy:

· *These same priests say, which does not seem credible to me, that the god himself comes to the chapel ...*

· *[The Egyptian king Rhampsinitus] ... what he did—so the story goes, but I find it unbelievable—was install his daughter in a room with instructions to accept all men indiscriminately ...*

· *The bald-headed [??] people say, which strikes me as improbable, that the mountains are inhabited by a goat-footed race, and when one passes them, one will find others, who sleep for six months at a time. I cannot believe that at all ...*

· (about the Neurians' ability to turn themselves into wolves): *Personally I do not believe this, but they make the claim despite its implausibility, and even swear that they are telling the truth.*

· (about statues that fell to their knees before people): *This thing does not seem credible to me, but perhaps to someone else—yes ...*

History's first globalist sneers and scoffs at the ignorance of his contemporaries: *I am amused when I see that not one of all the people who have drawn maps of the world has set it out sensibly. They show Ocean as a river flowing around the outside of the earth, which is as circular as if it had been drawn with a pair of compasses, and they make Asia and Europe the same size. I shall now briefly explain how big each of these continents is and what each of them should look like on the map.*

And after delineating Asia, Europe, and Africa, he ends his description of the world with the sentence: *I have no idea why the earth—which is, after all, single—has three separate names (each of which is the name of a woman)* ...

BEFORE HE IS TORN APART
BY DOGS AND BIRDS

The driver with whom I traveled about most frequently in
Ethiopia—which I had reached by a somewhat circuitous
route, through Uganda, Tanzania, and Kenya—was called Negusi.
He was a slight, thin man, on whose skinny neck swollen with
veins rested a disproportionately large yet shapely head. His eyes
were remarkable—enormous, dark, obscured by a shiny film, like
the eyes of a dreamy girl. Negusi was compulsively neat: at each
stop he carefully removed the dust from his clothes with a little
brush, which he always carried with him. This was not wholly
unjustified in this country, where in the dry season, there was no
place free of dust and sand.

My travels with Negusi—and we drove thousands of kilometers
together under difficult and hazardous conditions—were yet
another lesson in what an abundance of signs and signals any
human being is. All one has to do is make an effort to notice and
interpret them. Predisposed to thinking that another person communicates with us solely by means of the spoken or written word,
we do not stop to consider that there are many other methods of
conversation. Everything speaks: the expression of the face and
eyes, the gestures of the hand and the movements of the body, the
vibrations which the latter sends out, his clothing and the way it is

worn; dozens of other transmitters, amplifiers, and mufflers, which together make up the individual being and—to use the conceit of the Anglophone world—his personal chemistry.

Technology, which reduces human exchange to an electronic signal, impoverishes and mutes this multifarious nonverbal language with which, when we are together, in close proximity, we continually and unconsciously communicate. This unspoken language, moreover, the language of facial expression and minute gesture, is infinitely more sincere and genuine than the spoken or written one; it is far more difficult to tell lies without words, to conceal falsehood and hypocrisy. So that a man could truly camouflage his thoughts, the disclosure of which could prove dangerous, Chinese culture perfected the art of the frozen face, of the inscrutable mask and the vacant gaze: only behind such a screen could someone truly hide.

Negusi knew only two expressions in English: "problem" and "no problem."

But using this gibberish we communicated ably in the most fraught circumstances. In conjunction with the wordless signals particular to each human being and which can speak volumes if only we would observe him carefully—drink him in, as it were— two words sufficed for us to feel no chasm between us and made traveling together possible.

A military patrol stops us in the Goba mountains. Soldiers in these parts maraud with impunity, are spoiled, greedy, and frequently drunk. All around are craggy mountains, a desolate emptiness without a single living soul. Negusi gets into a negotiation. I can see that he is explaining something; he puts his hand to his heart. The others are also speaking. They adjust their automatic rifles, pull their helmets lower down on their foreheads, which only makes them look more menacing. "Negusi," I ask, "problem?" The answer can be twofold. He can reply, dismissively: "No problem!" and drive on, looking satisfied. Or he can say in a serious, even fearful voice, "Problem!," which signals that I must pull out ten dollars, which he will hand over to the soldiers so that they might let us pass.

All of a sudden, for reasons I cannot fathom, seeing nothing on the road as we drive through an unpopulated, lifeless area, Negusi becomes anxious, squirming and looking all around. "Negusi," I ask, "problem?" He doesn't answer and continues to peer in all directions, visibly nervous. The atmosphere in the car grows tense. His fear starts to rub off on me: who knows what lies in wait for us? An hour passes in this way, and then, after a turn in the road, Negusi relaxes and happily slaps the steering wheel to the rhythm of some Amharic song. "Negusi," I ask, "no problem?" "No problem!" he exclaims joyfully. I discover later in a nearby town that we had been driving a stretch of road notorious for armed bands that attack, rob, and even kill passersby on a regular basis.

People here have little awareness of the greater world, do not know Africa well, or even their own country, but on the circumscribed territory of their small homeland, of their own tribe, they are familiar with every path, every tree and stone. Such places hold no mystery for them, because they have come to know them from childhood, walking countless times at night in the darkness, touching with their hands the boulders and trees standing by the roadside, feeling with their bare feet where the invisible paths run.

It is thus during my travels over Amharic lands with Negusi. He is a poor man, but in some little corner of his heart he feels pride in this vast region, whose real boundaries only he can truly delineate.

I am thirsty, so Negusi stops by a stream and encourages me to sip its cold, crystalline water.

"No problem!" he calls, seeing that I am hesitating about whether this water is clean, and he submerges his large head in it.

Later, I want to sit down on some nearby rocks, but Negusi forbids it:

"Problem!" he warns, and indicates with a zigzagging motion of his hand that there might be snakes there.

Every expedition into the depths of Ethiopia is a luxury. Ordinarily, my days are spent gathering information, writing telegrams, and going to the post office, so the telegrapher on duty can forward my dispatches to the Polish Press Agency offices in London (this turns out to be less costly than sending them directly to Warsaw). The collecting of information is a time-consuming, difficult, and dodgy business—a hunting expedition that rarely results in capturing one's quarry. Only one newspaper is published here: four pages called the *Ethiopian Herald*. (I witnessed several times in the countryside a bus arriving from Addis Ababa, bringing not only passengers but a single copy of this publication as well. People gathered in the marketplace and the mayor or a local teacher read aloud the articles in Amharic and summarized those written in English. Everyone listened raptly and the atmosphere was almost festive: a newspaper had arrived from the capital!)

An emperor rules Ethiopia at this time; there are no political parties, trade unions, or parliamentary opposition. There are Eritrean guerrillas, but far away in the north, in mostly impenetrable mountains. A Somali opposition movement operates out in a region of equally difficult access, the desert of the Ogaden. Yes, I could somehow make my way to both places, but it would take months, and I am Poland's only correspondent in all of Africa. I cannot just suddenly go silent, disappear into the continent's uninhabited wastelands.

So how am I to gather my material? My colleagues from the wealthy news agencies—Reuters, AP, or AFP—hire translators, but I lack the funds for this. Furthermore, their offices are equipped with a powerful radio: an American Zenith, a Trans-Oceanic, from which one can tune in the entire world. But it costs a fortune, and I can only fantasize about it. So I walk, ask, listen, cajole, scrape, and string together facts, opinions, stories. I don't complain, because this method enables me to meet many people and find out about things not covered in the press or on the radio.

When there's a lull, I make arrangements with Negusi to go out into the field. One cannot venture too far, because out there in the vastness it is easy to get stuck for days on end, weeks even. I have in mind a distance of one hundred or two hundred kilometers, before the great mountains begin. Furthermore, Christmas is approaching, and all of Africa, even the Muslim part, is growing noticeably quieter, to say nothing of Ethiopia, which has been Christian for sixteen centuries. "Go to Arba Minch!" advise those in the know, and they say it with such conviction that the name begins to acquire a magical resonance for me.

Indeed, it turns out to be a truly extraordinary place. On a flat and empty plain, on a low isthmus between the lakes of Abaya and Chamo, stands a wooden, white-painted barracks—the Berkele Mole Hotel. Each room gives onto an open verandah which extends right to the edge of a lake—one can jump from the deck straight into the emerald water (which, depending on the angle of the sun's rays, can turn azure blue, green, almost purple, and, in the evenings, navy blue and black).

In the morning, a peasant woman in a white robe sets up on the verandah a wooden armchair, as well as a massive sculpted wooden table. Silence, water, several acacia trees, and in the far distance, in the background, the gigantic, dark green Amaro mountains. One feels like the king of the world here.

. . .

I've brought with me a bundle of periodicals with articles about Africa, but from time to time I also reach for the tome from which I am inseparable, which has become my accustomed refuge, a retreat from the tensions of the world and the nervous pursuit of novelty into a peaceful realm of sunshine and quiet that emanates from events that have already occurred, people now gone and sometimes who were never there, having been only contrivances of the imagination, fictions, shadows. But this time my hopes for escape come to naught. I can see that serious and dangerous things are happening in my Greek's world, I sense a historic storm brewing, a sinister hurricane approaching.

Until now I had wandered far and wide with Herodotus, to the edges of his universe—to the Egyptians and the Massagetae, to the Scythians and the Ethiopians. But it is time to cease these far-flung peregrinations, for events are now shifting from these distant borderlands to the eastern part of the Mediterranean Sea, to where Persia and Greece, or more generally speaking, Asia and Europe, meet—in short, to the very omphalos of the world.

It is as if in the first part of his oeuvre Herodotus constructed a massive open-air amphitheater in which he placed dozens, even hundreds of nations and tribes from Asia, Europe, and Africa— from all of humanity as he knew it—and said to them: Now observe carefully, because here before your very eyes will unfold the world's greatest drama! He wants everyone to watch carefully. And the action on the stage does indeed take an abrupt dramatic turn.

Old Darius, king of the Persians, is preparing a great war against Greece to avenge his defeats in Sardis and at Marathon (one of Herodotus's laws: Do not humiliate people, because they will thereafter subsist on dreams of revenge). He conscripts his entire empire, all of Asia, into the preparations. But in the midst of all this, in 485 B.C.E. (the presumed year, incidentally, of Herod-otus's birth), he dies, having ruled for thirty-six years. After vari-ous struggles and intrigues, his young son Xerxes assumes the throne—the beloved child of Darius's wife, now widow, Atossa, whom Herodotus credits with having exercised great influence in the empire.

Xerxes inherits his father's project—preparing for war against the Greeks—but he is of a mind to strike against Egypt first: the Egyp-tians have mutinied against the Persian occupation of their land and want independence. Xerxes believes that quelling the Egyp-tian uprising is a more pressing matter, and that the expedition against the Greeks can wait. But his older and very influential cousin, Mardonius, son of deceased Darius's sister, is of another opinion. Who cares about the Egyptians? he says. We must move against the Greeks! (Herodotus suspects Mardonius of being in a hurry to attain power probably as eventual satrap of a conquered Greece): "*Master, it's wrong for the Athenians to go unpunished for all the harm they've done Persia.*"

Herodotus tells us that with time Mardonius does indeed con-vince Xerxes of the necessity of the Greek war. The Persian king nonetheless sets off first against Egypt, suppresses the rebellion, subjugates the country once again, and only then turns his atten-tion to the Greeks. Still he is quite cognizant of the seriousness of the action at hand, which is why he *summoned the pick of the leading Per-sians to a meeting, because he wanted to hear what they had to say.* He shares with them his plans for world conquest: "*There would be no point in recounting all the victories Cyrus, Cambyses, and my father Darius won, and all the peoples they annexed, because you are already well aware of their achievements. But what about me? When I became the king of Persia, I began to wonder how to avoid being left behind by those who preceded me in this position of honour, and how I might increase the Persian empire just as much as they did. . . . The reason I have convened this meeting, then, is to tell you my plans.*

"*I intend to bridge the Hellespont and march an army through Europe and against Greece, so that I can make the Athenians pay for all that they have done to Persia and to my father. . . . I will not rest until I have captured Athens and put it to the torch.*

" *. . . If we conquer them and their neighbours . . . we will make Persian territory end only at the sky, the domain of Zeus, so that the sun will not shine on any land beyond our borders. . . . If my information is accurate, once we have eliminated those I have mentioned, there will be nobody left — no town or people — capable of offering us armed resistance. And so the innocent will bear the yoke of slavery along with those who have wronged us.*"

Next to speak is Mardonius. To win over Xerxes, he begins with flattery: "*Master, you are the greatest Persian there has ever been, nor will there ever be anyone to equal you in the future either.*" After this ritualistic introduction, he tries to assure Xerxes that there will be no difficulties in conquering the Greeks. "No problem!" the excited Mardonius seems to be saying. He then claims that "*the Greeks usually wage war in an extremely stupid fashion, because they're ignorant and incompetent. . . . So, my lord, who is going to oppose you? Who is going to threaten you with war when you come from Asia at the head of a massive army and with your whole fleet? I am sure that the Greeks are not so foolhardy.*"

Silence falls among the assembled Persians: *No one else had anything to say — certainly, no one dared to voice an opinion contrary to the one before them . . .*

It is quite understandable. Imagine the situation: We are in Susa, the capital of the Persian empire. In an airy, shadow-filled hall in the royal palace, young Xerxes sits on a throne, and all around on stone benches sits *the pick of the leading Persians.* The council is deliberating the world's ultimate battle: if victory is achieved, the whole world will belong to the king of the Persians.

Furthermore, the prospective field of battle is far away from Susa—agile messengers need more than three months to cross the distance between the Persian capital and Athens. There is something unreal about an operation taking place at such a remove. But that is not why the summoned Persians dare not express contrary views. Despite being important and influential, despite constituting the elite of the elites, they nevertheless know that they live in an authoritarian and despotic state, and that it takes only a nod from Xerxes for any one of them to lose his head. So there they sit, frightened, mopping their foreheads. They dare not speak. The atmosphere must have resembled that of the Politburo under Stalin: at stake in both instances not just one's career, but life itself.

There is someone, however, who can speak up without fear. It is old Artabanus, Darius's brother and Xerxes' uncle. Even so, he begins cautiously, making certain to offer justification for daring to voice his opinions: *"My lord, unless opposing views are heard, it is impossible to pick and choose between various plans and decide which one is best."* He also reminds Xerxes that he cautioned his father, and his own brother, Darius, not to undertake the expedition against the Scythians, because that one too, he had felt, would end badly. And so it did. And now the Greeks?! *"This campaign you're planning, my lord, is against men who are vastly superior to the Scythians; they have the highest reputation for bravery on both land and sea."*

He counsels prudence and long reflection. He attacks Mardonius for encouraging the king to go to war, and proposes to him: *"Let each of us gamble the lives of our children on the outcome. If matters turn out as you say they will for the king, let my children be put to death, and I will join them; but if things turn out as I am predicting, let your children suffer that fate, and you too, if you make it back home. If you aren't prepared to run the risk, but are still determined to take the army overseas to Greece, I can tell you what news of Mardonius will reach the ears of those who stay behind here: they will be told that Mardo-*

nius was the cause of a great disaster for Persia, and that you were then torn apart by dogs and birds somewhere in Athenian territory . . ."

Tensions rise as everyone reflects on the wager proposed. Xerxes becomes angry, calls Artabanus a coward, and as punishment forbids him to go with him to war. He explains: *"It is impossible for either side to withdraw now; the only question at stake is whether or not we actively take the initiative. And in the end either all Persia will be in Greek hands, or all Greece will be in Persian hands; there is no middle ground in this war."*

And he dissolves the council. *Later, during the night, Xerxes was still worried by the view Artabanus had expressed. He thought it over during the night and he became quite convinced that it was not in his best interests for him to march on Greece. After this change of heart, he fell asleep, and during the night he had the following dream, or so the Persians say. Xerxes dreamt that a tall, handsome man stood over him and said, "Are you changing your mind, Persian? Are you deciding against taking an expedition to Greece . . . ? . . . No, keep the course of action you decided on during the daytime." In Xerxes' dream, after delivering this speech, the man flew away.*

Come daylight, Xerxes once again convenes a council. Ignoring the dream, he announces that he has changed his mind and that there will be no war. *The Persians were delighted with what Xerxes said, and prostrated themselves before him.*

That night, however, when Xerxes was asleep, the same figure appeared to him again in a dream and said, ". . . if you do not go out on this campaign immediately, this is what will happen. You have risen rapidly to a position of prominence and importance, but you will be laid low again just as swiftly."

Terrified by this apparition, Xerxes jumps out of bed and sends a messenger for Artabanus. He confesses to him the nightmares that have plagued him from the moment he decided to recall the expedition against the Greeks: *". . . ever since I've backed down and changed my mind, I've been haunted by a dream figure who does not approve of what I'm doing at all. In fact he threatened me just now, and then disappeared. If this dream is being sent by a god and he will be satisfied only when the campaign against Greece takes place, the same dream should wing its way to you as well, and give you the same instructions as it did me."*

Artabanus tries to calm Xerxes: *"In actual fact, ... dreams don't come from the gods, my son. ... The visions that occur to us in dreams are, more often than not, the things we have been concerned about during the day. And, you see, we have been extremely occupied with this expedition for some days now."*

But Xerxes cannot calm down: the phantom continues to visit him, exhorting him to go to war. He proposes that since Artabanus does not believe him, he should put on the royal robes, sit on the royal throne, and then, at night, lie down on the royal bed. Artabanus does this *and while he was asleep the same dream figure came to him as had appeared to Xerxes. The figure stood over Artabanus and said, "So you're the one who has been trying to discourage Xerxes from attacking Greece, are you? ... Well, you will not escape punishment, either now or in the future, for trying to deflect the inevitable."* ...

Artabanus dreamt that as well as making these threats the phantom was about to burn his eyes out with red-hot skewers. He uttered a loud cry, jumped out of bed, and sat himself down next to Xerxes. First he described what he had seen in his dream, and then he said, ... "Since your impetuousness is god-given, and since the destruction overtaking the Greeks is apparently heaven-sent, it is my turn to back down and change my mind." ...

Later, with Xerxes all intent on his campaign, he had a third dream one night, in which he saw himself wearing a garland made out of sprigs of an olive-tree whose branches overshadowed the whole world, but then the garland disappeared from his head. He described the dream to the Magi and they interpreted its reference to the whole world as meaning that he would gain dominion over the whole human race.

"Negusi," I said in the morning and started to pack, "we're going back to Addis Ababa."

"No problem!" he answered cheerfully and smiled, showing his fantastically white teeth.

XERXES

The end is not apparent
From the very outset.

—Herodotus

Much like the phantom from Herodotus's account, this scene continued to haunt me long after our return to Addis Ababa. Its message is pessimistic, fatalistic: man has no free will. He carries his fate within him like his genetic code—he must go where, and do what, destiny has ordained. Predestination is the Supreme Being, an omnipresent and all-encompassing Cosmic Causal Force. No one is above it—not the King of Kings, not even the gods themselves. Which is why the apparition that visits Xerxes does not have the shape of a god. One could negotiate with a god, one could disobey and even try to fool him; with destiny, that is impossible. It is anonymous and amorphous, lacking a name or distinct features, and all it does is warn, command, or threaten.

When does it do this?

With his fate immutably inscribed, man has but to read the script and enact it faithfully, point by point. If he interprets it erroneously, or else attempts to alter it, then the phantom of fate will appear, at first to shake its finger at him, and failing that to bring misfortune and punishment down upon the braggart's head.

The condition for survival, therefore, is humility vis-à-vis one's destiny. Xerxes at first accepts his mission, which is to exact vengeance on the Greeks for their having insulted the Persians generally and his father in particular. He declares war against them and vows not to rest until he conquers Athens and sets it on fire. Later, however, listening to the voices of reason, he changes his mind. He suppresses thoughts of war, sets aside the invasion plans, pulls back. It is then that the phantom appears in his dreams: "Madman," it seems to be saying, "do not hesitate! It is your destiny to strike against the Greeks!"

Initially, Xerxes tries to ignore the nighttime visitant, to treat it as an illusion, to rise above it somehow. But by doing so he only further irritates and angers the phantom, which appears once more by his throne and bedside, this time seriously offended, menacing. Xerxes looks around for succor, wondering if perhaps the weight of his responsibility has not driven him mad—he must make a decision, after all, that will determine the fate of the world, and as will eventually become clear, determine it for the next thousand years. He summons his uncle, Artabanus. "Help!" he pleads. The latter at first counsels Xerxes to ignore the dream: we dream about what has preoccupied us during the day, that is all. The dream, Artabanus says, is but a chimera.

The king is not convinced, because the phantom does not relent; it becomes more importunate and implacable than ever. Finally even Artabanus—a sensible and a wise man, a rationalist and a skeptic—bows to the ghostly presence, not only abandoning his earlier position, but changing from doubter into ardent believer, an executor of the phantom-fate's decree: "Move against the Greek? Let's go—at once!" Man is in thrall to both the earthly and the spiritual world, and in this episode we can see that the power of spirits is greater than the power of material reality.

Hearing about these nightmares of Xerxes, the average Persian or Greek might murmur, "Gods, if such a mighty person, the King of Kings, the ruler of the world, is but a pawn in the hands of destiny, then what about me, an ordinary man, a nothing, a mote of dust!" There is cause for comfort in this thought, relief—even optimism.

Xerxes is an odd figure. Although he ruled the world quite some time (almost the entire known world, in fact, with the exception of two cities, Athens and Sparta, to his unremitting torment), we know little about him. He assumed the throne at age thirty-two. He was consumed by desire for absolute power—power over everything and everyone. I am reminded of the title of a newspaper story I once noticed, whose author I unfortunately do not recall: "Mother, will we have everything someday?" That is precisely what animated Xerxes: he wanted to have everything. No one opposed him, because one would have had to pay with one's head for doing so. But in such an atmosphere of acquiescence, it takes only one dissenting voice for the ruler to feel anxiety, to hesitate. It was thus with Artabanus's objection. Xerxes lost his nerve, grew so uncertain having heard his uncle that he decided to abandon his plans of conquest. But these are human impulses, conflicts, and doubts; a Higher Power, the Deciding One, now steps onto the earthly stage. And from here on all will follow its decree. Fate must be fulfilled; you cannot alter or avoid it, even if it leads into an abyss.

Therefore Xerxes, in accordance with the Voice of Destiny's commands, goes to war. He recognizes his greatest strength, the

East's strength, Asia's strength—numbers, the immeasurable human mass, and trusts that its weight and momentum will crush and pulverize the enemy. (Scenes from World War I come to mind: In Poland's lake district of Mazury, Russian generals storming German positions sent forth entire regiments in which only a portion of the soldiers had rifles—and those lacking ammunition.)

First, Xerxes spends four years creating his army—a worldwide military coalition into whose ranks will be recruited all the peoples, tribes, and clans of the empire. Just naming them all takes Herodotus several pages. He calculates that this army—infantry, cavalry, and naval crews—numbered some five million men. He exaggerates, of course. Even so, it was a gigantic fighting force. How to feed it? How to supply it with sufficient drinking water? These men and animals would imbibe entire rivers along the way, leaving empty beds behind them. Someone observes that, luckily, Xerxes ate only once a day. If the king, and with him the entire army, ate twice daily, they would have turned all of Thrace, Macedonia, and Greece into a desert, and the local populations would have died of hunger.

Herodotus is fascinated by this army's advance, by the vertiginous mighty river of men, beasts, and equipment, of uniforms and armor. Because each ethnic group has its own attire, the colorful diversity of this throng is difficult to describe. Two chariots form the center of the procession: *the sacred chariot of Zeus, which was drawn by eight white horses. Following them on foot (because no human being is allowed to mount the seat of this chariot) came the charioteer, with the reins in his hands. Behind him came Xerxes himself, seated on a chariot drawn by Nesaean horses. . . . He was followed by the 1,000 bravest and noblest Persian spearmen, . . . and then another 1,000 élite Persian horsemen, and after them came the 10,000 best remaining Persian soldiers on foot. . . . And finally the rest of the army brought up the rear, all massed together indiscriminately.*

But let us not be misled by the ornamentalism of this army marching off to war. This is no carnival, no holiday party. On the contrary. Herodotus notes that the troops, walking with difficulty and in silence, had to be driven on now and then by whips.

He describes in detail the behavior of the Persian king. Xerxes is unbalanced, unpredictable, an astonishing bundle of contradictions (in this he resembles Stavrogin).

Here he is, making his way to Sardis with his army. He spots a plane-tree along the road *which was so beautiful that he presented it with golden decorations and appointed one of the Immortals as guardian to look after it.*

He is still under the spell of the tree's charms when news reaches him that a great storm in the straits of the Hellespont has destroyed the bridges which he had ordered built so that his army could cross from Asia into Europe in its advance on Greece. Upon hearing this, Xerxes flew into a rage. *He ordered his men to give the Hellespont three hundred lashes and to sink a pair of shackles into the sea. I once heard that he also dispatched men to brand the Hellespont as well. Be that as it may, he did tell the men he had thrashing the sea to revile it in terms you would never hear from a Greek. "Bitter water," they said, "this is your punishment for wronging your master when he did no wrong to you. King Xerxes will cross you, with or without your consent. People are right not to sacrifice to a muddy, brackish stream like you!" So the sea was punished at his orders, and he had the supervisors of the bridging of the Hellespont beheaded.*

We do not know how many of these heads were cut off. We do not know if the condemned builders meekly offered up their necks, or if they fell on their knees and begged for mercy. The carnage must have been horrific, because such bridges were built by thousands upon thousands of people. In any event, the punishments satisfy Xerxes, help him regain his mental equilibrium. His people build new bridges across the Hellespont, and the Magi announce that all omens are auspicious.

The king, overjoyed at this news, decides to press on when a Lydian he knew, Pythius, comes to him and begs for a favor: *"Master, I have five sons, all of whom have to march with you against Greece. Please, my lord, take pity on me in my old age and release one of my sons, the eldest one, from military service, so that he can look after me and manage my property as well. But take the other four with you—and may you return home with all your objectives attained!"*

At these words Xerxes once again falls into a fury: *"Damn you!"* Xerxes shouts at the old man. *". . . How dare you mention a son of yours, when you are no more than my slave, and should follow in my train with your whole household, wife and all? . . ."* As soon as Xerxes had given Pythius this answer, he ordered those of his men who were responsible for such matters to find the eldest of Pythius' sons and to cut him in half. Then they were to place one half on the right of the road and the other half on the left, so that the army would pass between them.

And that is what happened.

The unending river of troops filed down the road, urged along by the crack of the whips, and all the soldiers saw lying on either side of them the bloody remains of Pythius's eldest son. Where was Pythius at that moment? Did he stand by the corpse? By which part of it? How did he behave when Xerxes approached in his chariot? With what expression on his face? This is unknowable, because, being a slave, he had to kneel with his face to the ground.

An uncertainty afflicts Xerxes. It gnaws at him. He hides it with a show of haughtiness and pride. In order to feel stronger, internally shored up, assured of his power, he organizes a review of his army and fleet. The immensity of this mass cannot but impress, cannot but take one's breath away. So great is the number of arrows released simultaneously from all the bows that it obscures the sun. The ships are so many that one cannot see the waters of the bay: *While they were in Abydus, Xerxes decided that he would like to survey his whole army. A dais of white stone had already been made especially for him . . . and set up on a hill there. From this vantage-point he could look down on to the sea-shore and see both the land army and the fleet. As he watched them he conceived the desire to see the ships race . . . Xerxes took great pleasure in the race, and indeed in the whole army.*

The sight of the Hellespont completely covered by his ships and the coast and plains of Abydus totally overrun by men first gave Xerxes a feeling of deep self-satisfaction, but later he began to weep.

The king crying?

His uncle, Artabanus, seeing Xerxes' tears, spoke to him thus: *"My lord, a short while ago you were feeling happy with your situation and now you are weeping. What a total change of mood!"*

"Yes," Xerxes answered. "I was reflecting on things and it occurred to me how short the sum total of human life is, which made me feel compassion. Look at all these people—but not one of them will still be alive in a hundred years' time."

They converse thus about life and death for a long while still, after which the king sends his old uncle back to Susa and, having waited for the dawn, orders the crossing of the straits of the Hellespont to the other side—to Europe: *At sunrise, Xerxes poured a libation from a golden cup into the sea and, facing the sun, asked the sun-god to avert any accidents which might stop him from reaching the outer limits of Europe and conquering the whole continent.*

Xerxes' army, drinking the rivers dry, consuming whatever food it comes across, and keeping to the northern shores of the Aegean Sea, crosses Thrace, Macedonia, and Thessaly, and reaches Thermopylae.

Every school curriculum includes Thermopylae; it is not usual to devote an entire class to it.

Thermopylae is a narrow isthmus, a passage between the sea and a high mountain lying to the northwest of today's Greek capital. To seize this passage is to have an open road to Athens. The Persians understand this, as do the Greeks, of course. Which is why both will wage a fierce battle here. The Greek combatants will all perish, but Persian losses will also be immense.

Initially, Xerxes counted on the handful of Greeks defending Thermopylae simply to flee at the sight of the gigantic Persian army, and so calmly waited for that to occur. But the Greeks, under the command of Leonidas, do not retreat. Impatient, Xerxes sends out a scout on horseback on a mission of reconnaissance. *The scout approached the Greeks' camp and kept them under close surveillance . . . He watched them in a variety of occupations, such as exercising naked and combing their hair; this surprised him, but he took careful note of their numbers and then made his way back to Xerxes, without meeting any opposition. No one set out after him, and in fact he met with total indifference. When he got back he gave Xerxes a thorough report on what he had seen.*

Xerxes listened to what the scout had to say, but he could not understand that in actual fact the Greeks were getting themselves ready to kill or be killed to the best of their ability.

The battle lasts several days, and the balance is tipped only by a traitor who shows the Persians the path through the mountains. They surround the Greeks, all of whom are killed. After the battle, Xerxes walks over the battlefield strewn with corpses, looking for the body of Leonidas. *When he came to Leonidas' corpse, . . . he told his men to cut off his head and stick it on a pole.*

Xerxes lost all of his subsequent battles. *When Xerxes realized the extent of the disaster that had taken place, he became afraid. What if the Greeks got the*

idea ... of sailing to the Hellespont and demolishing his bridges? In that case, he
would be trapped in Europe, and would probably be wiped out. And so Xerxes'
thoughts turned to flight.

And flee he does, abandoning the theater of war before the war's end. He returns to Susa. He is thirty-something years old. He will be king of the Persians for another fifteen years, during which time he will occupy himself with expanding his palace in Persepolis. Perhaps he felt internally spent? Perhaps he suffered from depression? In any event, insofar as the world was concerned, he disappeared. The dreams of might, of ruling over everything and everyone, faded away. It is said that he was interested only in women; he constructed for them an immense, imposing harem, whose ruins I have seen.

He was fifty-six years old when, in 465 B.C.E., he was murdered by Artabanus, the commander of his security guard. This Artabanus put up Xerxes' younger brother, Artaxerxes, to be king. Artaxerxes in turn later murdered Artabanus, during a fight that broke out in the palace. The son of Artaxerxes, Xerxes II, was murdered in 425 by his brother Sogdians, who was later murdered by Darius II, etc., etc.

THE OATH OF ATHENS

Before the defeated Xerxes pulls out of Europe and returns to Susa with his emaciated, sick, and starving forces (*wherever they went and whatever people they encountered, they stole and ate their crops. If there were no crops to be had, they ate grass and herbs they found growing in the ground, and bark and leaves they peeled or pulled off both wild trees and cultivated ones. They were so hungry that they left nothing untried. Moreover, they were ravaged by disease, and men were dying of dysentery throughout the journey. Xerxes also left sick troops in the care and maintenance of whichever community they had reached at that particular point of the march . . .*), before all this happens, many other things will come to pass and much blood will be spilled.

There is a war going on, after all, one in which Persia is to conquer Greece—meaning, Asia is to seize Europe, despotism is to destroy democracy, and slavery is to prevail against freedom.

At first, everything suggests that this will in fact occur, that it will be thus. The Persian army marches hundreds of kilometers into Europe without meeting any resistance. What is more, several small Greek states, fearing that such a great army's victory is inevitable, surrender without a fight and join the Persian side. So Xerxes' army grows even larger and more powerful as it advances. Having seized the barrier that was Thermopylae, Xerxes reaches Athens. He occupies and burns down the city. Yet while Athens lies in ruins, Greece still exists—and it will be saved by the genius of Themistocles.

Themistocles has just been chosen leader of Athens. This takes place at a difficult time, during a moment of great tension, because it is known that Xerxes is preparing an invasion. It so happens that just at that moment, Athens receives a large influx of funds generated by its silver mines in Laurium. The populists and the demagogues instantly feel the wind in their sails and come out with a slogan: Distribute it to all equally! Finally, everyone will have something, everyone will feel strong and secure.

But Themistocles acts sensibly and courageously: Athenians, he calls, come to your senses! The danger of annihilation hangs over our heads. Our only salvation, instead of spreading that money about, is to build with it a strong fleet capable of resisting the Persian force!

Herodotus paints the picture of this great war of antiquity by means of contrasts: On the one side, from the East, comes surging an immense, powerful steamroller, a blind force subject to the despotic will of a king-master, a king-god. On the other side sprawls the scattered, internally quarrelsome Greek world, rife with disputes and antagonisms, a world of tribes and independent cities without a common government to bind them. Two urban centers, Athens and Sparta, rise to the top of this incoherent amalgam, and taken together, their relations and arrangements will determine the principal axis of ancient Greek history.

Two individuals also face each other in this war. The young Xerxes, with a strong sense of boundless power, and Themistocles, older, convinced his cause is just, courageous in thought and in deed. Their situations are not comparable: Xerxes rules absolutely, issuing orders at will; before Themistocles can issue an order, he must first secure the consent of military commanders who only nominally answer to him, and he must also win the approval of the populace. Their roles, too, are different: one rides at the head of an army advancing like an avalanche, in a hurry to attain a decisive victory; the other is merely a *primus inter pares*, and spends his time convincing, debating, and discussing with the continually convening disputatious Greeks.

The Persians face no dilemmas—their single goal is to please their king. They are like Russian soldiers from the poem "Ordon's Redoubt" by Adam Mickiewicz.

> How the soldiers fall, whose God and faith
>   is the Czar.
> The Czar is angry: let us die, and make the
>   Czar happy.

The Greeks by contrast are by nature divided. On the one hand, they are attached to their small homelands, their city-states, each with its distinct interests and separate ambitions; on the other hand, they are united by a common language and common gods, as well as by a vague feeling—which nevertheless resonates forcefully at times—of a greater Greek patriotism.

The war is taking place on two fronts: on land and at sea. After seizing Thermopylae, the Persians encounter no resistance for a long time. Their fleet, however, keeps suffering dramatic setbacks. To begin, it sustains large losses as a result of storms and gales. Sudden violent winds propel Persian ships onto coastal rocks, where they shatter like matchboxes and their crews drown.

Initially, the Greek fleet is a lesser danger than the storms. The Persians have many times more ships and this numerical superiority depresses Greek morale; time and again they fall into a panic, lose heart, think of escaping. They are far from being born killers. They do not have a taste for soldiering. If there is an opportunity to avoid a clash, they eagerly seize it. Sometimes they will go to great lengths just to avoid a skirmish. Unless the opponent is another Greek, of course—in which case they will wrestle with him ferociously.

Now too, under Persian pressure, the Greek fleet keeps retreating. Its commander, Themistocles, tries as far as he can to restrain it. Hold on, he exhorts the crews of the ships, try to maintain your positions! Sometimes they listen to him, but not always. The withdrawal continues, until at last the Greek ships find harbor in the bay of Salamis, near Athens. The Greek captains feel safe here. The entrance to the bay is so narrow that the Persian king will think twice before sailing in with his gigantic fleet.

Both Xerxes and Themistocles now ponder their situations. Xerxes: To go in or not to go in? Themistocles: If I can draw Xerxes into the little bay, its surface is so small that his numbers will prove a disadvantage. Xerxes: I will win, because I will sit on the throne at the edge of the sea, and the Persians, seeing that their king is watching, will fight like lions! Themistocles doesn't yet know what Xerxes is thinking, and to make certain that the Persians enter the bay, he resorts to a trick: He ... briefed one of his men (a house-slave of his—his children's attendant, to be precise—whose name was Sicinnus), and sent him over to the Persian camp in a boat. ... Sicinnus sailed over and said to the Persian commanders, "I am on a secret mission for the Athenian commander, who is in fact sympathetic to Xerxes' cause and would prefer you to gain the upper hand in the war rather than the Greeks. None of the other Greeks know that I am here. The message from my master is that the Greeks are in a state of panic and are planning to retreat. Unless you just stand by and let them escape, you have an opportunity here to achieve a glorious victory. They are disunited, in no *position to offer you resistance; in fact you'll see them pitting their ships against one another, those who are on your side fighting those who are not." After delivering this message, Sicinnus left.*

Themistocles turned out to be a good psychologist. He knew that Xerxes, like every ruler, was a vain man, and that vanity makes one blind, impairs one's ability to think rationally. And so it was this time. Encouraged by the disinformation about Greek squabbling, instead of steering clear of the trap that a small bay always poses for a large fleet, he gives the order to sail into Salamis and block the Greeks' escape route. The Persians execute this maneuver, under the cover of darkness.

That same evening, even as the Persians are secretively and quietly approaching the bay, another dispute flares up among the Greeks, who do not realize what is transpiring: *So the commanders at Salamis were furiously hurling arguments at one another. They were still unaware that they had been surrounded by the Persian fleet, and continued to assume that the enemy had remained where they had seen them stationed during the day.*

When they hear of the Persians' approach, they initially give the news no credence, but finally accept the information and, spurred on by Themistocles, prepare themselves for combat.

The battle begins at dawn, so that Xerxes, sitting on a throne at the foot of the mountains which lie opposite Salamis and are called the Aegaleos, can observe it. *Whenever anything went well for his side, he asked who the captain of the ship in question was, and his scribes wrote down the name of the man, his father, and the town he came from.* Xerxes, confident of victory, wants to be able to reward his heroes later.

Faithful descriptions of battles which can be found in the literature of every epoch have one thing in common: they paint a picture of tremendous chaos, monstrous confusion, spectacular disorder. Even the most carefully orchestrated engagement in the moment of frontal collision descends into a bloody, quivering vortex, in which it is difficult to get one's bearings let alone to gain control. There are those hell-bent on killing others, and those looking for a means to slip away, or at the very least to duck the blows, and everything is overlaid with shouts, moans, and yelps, amidst turmoil and smoke.

So it was at Salamis. Whereas in the combat between two individuals one may discern agility, even grace, the collision in tight quarters of two fleets consisting of wooden ships and propelled by thousands of oars must have resembled a great bucket into which someone has thrown hundreds of sluggishly creeping, clumsily clambering, and chaotically entangled crabs. One ship rammed another, one listed on its side, another sank to the bottom with its entire crew, yet another attempted retreat, somewhere else several struggled against one another, permanently locked together it would have seemed, somewhere else a ship was trying to turn around, another was attempting to slip out of the bay, and in the general confusion Greeks fell upon Greeks, Persians upon Persians, until at last, after hours of this maritime hell, the Persians gave up and those of them who were left—those not drowned or otherwise killed—escaped.

Xerxes' first reaction to the defeat is fear. The first thing he undertakes is to send *his children to Ephesus (some illegitimate children of his had come along on the expedition)*. He gives them as a guardian Hermotimus, a high-ranking court eunuch who was born in Pedasa.

Herodotus is very interested in this man's fate and writes about it in detail: *No one we know of has ever exacted a more total retribution for a wrong done to him than Hermotimus. He was taken prisoner in a war, put up for sale, and bought by a man from Chios called Panionius. Now, Panionius made a living in the most atrocious way imaginable. What he used to do was acquire good-looking boys, castrate them, and take them to Sardis and Ephesus, where he would offer them for sale at very high prices; in foreign countries eunuchs command higher prices than whole men on account of their complete reliability. One of Panionius' victims—one among a great many, because this was the way he made a living—was Hermotimus. In fact, however, Hermotimus' luck was not all bad: he was sent from Sardis to Xerxes' court as one of a number of gifts, and eventually became the king's most valued eunuch.*

Now, when Xerxes was in Sardis, in the course of setting out with his army against Athens, Hermotimus went down on some business or other to the part of Mysia called Atarneus, where people from Chios live, and he met Panionius there. He entered into a long, friendly conversation with him, first listing all the benefits that had come his way thanks to Panionius, and then offering to do as much good to him in return; all he had to do, he said, was move his family to Atarneus and live there. Panionius gladly accepted Hermotimus' offer and moved his wife and children there. So when Hermotimus had Panionius and his whole family where he wanted, he said, "Panionius, there is no one in the world who makes a living in as foul a way as you do. What harm did I or any of my family do to you or any of yours? Why did you make me a nothing instead of a man? You expected the gods not to notice what you used to do in those days, but the law they follow is one of justice, and for your crimes they have delivered you into my hands. As a result, then, you should have no grounds for complaint about the payment I am going to extract from you." When he had finished this rebuke, he had Panionius' sons brought into the room and proceeded to force him to castrate all four of them. The deed was done, under compulsion, and afterwards Hermotimus forced the sons to castrate their father. And that is how vengeance and Hermotimus caught up with Panionius.

Crime and punishment, injustice and revenge—one always follows the other, sooner or later. As it is in relations between individuals, so it is between nations. Whoever first starts a war, and therefore, in Herodotus's opinion, commits a crime, will be revenged upon and punished, be it immediately or after the passage of time. This relation, this inexorable pairing, is the very essence of fate, the meaning of irreversible destiny.

Panionius experienced it, and now it was Xerxes' turn. In the case of the King of Kings, the matter is more complicated, because he is also the symbol of the nation and of the empire. The Persians in Susa, having learned about the annihilation of the fleet at Salamis, do not rend their garments; rather, they tremble for the fate of their king and hope that nothing untoward happens to him. Which is why, when he finally does return to Persia, his homecoming is a grand and magnificent occasion—the people are happy, relieved. Who cares about the thousands of dead and drowned, about the shattered ships—what matters most is that the king is alive and that he is once again with us!

Xerxes escapes from Greece, but leaves part of his army there. As its commander he designates his cousin, Darius's nephew—Mardonius.

Mardonius begins cautiously. First, without hurrying, he calmly winters in Thessaly. Then he sends a special messenger to the various oracles, to learn their prophecies. Guided by these, *he sent a Macedonian, Alexander . . . , off to Athens with a message. One reason he chose Alexander for this mission was because Alexander had family ties with Persia . . . He considered Alexander his best bet for winning over the Athenians, which he wanted to do because he had apparently heard that they were a populous and warlike race, and he was aware that the defeat the Persians had met at sea was due mainly to them. With the Athenians on his side, Mardonius was sure—an entirely justified confidence—that he would have no difficulty in gaining control of the sea, while he already had a considerable advantage on land, as far as he could see. So this was his plan for overcoming the Greeks.*

Alexander arrives in Athens and tries to convince its inhabitants that they should not wage war against the Persians but instead should enter into an agreement with them, for otherwise they will perish, seeing as how *the king has incredible power at his command and a very long reach.*

The Athenians nevertheless reply as follows: "*In actual fact, we were already aware of the disparity between the resources at our disposal and Xerxes' enormous power, so there was no need for your pointed reminder. Nevertheless, we are so focused on freedom that we will fight for it however we can.... Go and take this message from the Athenians to Mardonius: as long as the sun keeps to its present course, we will never come to terms with Xerxes. On the contrary, we will take to the field and fight against him, confident of the support of the gods and heroes for whom he felt such utter contempt that he burnt their homes and statues.*"

And to the Spartans, who had arrived in Athens fearing that the city would come to terms with the Persians, they said this: "*You are perfectly well aware of the Athenian temperament. You should have known that there isn't enough gold on earth, or any land of such outstanding beauty and fertility, that we would accept it in return for collaborating with the enemy and enslaving Greece.... So if you didn't know it before, we can assure you that so long as even a single Athenian remains alive, we will never come to terms with Xerxes.*"

After hearing these words, Alexander and the Spartans departed from Athens.

TIME VANISHES

This was no longer Addis Ababa but Dar es-Salaam, a city on a bay that had been sculpted into such a perfect semicircle that it seemed like one of hundreds of gentle Greek coves—this one somehow transported here, to the eastern shore of Africa. The sea was always calm; slow little waves, creating a quiet, rhythmic splash, sank without a trace into the warm sand of the shore.

Although the city numbered no more than two hundred thousand, it seemed now as if half the world had converged upon it and was calling it home. Its name alone, Dar es-Salaam, which in Arabic means "House of Peace," spoke of its ties to the Middle East (infamous ties, to be sure, because Arabs shipped out African slaves through here). The center of town was occupied largely by Indians and Pakistanis, with all the permutations of language and faith their civilization has produced: Among them were Sikhs, followers of the Aga Khan, Muslims, and Catholics from Goa. There were colonies of immigrants from the Indian Ocean islands—from the Seychelles and the Comoros, Madagascar and Mauritius—an attractive, even beautiful group that came into being from the mingling of various peoples of the South. And there were the more recently arrived Chinese, who had come here to build the Tanzania–Zambia railroad.

Encountering for the first time such a diversity of peoples and cultures as were in evidence in Dar es-Salaam of the 1960s, the European was struck not so much by the realization that all manner of other worlds existed beyond Europe's boundaries—he had been aware of this, at least theoretically, for quite some time—but above all by the fact that these worlds met, mixed, and coexisted without the mediation and, to some degree, without the knowledge and consent of Europe. For many centuries, Europe was the center of the world in such a literal and obvious way that it now dawned upon the European with difficulty that, without him and beyond him, other peoples and civilizations carried on with their respective traditions and their distinct problems. It was moreover he who was the newcomer here, the foreigner, and *his* universe but a distant and abstract reality.

The first to realize the world's essential multiplicity was Herodotus. "We are not alone," he tells Greeks in his opus, and to prove this he undertakes his journeys to the ends of the earth. "We have neighbors, they in turn have their neighbors, and all together we populate a single planet."

For a human being who until then had lived within the confines of a small homeland whose territory he could easily cover on foot, this unprecedented, planetary survey was an awakening, one that transformed his understanding, imparting to it hitherto unknown dimensions, an entirely new scale of values.

Traveling and encountering various tribes and peoples, Herodotus observes and records that each of them has its own history, which unfolds independently from yet parallel to other histories—in other words, that far from being one story, human history in its aggregate resembles a great cauldron whose perpetually simmering surface sees incessant collisions of innumerable particles, each moving in their own orbits, along trajectories that intersect at an infinite number of points.

Herodotus discovers something else as well, namely, the multi-formity of time, or, more precisely, the multiplicity of methods of measuring it. For in the old days, peasants calculated time by the seasons of the year, city dwellers by generations, the chroniclers of ancient states by the length of the ruling dynasties. How does one compare these measurements, how does one find a means of conversion or a common denominator? Herodotus wrestles with this issue constantly, searches for solutions. Accustomed to an exacting mechanical measurement, we do not realize what a problem the computation of time once presented, how much difficulty lurked therein, how many riddles and mysteries.

At times, when I had a free afternoon or evening, I would drive in my beat-up green Land Rover to the Sea View Hotel, where one could sit on the verandah, order a beer or some tea, listen to the sigh of the sea or, beginning at dusk, to the chirping of the cicadas. It was one of Dar es-Salaam's most popular meeting places, and colleagues from other agencies or publications would often drop by. During the day, we all cruised about town, trying to find things out. There was not much happening in this remote, provincial city, and to collect any information at all we had to cooperate, not compete. One of us had a better ear than others, one a better eye, another more journalistic luck. Every now and then—in the street, in one of the air-conditioned cafés, or here at the Sea View Hotel—the exchange of loot took place. Someone had heard that there had been a coup against Mobutu; others dismissed this as gossip—and how could one verify it, anyway? From such rumors, whispers, conjectures—and facts, too—we cobbled together our reports and sent them back home.

Sometimes no one appeared on the verandah, and if I happened to have Herodotus with me, I would open the book at random. *The*

Histories is full of stories, digressions, observations, hearsay. *The population of Thrace is the largest in the world, after the Indians, of course. If they were ruled by a single person or had a common purpose, they would be invincible and would be by far the most powerful nation in the world, in my opinion. This is completely impossible for them, however—there is no way that it will ever happen—and that is why they are weak. . . . They have the practice of selling their children for export abroad. They do not restrict the behaviour of their young women, but let them have sex with any men they want; however, they keep a very strict eye on their wives. They buy their wives from the woman's parents for a great deal of money. Being tattooed is taken by them to be a sign of high birth, while it is a sign of low birth to be without tattoos. They consider it best not to work, and working the land is regarded as the most dishonourable profession. The best way to make a living, in their judgement, is off the spoils of war. These are their most remarkable customs.*

I raise my eyes and notice that in the colorfully illuminated garden a white-clad waiter—a Hindu called Anil—is feeding a banana to a tame monkey hanging from the branches of a mango tree. The animal is making comical faces, and Anil is roaring with laughter. The waiter, the evening, the warmth, the cicadas, the banana, and the tea, all remind me of India, of my days of fascination and confusion; both here and there, the tropics penetrate with the same intensity every fiber of one's being. It even seems to me that the scents of India are reaching me here, but it's just the aroma of Anil, with his betel, anise, and bergamot. And India, in a sense, is all around—one keeps seeing Hindu temples, restaurants, sisal and cotton plantations.

I return to Herodotus.

The frequent reading of his work and even a certain kind of intimacy with it—a familiarity, a habit, a dependence, even—

started to exert an odd indefinable influence on me. What is certain is that I was no longer conscious of a barrier of time, of being separated from the events the Greek describes by two and a half thousand years—a veritable abyss in which lie Rome and the Middle Ages, the birth and development of the Great Religions, the discovery of America, the Renaissance and the Enlightenment, the steam engine and electricity, the telegraph and the airplane, hundreds of wars, including two world wars, the discovery of antibiotics, the population explosion, thousands upon thousands of things and events which, when we read Herodotus, vanish as if they didn't exist, or at least recede into the background, moving from the fore into the shadows.

Could Herodotus, who was born, lived, and worked on the other side of this chronological chasm, feel impoverished as a result? We can make no reasoned inference that he did, and he gives no indication. On the contrary: he lives fully, explores the whole world, meets numerous people, listens to hundreds of tales; he is an active, energetic, and tireless man, constantly searching, constantly busy with something. He would like to learn about many more things, issues, mysteries, solve many more riddles, find the answers to a long litany of questions, but he simply does not have time enough—enough time or strength. He simply cannot manage it all, just as we cannot manage it all—man's life is so brief! Is he bothered that there are no high-speed trains or planes yet, or even bicycles? One can reasonably doubt that. If he had a train or plane at his disposal, would he have gathered and left us even more information? One should doubt that as well.

I have the impression that Herodotus's problem was altogether different: He decides, probably toward the end of his life, to write a book because he realizes that he has amassed such an enormous trove of stories and facts that unless he preserves them, they will simply vanish. His book is yet another expression of man's struggle against time, against the fragility of memory, its ephemerality, its perpetual tendency to erase itself and disappear. The concept of the book, any book, arose from just this battle. The written word has a durability, one would even like to say "eternality." Man knows, and in the course of years he comes to know it increasingly well, feeling it ever more acutely, that memory is weak and fleeting, and if he doesn't write down what he has learned and experienced, that which he carries within him will perish when he does. This is why it seems everyone wants to write a book. Singers and football players, politicians and millionaires. And if they themselves do not know how, or else lack the time, they commission someone else to do it for them. That is how it is and always will be. Engendering this reality is the impression of writing as an easy and simple pursuit, though those who subscribe to that view might do well to ponder Thomas Mann's observation that "a writer is a man for whom writing is more difficult than it is for others."

As a result of Herodotus's desire to preserve for others as much as possible of what he has found out and lived through, his book is not a simple recording of the histories of dynasties, kings, and palace intrigues—though he does write a great deal about rulers and power, he tells us also about the life of simple people, about their religious beliefs and agricultural practices, about illnesses and natural disasters, about mountains and rivers, plants and animals. For example—about cats: *If a house catches fire, what happens to the cats is quite extraordinary. The Egyptians do not bother to try to put the fire out, but position themselves at intervals around the house and look out for the cats. The cats slip between them, however, and even jump over them, and dash into the fire. This plunges the Egyptians into deep grief. In households where a cat dies a natural*

death, all the people living there shave off their eyebrows—nothing more. In house-
holds where a dog dies, they shave their whole bodies, head and all.

Or about crocodiles:

This is what crocodiles are like. They eat nothing during the four winter months.
They are four-footed, and amphibious ... As far as is known, there is no mortal
creature which grows so big from such small beginnings. The eggs it lays are not
much bigger than a goose's eggs, and the size of a new-born crocodile corresponds to
that of its egg, but a fully grown adult can be at least seventeen cubits long, and
maybe more. It has eyes the size of a pig's, but huge teeth and tusks. ... With the
exception of the sandpiper, all other birds and animals run away from it. The sand-
piper, however, is on good terms with it, because it is of use to the crocodile. When the
crocodile climbs out of the water and on to land, it yawns widely (usually when fac-
ing west), and then the sandpiper slips into its mouth and swallows the leeches. This
does the crocodile good and gives it pleasure, so it does not harm the sandpiper.

I did not notice these cats and crocodiles at first. They appeared
to me only upon successive readings, when I suddenly noticed, to
my horror, the crazed cats leaping into the fire, and when it
seemed to me, as I was sitting at the edge of the Nile, that I spotted
nearby the opened jaws of a crocodile and a small, fearless bird
rummaging around inside them. This is natural: one must read
Herodotus's book—and every great book—repeatedly; with each
reading it will reveal another layer, previously overlooked themes,
images, and meanings. For within every great book there are several others.

Herodotus lives fully; he is not bothered by the lack of the telephone or the airplane, nor does he worry about not having a
bicycle. These machines will appear only thousands of years
later—and so what? It doesn't occur to him that such things might
have been useful to him, perhaps because he manages excellently
without them. His world, his life have their own strength, their

own undiminishing and self-sufficient energy. He senses it, and it gives him wings. He must have been a cheerful, relaxed, kind man, because it is only to such people that strangers reveal their secrets. They do not open up to someone withdrawn and gloomy; pessimistic dispositions awaken in others the desire to move away, the need for distance, and can even elicit fear. If such had been Herodotus's personality, he would have been unable to accomplish what he did, and we wouldn't have his book.

I thought about this frequently, sensing at the same time, not without surprise and even a measure of anxiety, that as I immersed myself increasingly in Herodotus's book, I identified more and more, emotionally and cognitively, with the world and events that he recalls. I felt more deeply about the destruction of Athens than about the latest military coup in the Sudan, and the sinking of the Persian fleet struck me as more tragic than yet another mutiny of troops in Congo. The world that I was experiencing was not only the African one, about which I was supposed to be writing as the correspondent of a press agency, but also that one far from here which vanished hundreds of years ago.

And so there was nothing strange about the fact that, sitting of a steamy tropical evening on the verandah of the Sea View Hotel in Dar es-Salaam, I was thinking about the freezing soldiers of Mardonius's army, who on a frosty night—for it was winter in Europe then—tried to warm their numb hands by the fire.

THE DESERT AND THE SEA

I set aside for a while the Greco-Persian war, with its endless processions of barbarian armies and the arguing of the quarrelsome Greeks—over who among them is most important, whose leadership should be recognized—because the Algerian ambassador, Judi, has just called, saying that "it would be worthwhile to meet." The expression "it would be worthwhile to meet" has a subtext, and usually implies a promise of some sort, a hopeful eventuality, something worthy of interest and closer attention; it is as if someone said, "Come meet me, I have something for you—you won't regret it."

Judi had a magnificent residence—a white, airy villa, in the grand old Mauritanian style, constructed in such a way as to create shade everywhere, even in those places which, logically, should be in direct sunlight. We sat in the garden, and from behind the high wall the sounds of the ocean washed over us. It was high tide, and from somewhere in the watery depths, from far beyond the horizon, enormous waves moved toward us and crashed nearby, for the villa stood right on the water, on a low, rocky shore.

We spoke about everything, but about nothing important, and just as I was beginning to wonder why he had invited me here, he suddenly said:

"I think that it would be worth your while to go to Algiers. It might be interesting there now. If you want, I'll give you a visa."

I was taken aback. It was 1965, and there was nothing of note happening in Algeria. It had been an independent country for three years now, and had an intelligent, popular young leader: Ahmed Ben Bella.

Judi would say no more, and because the hour of Muslim evening prayers was approaching and he had begun to finger his emerald prayer beads, I realized it was time for me to go. I faced a dilemma. If I were to approach my superiors for permission to take this trip, they would start asking me questions. I had no idea why I should be going there. At the same time, traveling halfway across Africa for no good reason would be a grave insubordination—not to mention a financial risk, especially given that my employer was a press agency so short of funds one had to justify at length the smallest expenditure.

But there was something so convincing, insistent even, in Judi's manner, in the encouraging tone of his voice, that I decided to take the chance. I flew from Dar es-Salaam through Bangui, Fort Lamy, and Agadez, and on these routes the planes are small and slow and even the upper limit of their flight paths are low, affording one an excellent view of the route over the Sahara, which is full of captivating images—either joyfully colorful or monotonously bleak, though even in the latter, there will suddenly appear, amidst a lunar lifelessness, a bright and crowded oasis.

The airport in Algiers was empty, closed, in fact. Our plane was allowed to land because it belonged to the domestic carrier. Soldiers in gray-green camouflage jackets immediately surrounded it and escorted us—several passengers—to a glass building. The passport control was not onerous and the soldiers were courteous, although reticent. They would say only that there had been a coup d'état during the night, that "the tyrant had been removed," and that power had been seized by the general staff. "Tyrant?" I wanted to ask, "what tyrant?" I had seen Ben Bella two years earlier in Addis Ababa. He seemed a polite, even pleasant man.

The city is large, sunny, spread out broadly, amphitheatrically, around the bay. One must constantly climb uphill or down. There are stylish French streets and bustling Arab ones. All about is a Mediterranean mixture of architectural styles, clothing, and customs. Everything sparkles, smells, intoxicates, exhausts. Everything arouses curiosity, draws one in, fascinates—but also makes one anxious. If you are tired, you can sit down in one of the hundreds of Arab or French cafés. You can eat in one of the hundreds of bars or restaurants. Because the sea is close by, there are plenty of fish on the menus, and untold delicacies of *frutti di mare*—crustaceans, clams, cephalopods, octopi, oysters.

But Algiers is first and foremost a place where two cultures meet and coexist—the Christian and the Arab. The history of this coexistence is the history of this city (although, of course, it also has other, much older historical chapters—Phoenician, Greek, Roman). Moving inevitably in the shadow of either a church or a mosque, the Algiers resident is continually made aware of the winding borderline between the two realms.

Take downtown. Its Arab section is called the Casbah. You enter it walking uphill, along wide stone steps—dozens of them. But the stairs are not the problem; the difficulty is the sense of intrusion we feel as we venture deeper into the Casbah's recesses. But do we really look into, try to penetrate those hidden corners? Or do we instead hurry along, intent on extricating ourselves from an uncomfortable, somewhat awkward situation—for we have noticed dozens of pairs of motionless eyes, importunately attentive, watching us as we walk? Are we perhaps only imagining it? Could it be that we are oversensitive? Why are we indifferent when someone stares at us on a French street? Why does it not bother us then, or cause us discomfort, whereas here in the Casbah it does? The eyes are similar, after all, likewise the act of observing, and yet we react to the two situations in such dissimilar ways.

When we finally emerge from the Casbah and find ourselves once more in a French neighborhood, we may not breathe an audible sigh of relief, but we certainly feel lighter, more at ease, more natural. Why can we not control these latent, even subconscious attitudes and emotions? For thousands of years, all over the world—nothing?

A foreigner who might have arrived in Algiers on the same day as I did would not have realized that something as important as a coup d'état had taken place the previous night, that the internationally popular Ben Bella had been ousted by an unknown who, as would soon become apparent, was the introverted, taciturn commander of the army, Houari Boumedienne. The entire business was carried out at night, far from the center of town, in an exclusive villa neighborhood called Hydra, and in that part of it, moreover, that is occupied by the government and the generals and thus inaccessible to ordinary pedestrians.

One could not hear the shots or explosions in the city itself; there were no tanks in the streets, no marching troops. In the morning, people drove or walked to work as usual, shopkeepers opened their shops, vendors set up their stalls, and bartenders invited one in for morning coffee. Superintendents doused the sidewalks to give the city a bit of moist freshness in advance of the noontime heat. Buses roared terrifyingly as they struggled to scale steep streets.

I walked around crushed—and furious at Judi. Why did he encourage me to make this trip? What did I come here for? What would I write about from here? How would I justify the expenditure? Dejected, I suddenly noticed a crowd gathering on the avenue Mohammed V. Unfortunately, they were merely gawkers drawn by the quarrel of two drivers who had collided at the intersection. At the other end of the street I saw another small gathering. I ran there. But they were merely people patiently waiting for the post office to open. My notebook was empty, and I had not witnessed a single event worth describing.

But it was here in Algiers, several years after I had begun working as a reporter, that it slowly began to dawn on me that I had set myself on an erroneous path back then. Until that awakening I had been searching for spectacular imagery, laboring under the illusion that it was compelling, observable tableaux that somehow justified my presence, absolving me of responsibility to understand the events at hand. It was the fallacy that one can interpret the world only by means of what it chooses to show us in the hours of its convulsions, when it is rocked by shots and explosions, engulfed in flames and smoke, choked in dust and the stench of burning, when everything collapses into rubble on which sit people despairing over the remains of their loved ones.

How did this spectacle come about? What do these scenes of destruction, replete with shouts and blood, mean to express? What forces—subcutaneous and invisible, yet powerful and unrestrainable—brought them about? Are these scenes the end or beginning of something, portents of tensions and conflicts still to come? And who will monitor them? We, the correspondents and reporters? No. The dead will barely have been buried, the wrecks of incinerated cars will have just been cleared away and the streets swept of the broken glass, and we will have already packed our bags and moved on, to where others are burning cars, shattering shop windows, and digging graves for the fallen.

But might it not be possible to pierce that spectacular stereotype, to move beyond imagery, attempt to reach deeper? It seemed only practical to try. Unable to write about tanks, burned cars, and looted stores—having seen nothing of the sort—and wanting to justify my unauthorized journey, I went in search of the background and the wellspring of the Algerian coup, to try to determine what lay behind it and what it signified; to talk, to observe people and places, and to read—in short, to try to understand.

It was only then that I began to see Algiers as one of the most fascinating and dramatic places on earth. In the small space of this beautiful but congested city intersected two great conflicts of the contemporary world. The first was the one between Christianity and Islam (expressed here in the clash between colonizing France and colonized Algeria). The second, which acquired a sharpness of focus immediately after the independence and departure of the French, was a conflict at the very heart of Islam, between its open, dialectical—I would even venture to say "Mediterranean"—current and its other, inward-looking one, born of a sense of uncertainty and confusion vis-à-vis the contemporary world, guided by fundamentalists who take advantage of modern technology and organizational principles yet at the same time deem the defense of faith and custom against modernity as the condition of their own existence, their sole identity.

Algiers, which at its beginnings, in Herodotus's time, was a fishing village, and later a port for Phoenician and Greek ships, faces the sea. But right behind the city, on its other side, lies a vast desert province that is called "the *bled*" here, a territory claimed by peoples professing allegiance to the laws of an old, rigidly introverted Islam. In Algiers one speaks simply of the existence of two varieties of Islam—one, which is called the Islam of the desert, and a second, which is defined as the Islam of the river (or of the sea).

The first is the religion practiced by warlike nomadic tribes struggling to survive in one of the world's most hostile environments, the Sahara. The second Islam is the faith of merchants, itinerant peddlers, people of the road and of the bazaar, for whom openness, compromise, and exchange are not only beneficial to trade, but necessary to life itself.

Under colonialism, both these strains of Islam were united by a common enemy; but later they collided.

Ben Bella was a Mediterranean man, educated in French culture, open-minded and conciliatory by nature. Local Frenchmen referred to him in conversation as a Muslim of the river and of the sea. Boumedienne, on the contrary, was the commander of an army which for years had fought in the desert, had its bases and camps there, drew its recruits from there, and took advantage of the support and help proffered by the nomads, people of the oases and of desert mountains.

The two men differed even in their appearance. Ben Bella was always well-groomed, elegant, refined, courteous, smiling amiably. When Boumedienne appeared for the first time in public after the coup, he looked like a tank commander who had just stepped out of his conveyance covered in the sands of the Sahara. He did try to smile, but without much success—it was simply not his style.

In Algiers I saw the Mediterranean Sea for the first time. I saw it up close—I could dip my hand into it, feel its touch. I didn't have to ask for directions; I knew that just by walking downward, then down some more, I would eventually reach it. It was everywhere, visible from afar, glimmering from behind various buildings, appearing at the bottoms of steep streets.

At the very bottom was the port district, with simple wooden bars all in a row, smelling of fish, wine, and coffee. But it was the tart scent of the sea that was most noticeable, a gentle, calming refreshment carried on each gust of the wind.

I had never been in a city where nature is so kind to man. For it offered everything all at once—the sun, a cooling breeze, the brightness of the air, the silver of the sea. The sea seemed familiar to me, perhaps because I had read so much about it. Its smooth waves signified fine weather, peace, something like an invitation to travel and experience. One had the urge to join those two fishermen over there, who were just setting sail.

I returned to Dar es-Salaam, but Judi had left. I was told that he had been recalled to Algiers and assumed, because he was a participant in the victorious conspiracy, that the move meant a promotion. In any event, he did not return here. I never met him again, in fact, and so was unable to thank him for having incited me to take the trip. The military coup in Algeria was the start of an entire series, a whole chain of similar revolts, which for the next quarter century would decimate the continent's young postcolonial states. Those states turned out to be weak from the start, and many of them have remained so to this day.

Not least, thanks to this journey, I stood for the first time on the shore of the Mediterranean Sea. It seems to me that from that moment on I understood Herodotus even better than before. His thoughts, his curiosity, how he saw the world.

THE ANCHOR

We are still by the Mediterranean, Herodotus's sea, only now on its eastern end, where Europe adjoins Asia and where the two continents meet across a chain of gently contoured, sunny isles, whose quiet, calm bays encourage sailors to visit and to stay awhile.

The commander of the Persians, Mardonius, leaves his winter lair in Thessaly and heads south *at the head of his army to attack Athens.* When he reaches the city, however, he finds it uninhabited. Athens is destroyed and deserted. The population has moved away, taking shelter in Salamis. He sends an envoy there, a certain Murichides, whose mission is to once again propose to the Athenians that they surrender without a fight and recognize King Xerxes as their ruler.

Murichides presents this proposal to the highest Athenian authority, the Council of Five Hundred, and a crowd of Athenians listens in on the assembly's deliberations. One member of the council, Lycides, argues that it would be best to accept Mardonius's conciliatory offer and come to some kind of an agreement with the Persians. Hearing this, the Athenian audience erupts in anger, surrounds the speaker, and stones him to death on the spot.

Let us pause a moment at this scene.

We are in democratic Greece, proud of its freedom of speech

and of thought. One of its citizens publicly expresses his views—and what happens? There is an instant outcry. Lycides simply forgot that there was a war going on, and that in wartime all democratic freedoms, including the freedom of speech, are typically put on the shelf. War engenders its own, distinct laws, and the normally complex code of governing principles is reduced to a single fundamental imperative: victory at any cost!

Lycides has barely finished his speech when he is put to death. One can imagine how rattled, agitated, and near hysteria the crowd listening to him must have been. The Persian army is hot on their heels, they have already lost half their country, they have lost their city. It is not difficult to find stones in the spot where the council deliberated and the onlookers gathered. Greece is a country of stones; they are everywhere. Everyone walks on them. You need only bend down. And that is exactly what happens. People reach for the nearest stone, the one closest at hand, and hurl it at Lycides. At first, he probably shouts in terror; later, already dripping with blood, he moans from pain, cowers, wheezes, begs for mercy. In vain. The throng, furious, in a state of mad frenzy, no longer hears, no longer thinks, and is incapable of stopping itself. It will come to its senses only after the last stone has extinguished the life of Lycides, turned him to pulp, silenced him forever.

But that is not the end of it!

Herodotus writes that *the uproar in Salamis over Lycides alerted the Athenian women to what was happening. With every woman arousing and enlisting the support of her neighbor, they spontaneously flocked to Lycides' house, where they stoned his wife and his children to death.*

His wife and children! How were the Athenian tots guilty of their daddy's advocacy of a compromise with the Persians? Did they even know anything about these Persians, much less that the mere suggestion of talking to them was punishable by death?

Were the youngest among them even able to imagine what death looks like? How terrible it is? At what point did they realize that the grandmothers and aunts whom they suddenly saw in front of their house were not bringing them sweets and grapes, but rather stones, with which they would now start to crack open their heads?

Lycides' fate demonstrates the Greeks' deeply felt pain of even contemplating collaboration with the invader, what great angst it aroused. What should one do? How should one behave? What choice should one make? Cooperate or resist? Enter into talks or boycott? Come to an arrangement and try to survive, or opt for heroism and go out in a blaze of glory? Difficult, rankling questions, tormenting dilemmas.

The Greeks are divided over these alternatives, and their disagreements are not confined to discussions and verbal sparring. They fight one another with weapons, on battlefields—the Athenians with the Thebans, the Phocians with the Thessalians; they go for one another's throats, gouge out one another's eyes, cut off one another's heads. No Persian provokes so much hatred in a Greek as another Greek does—just so long as he is from an opposing camp or from a tribe that is at odds with his. Perhaps various complexes contribute to this, feelings of guilt, disloyalties, treacheries? Hidden fears, terror at the thought of a divine curse?

A fresh confrontation is about to take place, in the last two battles of this war, which will be fought at Plataea and Mycale.

First, Plataea. After Mardonius determined that the Athenians and the Spartans would not bend to come to terms with him, he leveled Athens and withdrew to the north, to the territories of the Thebans, who were collaborating with the Persians and whose flat, even lands were well suited to heavy cavalry, the signature Persian military formation. The pursuing Athenians and Spartans now also arrived at this plain in the vicinity of Plataea. Both armies took up positions facing each other, formed into lines—and waited. All sensed that a great moment was approaching, a decisive and deadly one. Days passed, and both sides remained in a disconcerting and enervating motionlessness, asking the gods—each side its own—if the time was right to begin the battle. But the answers were no and no.

During one of those days, a Theban, the Greek collaborator Attaginus, organizes a banquet for Mardonius to which he invites fifty of the most eminent Persians and as many of the most distinguished Thebans, seating each Persian-Theban pair on a separate couch. One of the couches is occupied by Thersander, a Greek, and a Persian whose name Herodotus does not provide. They eat and drink together, and at a certain moment the Persian, clearly in a reflective mood, says to Thersander, *"Look at these Persians here at the banquet, and consider also the army which we have left encamped on the river."* He has been tormented by premonitions, as is clear from what he says next: *"Before much time has passed you'll see few of them left alive."* The Persian was weeping as he spoke. Thersander, still sober, tries to end the sobbing of his dejected and drunk couchmate by saying, quite sensibly: *"Shouldn't you be telling this to Mardonius and the next highest–ranking Persians?"* To which the Persian replies with a tragic-sounding wisdom: *"My friend, an event which has been decreed by the god cannot be averted by man, for no one is willing to believe even those who tell the truth. A great many Persians are well aware of what I've just said, but we follow our leaders because we have no choice. There's no more terrible pain a man can endure than to see clearly and be able to do nothing."*

The great battle of Plataea, which will end with the defeat of the Persians and will establish Europe's long-lasting hegemony over

Asia, is preceded by minor skirmishes in which the Persian cavalry attacks the defending Greeks. In one of them, the de facto commanding officer of the Persian army, Masistius, perishes. *Masistius' horse, which was out in front of the rest, was hit in the side by an arrow, and the pain of the wound made it rear up and unseat him. As soon as Masistius landed on the ground, the Athenians sprang forward, seized the horse and killed Masistius, although he fought back. At first, in fact, they failed to kill him: next to his skin he was wearing a breastplate made of gold scales, with a red tunic on top, so the Athenians' blows kept hitting the breastplate and achieving nothing. Eventually, however, one of them realized what was happening and struck Masistius in the eye. Only then did he fall to the ground and die.*

A fierce struggle then erupted over the body. The corpse of a leader is a sacred thing. The fleeing Persians fought for its possession as they retreated. But they fought in vain, returning in empty-handed defeat to their camp. *When the cavalry got back to the Persian encampment, Mardonius and the whole of his army were deeply upset to hear of Masistius' death. They shaved off not only their own hair, but also that of their horses and their yoke-animals, and gave themselves over to unending lamentation. The whole of Boeotia echoed with the sound of mourning, since, after Mardonius, there was no one in Persia who was more highly respected by the Persians in general and the king in particular.*

Whereas the first thing the Greeks did, having managed to hold on to Masistius's body, was to *load the corpse on to a cart and parade it past their lines. Masistius had been remarkably tall and good-looking (which is in fact why they did this with the body), and the men broke ranks to go and see him.*

All this takes place several days before the great and conclusive battle, which neither side dares initiate because the omens continue to be unfavorable. On the Persian side, the fortune-teller is a certain Hegesistratus, a Greek from the Peloponnese but an enemy of the Spartans and the Athenians. *Hegesistratus had once been arrested and imprisoned by the Spartiates to await execution for the terrible and horrific treatment they had suffered at his hands. In this desperate situation, because his life was in danger and he was prepared to suffer gruesome agonies rather than die, he did something that defies description. He was being kept in stocks made of wood bound with iron, and somehow got hold of a blade which had been smuggled into the prison. What he then immediately set about doing must have taken more courage than anything else we have ever heard of. He worked out that the rest of his foot would get free of the stocks if he cut off the bulk of his foot, so he proceeded to do so. Then since he was under guard, he dug a hole through the wall and ran away to Tegea, travelling by night and resting by day under the cover of woodland. Although the Lacedaemonians were out looking for him in full force, he managed to reach Tegea two nights after escaping. The Lacedaemonians were amazed by his courage when they found half of his foot lying there, but they could not find him.*

How did he do that?

Cutting off one's own foot is hard work indeed.

It is not enough to sever the muscles. One also has to saw through the tendons and bones. Self-mutilations have occurred in our times as well: witnesses claim that in the gulags people occasionally cut off their own hands or pierced their stomachs with knives. An incident is even described in which a prisoner nailed his member to a wooden board. The goal was always to free oneself at any cost from the backbreaking labor, to go to the hospital, and there to be able to lie down awhile, to rest. But to cut off one's foot and then run off immediately?

To escape?

To hurry?

How was this even possible? Most likely by crawling on one's hands and the other leg. But that mutilated leg must have hurt fiendishly and bled profusely. How did he stanch the blood? Did he not faint from exhaustion during the flight? From thirst? From pain? Did he not feel himself on the verge of madness? Would he not have seen ghosts? Was he not plagued by hallucinations? Apparitions? Vampires? And did the wound not get infected? After all, he had to scrape that stump over the ground, through dust and dirt—for how else could he drag it along? Did that leg therefore not start to swell? Fill with pus? Turn blue?

And yet despite all this he escapes the Spartans, recovers, whittles himself a wooden prosthesis, and even becomes the soothsayer of Mardonius, commander of the Persians.

Tensions mount near Plataea. After a dozen days of fruitless offerings to the gods, the signs become slightly more favorable and Mardonius decides to commence hostilities. It is an ordinary human weakness: he is in a hurry to rout the enemy, wants to become the satrap of Athens and of all of Greece as quickly as possible. Now *every unit of the Greek army took casualties from the javelins and arrows of the Persian cavalry as they bore down on them.* And when the quivers are emptied, the two armies resort to terrifying hand-to-hand combat. Several hundred thousand men wrestle with one another, grip one another in murderous holds, choke one another in deadly embraces. Whoever has something at hand pounds his opponent over the head with it, or sticks a knife between his ribs, or kicks him in the shins. One can almost hear the collective panting and groaning, the moans and wheezes, the curses and cries!

In this bloody tumult, the most courageous man, according to Herodotus, turned out to be the Spartan Aristodamus. He had been the last of the three hundred soldiers of Leonidas's regiment, which perished defending Thermopylae. Aristodamus, no one really knows how, survived, but for that piece of luck he suffered shame and contempt. According to the code of Sparta, one could not have honorably survived Thermopylae: whoever was there, and truly fought in the defense of his homeland, would surely have died. Hence the inscription on the collective tombstone of Leonidas's regiment: "Passerby, tell Sparta that we who perished here were faithful to its laws."

Evidently, Sparta's strict laws did not envisage different categories of combatants on the losing side. Whoever went into battle could survive only if he were victorious; defeated, one had to die. And here was Aristodamus, sole survivor. This distinction plunges him into infamy and ignominy. No one wants to speak to him, everyone turns away with disdain. His miraculous salvation soon starts to rankle, smother him, burn. It weighs upon him, becoming increasingly difficult to bear. He searches for a solution, for some relief. And along comes a chance to remove the humiliating brand, or, rather, to end heroically the life so branded: the battle of Plataea. Aristodamus accomplishes miracles of bravery: he *had clearly wanted to die, because of the slur against his name, and so had recklessly broken rank and achieved such heroic exploits.*

In vain. The laws of Sparta are implacable. There is no pity in them, no human feeling. A fault once committed remains a fault forever, and whoever tainted himself can never be cleansed. And so Aristodamus's name is not among the heroes of this battle recognized by the Greeks—*among those who fell in this battle, all the men I mentioned, apart from Aristodamus, received special honours. Aristodamus did not, for the reason already mentioned—that he wanted to die.*

The outcome of the battle of Plataea was decided by the death of the Persian commander, Mardonius. In those times, commanders did not hide behind the lines in camouflaged bunkers, but went into battle at the head of their armies. When a commander died, however, his troops would disperse and flee the field. The commander therefore had to be visible from afar (most frequently, he sat on a horse), because the conduct of his soldiers depended on what he himself was doing. And so it was at Plataea—*Mardonius rode into battle on his white horse . . . But after he had been killed and the men of his battalion, the most effective troops on the Persian side, had been cut down, all the others turned and fled before the Lacedaemonians.*

Herodotus notes that one man on the Greek side stood out because of his exemplary inflexibility. He was an Athenian, Sophanes: *he used to carry an iron anchor, attached with a bronze chain to the belt of his breastplate, and whenever he reached a spot near the enemy he would drop anchor, so that as the enemy charged at him from their ranks they could not make him move; if they turned and fled, however, it was his plan to pick up the anchor and go after them.*

What a great metaphor! Rather than a lifeline, which allows us to float passively upon the surface, how much greater that which can chain us to our labors.

BLACK IS BEAUTIFUL

It takes less than half an hour for the local ferry to sail from the dock of Dakar to the island of Goree. Standing at its stern, one can see the city, which seems to bob on the crests of the waves created by the propeller as it grows smaller and smaller, and finally is transformed into a bright, rocky bank stretching along the horizon. At just that moment, the ferry turns its stern toward the island and, amidst the din of rumbling engines and rattling iron, scrapes its side on the concrete edge of the marina.

I walk first along a wooden pier, then a sandy beach, then a twisting, narrow little street until I reach the *pension de famille*, where I am awaited by Abdou, the watchman, and Mariem, the boardinghouse's quiet, always busy landlady. Abdou and Mariem are married, and, judging by Mariem's figure, will shortly have a child. Although they are both still very young, this will be their fourth. Abdou looks with satisfaction at his wife's clearly protruding abdomen: it is proof that all is well in their home. If a woman walks about with a flat stomach, says Abdou—and Mariem nods in assent—it means that something untoward is happening, something contrary to the order of nature. Anxious family and friends start asking questions, prying, spinning various frightening and sometimes also malicious tales. Everything should take place in accordance with the world's natural rhythms—and this means that a woman should once a year give visible proof of her generous and indefatigable fertility.

Abdou and Mariem both belong to the Peul community, which is the largest ethnic group in Senegal. Peul speak the Wolof language and have a paler skin than other West Africans—which is why one theory has it that they arrived in this part of the continent from the banks of the Nile, from Egypt, long ago when the Sahara was awash in green and one could wander safely over what today is desert.

From this stems a more general theory, developed in the 1950s by the Senegalese historian and linguist Cheih Anta Diop, about the Afro-Egyptian roots of Greek civilization and, by the same token, of European and Western civilization. Just as humankind arose physically in Africa, so European culture, too, he maintained, could trace its beginnings to this continent. For Anta Diop, who created a large comparative dictionary of the Egyptian and Wolof languages, the great authority was Herodotus, who had argued in his book that many elements of Greek culture were gathered and assimilated from Egypt and Libya—in other words, that European culture, especially its Mediterranean manifestations, had an African ancestry.

Anta Diop's thesis dovetailed with the popular movement of Négritude, developed in Paris at the end of the 1930s. Its authors were two young poets, the Senegalese Léopold Senghor, and Aimé Césaire, a descendant of slaves from Martinique. In their poetry and in their manifestos, they promulgated black pride—pride in their race, which for centuries had been humiliated by the white man—and praised the accomplishments and values of black people and their contributions to world culture.

. . .

All this occurred more or less in the middle of the twentieth century, when a non-European consciousness was awakening, when the people of Africa and of the so-called Third World in general were searching for their own identity, and the inhabitants of Africa in particular wished to rid themselves of the complex of slavery. Anta Diop's thesis and Senghor and Césaire's advocacy of Négritude—echoes of which can be found in the writings of Sartre, Camus, and Davidson—contributed to a European realization that our planet, dominated for centuries by Europe, was entering a new, multicultural epoch, and that non-European communities and cultures would have their own ambitions for dignity and respect in the family of man.

This is the context in which the problem arises of the Otherness of the Other. Until now, when we pondered our relation with the Other, the Other was always from the same culture as us. Now, however, the Other belongs to an altogether foreign culture, an individual formed by and espousing its distinct customs and values.

In 1960 Senegal gains its independence. The aforementioned poet, Léopold Senghor, a habitué of the clubs and cafés of the Latin Quarter in Paris, becomes its president. That which for years had been a theory, a plan, a dream harbored by him and by his friends from Africa, the Caribbean, and both Americas—the dream of a return to symbolic roots, to lost sources, to a world from which they had been brutally torn by hordes of slave traders and cast for entire generations into an alien, debasing, and hostile captivity—now for the first time can be put into practice, translated into ambitious projects, bold and far-reaching initiatives.

From the first days of his presidency, Senghor starts preparing the first-ever world festival of black art (Premier Festival Mondial des Arts Negres). Exactly—world festival: because the goal here is the art of all black people, not just Africans; the ambition is to show that art's immensity, greatness, universality, diversity, and vitality. Yes, Africa was its source, but it spans the globe.

Senghor inaugurates the festival in 1963 in Dakar; it is to last several months. Because I am late to the opening ceremonies and all the hotels in town are already full, I secure a room on the island, in the *pension de famille* run by Mariem and Abdou, Senegalese from Peul, perhaps the descendants of some Egyptian fellahin or—who knows?—even of one of the pharaohs.

In the morning Mariem sets down before me a piece of juicy papaya, a cup of very sweet coffee, half a baguette, and a jar of preserves. Although she likes silence best, custom dictates serving up a ritual morning portion of inquiries: how did I sleep, am I rested, was it too hot for me, was I not bitten by mosquitoes, did I have dreams? What if I had no dreams? I ask. That, says Mariem, is impossible. She always has dreams. She dreams about her children, about good times, about visiting her parents in the countryside. Very good and pleasant dreams.

I thank her for breakfast and go to the harbor. The ferry takes me to Dakar. The city lives and breathes the festival. Exhibitions, lectures, concerts, plays. Eastern and western Africa are represented here, as well as southern and central; there are also Brazil and Colombia, and all of the Caribbean, with Jamaica and Puerto Rico at the fore; there are Alabama and Georgia, and the islands of the Atlantic and of the Indian Ocean.

Theatrical performances abound in the streets and squares. African theater is not as formalistic as the European. A group of people can gather someplace extemporaneously and perform an impromptu play. There is no text; everything is the product of the moment, of the passing mood, of spontaneous imagination. The subject can be anything: the police catching a gang of thieves, merchants fighting to keep the city from taking away their marketplace, wives competing among themselves for their husband, who is in love with some other woman. The subject matter must be simple, the language comprehensible to all.

Someone has an idea and volunteers to be director. He assigns roles and the play begins. If this is a street, a square, or a courtyard, a crowd of passersby soon gathers. People laugh during the performance, offer running commentary, applaud. If the action unfolds in an interesting way, the audience will stand there attentively despite the punishing sun; if the play does not jell, and the ad hoc troupe proves unable to communicate and move the action forward effectively, the performance is soon over and the spectators and actors disperse, making way for others who may have better luck.

Sometimes I see the actors interrupt their dialogue and begin a ritual dance, with the entire audience joining in. It can be a cheerful and joyous dance, or the opposite—with the dancers serious, focused, and collective participation in the common rhythm an evidently profound experience for them, something meaningful touching their core. But then the dancing ends, the actors return to their spoken parts, and the spectators, for a moment still as if entranced, laugh once again, happy and amused.

Street theater includes not just dance. Its other important, even inseparable element is the mask. The actors sometimes perform in masks, or, because it is difficult in this heat to wear one for long, simply hold them near—in their hands, under their arms, even strapped to their backs. The mask is a symbol, a construct full of emotion and resonance that speaks of the existence of some other universe, whose sign, stamp, or presence it is. It communicates something to us, warns us about someone; seemingly lifeless and motionless, it attempts by means of its appearance to arouse our feelings, put us under its spell.

Borrowing from various museums, Senghor collected thousands upon thousands of such masks. When seen in the aggregate, they evoke a separate, mysterious world. Walking through that collection was a singular experience. One began to understand how masks acquired such power over people, how they could hypnotize, overwhelm, or lead people into ecstasy. It became clear why the mask—and faith in its magical efficacy—united entire societies, enabled them to communicate across continents and oceans, gave them a sense of community and identity, constituted a form of tradition and collective memory.

Walking from one theatrical performance to another, from one exhibit of masks and sculptures to others, I had the sense of being witness to the rebirth of a great culture, to the awakening of its sense of distinctness, importance, and pride, the consciousness of its universal range. Here were not only masks from Mozambique and Congo, but also lanterns for macumba rituals from Rio de Janeiro, the escutcheons of the guardian deities of Haitian voodoo, and copies of the sarcophagi of Egyptian pharaohs.

But this joy at the renaissance of a worldwide community was accompanied also by a sense of disappointment and disillusion. Example: It is in Dakar that I read *Black Power*, the affecting and then recently published book by Richard Wright. At the start of the 1950s, Wright, an African American from Harlem, moved by the desire to return to Africa, the land of his ancestors, went on a trip to Ghana. Ghana was fighting for its independence just then, and there were constant meetings, demonstrations, protests. Wright took part in these, got to know the daily life in cities, visited the marketplaces in Accra and Takoradi, conversed with merchants and planters—and concluded that despite his sharing with them the same black skin, they, the Africans, and he, the American, were total strangers to each other, had no common language, and what was important to them was of utter indifference to him. In the course of the African journey the alienation Wright felt became for him increasingly difficult to bear, a curse and a nightmare.

In the *pension de famille* I have a room on the second floor. It is immense, all hewn out of stone, with two openings in the place of windows and a single large one, proportioned like an entrance gate, where the door would be. I also have a wide terrace, from which one can see the Atlantic stretching to the horizon. Ocean and more ocean. A cool breeze wafts constantly through the room, and I have the sensation of living on a ship. The island is motionless and in a sense the continuously calm sea is also motionless, whereas the colors are always changing—the colors of the water, of the sky, of day and night. Of everything, really—of walls and rooftops, of the neighboring village, of the sails of fishermen's boats, of the sand on the beach, of the palm and mango trees, of the wings of the seagulls and terns that always circle here. This sleepy, even lifeless place can render anyone sensitive to color dizzy, can enthrall, stun, and after a time numb and exhaust him.

Not far from my boardinghouse, between large waterfront boulders and thick vegetation, one can see remnants of calcified walls ruined by time and salt. These walls—and all of Goree, in fact—are infamous. For two hundred years, perhaps even longer, the island was a prison, a concentration camp, and the port of embarkation for African slaves being sent to the other hemisphere—to North and South America and the Caribbean. According to various estimates, several million, twelve million, perhaps as many as twenty million young men and women were deported from Goree. Those were staggering numbers in those days. The mass abductions and deportations depopulated the continent.

Africa emptied out, became overgrown with bush and weeds.

For years on end, uninterruptedly, columns of people were driven from the African interior to where Dakar lies today, and from there were conveyed by boats to this island. Some died of hunger, thirst, and disease while awaiting the ships meant to transport them across the Atlantic. The dead were tossed at once into the sea, where sharks got them. The environs of Goree were their great feeding ground. The predators circled the island in packs. Attempting escape was useless—the fish lay in wait for such daredevils, no less vigilant than the white, human guards. According to historians' calculations, half of those who made it onto the sailing ships died en route. It is more than six thousand kilometers by sea from Goree to New York. Only the strongest would endure that distance and the journey's horrific conditions.

How often do we consider the fact that the treasures and riches of the world were created from time immemorial by slaves? From the irrigation systems of Mesopotamia, the Great Wall(s) of China, the pyramids of Egypt, and acropolis of Athens, to the plantations of sugar on Cuba and of cotton in Louisiana and Arkansas, the coal mines on Kolyma and Germany's highways? And wars? From the dawn of history they were waged in order to capture slaves. Seize them, chain them, whip them, rape them, feel satisfaction at having another human being as one's property. The acquisition of slaves was an important, and frequently sole, cause of wars, their powerful and even undisguised prime motivation.

Those who managed to survive the transatlantic journey (it was said that the ships carried "black cargo") brought with them their own Afro-Egyptian culture, the same one that had fascinated Herodotus and which he had described so tirelessly in his book long before that culture reached the Western Hemisphere.

And what of Herodotus himself, what sort of slaves did he have? How many? How did he treat them? I think that he was a kind-hearted man, and gave them little reason to complain overly much. They visited a huge expanse of the world with him, and later perhaps, when he settled in Thurii to write his *Histories,* they served him as living memories, as walking encyclopedias, reminding him of names, places, and details of stories which he needed help remembering as he began writing them down, and in this way they contributed to the astonishing richness of his book.

What happened to them after Herodotus's death? Were they put up for sale in the marketplace? Or were they maybe as aged as their master and likely to have followed him shortly after into the next world?

SCENES OF PASSION
AND PRUDENCE

The most pleasant thing I can imagine to do in Goree would be to sit in the evening on the terrace, next to a table with a lamp, and to read Herodotus while listening to the murmur of the sea. But this is extremely difficult, because the instant you light the lamp, the darkness comes to life and billowing swarms of insects begin to move closer. The most excited and inquisitive specimens, seeing a brightness before them, rush blindly in its direction, slam their heads against the burning bulb, and fall dead to the ground. Others, still only half-awake, circle more cautiously, although unceasingly, tirelessly, as if the light infused them with a kind of inexhaustible energy. The greatest nuisance is a type of tiny fly, so fearless and fierce that it cares not at all about being chased away and killed—one wave of them perishes and another is already waiting impatiently to attack. Beetles and various other intrusive and malicious insects whose names I do not know exhibit a comparable zeal. But the greatest obstacle to reading are certain moths, which, apparently alarmed and irritated by something about human eyes, try to cluster around and cover them, papering them over with their dark gray, fleshy wings.

From time to time, Abdou comes to my rescue. He brings a beat-up little kiln with glowing coals inside, on which he sprinkles a mixture of bits of resin, roots, rinds, and berries, before blowing on the sizzling grate with all the might of his powerful lungs. A sharp, heavy, choking odor begins to waft through the air. As if on command, the majority of the buggy crew makes a panicked run for it, and the rest, all those that weren't paying attention, become stupefied, crawling over me and the table for a while, then, suddenly growing paralyzed and motionless, drop to the ground.

Abdou walks away with a look of satisfaction and I can read in peace for a while. Herodotus is slowly approaching the end of his opus. His book closes with four scenes:

1. A battle scene (the last battle—Mycale)

The very day that the Greeks routed the Persian forces at Plataea and what was left of them began their homeward retreat, on the other, eastern shore of the Aegean Sea, at Mycale, the Greek fleet crushed another division of the Persian army, thereby bringing to an end Greece's (that is, Europe's) victorious war with the Persians (that is, with Asia). The battle at Mycale was short. The two armies stood facing each other. *The Greeks completed their preparations and set out towards the Persian lines.* As they were beginning their assault, they suddenly learned that their kinsmen had just defeated the Persians at Plataea!

Herodotus does not say how exactly they received the message. It is a mystery, since the distance between Plataea and Mycale is great—at least several days' sailing. Some today speculate that the victors could have passed the news through a chain of bonfires lit on separate islands—whoever saw a distant fire stoked his own, the next in line saw it and did likewise, and so on; each neighbor has his neighbors in turn. *But once the mysterious rumour had sped its way to them, [the Greeks] advanced into the attack with more energy and speed.* The battle was fierce, the Persian resistance firm, but the Greeks prevailed in the end. *After the Greeks had killed most of the enemy, either while fighting in the battle or while trying to escape, they set fire to the Persian ships and to the entire stronghold—but not before they had brought the booty out on to the beach* . . .

II. A love scene (a love story and an inferno of jealousy)

At the same time that the Persian armies are bleeding and dying at Plataea and Mycale, and their survivors, pursued and murdered by the Greeks, are trying to reach the Persian city of Sardis, King Xerxes, hiding in that very city, is not thinking about the war at all, or about his ignominious flight from Athens, or about the total collapse of his empire. He immerses himself instead in perverse and risky amorous escapades. Psychology is well acquainted with the concept of denial—someone who has had unpleasant experiences and subsequent painful memories denies them, erases them, and thereby achieves inner peace and spiritual equilibrium. Clearly, such a process must have occurred in Xerxes' psyche. One year, puffed up and imperious, he leads the world's greatest army against the Greeks; and the next, having lost, he forgets about everything and henceforth is interested in one thing only—women.

After fleeing from Greece and taking refuge in Sardis, *Xerxes had fallen in love with [his brother] Masistes' wife, who was also there. She proved impervious to his messages, however . . . Under these circumstances, with all other options closed off, Xerxes arranged for his son Darius to marry the daughter of this woman and Masistes, since he expected to have a better chance of seducing the woman in this situation.* At first, therefore, the king preys not on a young girl, but on her mother, his own sister-in-law, who struck him, at least while they were still in Sardis, as more attractive than her own daughter.

However, when Xerxes returns from Sardis to the royal palace in Susa, the imperial capital, his tastes change. *After he had arrived and had received Darius' wife into his house, he dropped Masistes' wife and began to desire Darius' wife, Masistes' daughter, instead. Her name was Artaynte, and he was successful with her.*

After a while, however, the secret got out. What happened was that Amestris, Xerxes' wife, wove a wonderful shawl, long and colourful, as a present for Xerxes. He liked it a lot, and wore it when he went to visit Artaynte. She gave him pleasure too—so much so that he told her he would give her anything she wanted in return for the favours she had granted him; whatever she asked for, he assured her, she would get.

Without hesitation, his daughter-in-law said the shawl. Frightened, Xerxes tries to dissuade her, for one simple reason: if he gives her the shawl, Amestris's suspicions about his misdeeds will be confirmed. So he offers the girl *cities, unlimited gold, and sole command of any army.* But the spoiled little mule says no. She wants the shawl, only the shawl, and nothing else.

And the sovereign of a world empire, who rules over millions of people, holding their life and death in his hands, must yield. *Eventually, then, he gave her the shawl, which she liked so much that she used to wear it and show it off.*

Amestris heard that Artaynte had the shawl, but this information did not make her angry with Artaynte. Instead she assumed that her mother was to blame and was responsible for the whole business, and so it was Masistes' wife whose destruction she started to plot. She waited until her husband Xerxes was holding a royal banquet—that is, the banquet which is prepared once a year on the king's birthday.... This is the only time of the year when the king anoints his head with oil, and he also distributes gifts among the Persians. So when the day arrived, Amestris told Xerxes what she wanted her gift to be—Masistes' wife. Xerxes under-

stood the reason for her request, and was shocked and horrified, not only at the thought of handing over his brother's wife, but also because she was innocent in this matter.

His wife was implacable, however, and he was constrained by the tradition that on the day of the royal banquet no request could be refused, so he agreed, with extreme reluctance. He turned the woman over to his wife and told her to do with her what she liked, and also sent for his brother. When he arrived, he said, "Masistes, . . . you are a good man. I want you to divorce your present wife, and I'll give you my daughter instead. You can have her as your wife. But get rid of the present one; the marriage displeases me."

Masistes was astonished at the king's words. "Master," he said, "what a cruel thing to say! Can you really be telling me to get rid of my wife and marry your daughter? I have grown-up sons and daughters by my wife . . . Besides, she suits me perfectly well. . . . Please let me stay married to my wife."

This reply of his made Xerxes angry, and he said, "Do you want to know what you've done, Masistes? I'll tell you. I withdraw the offer of marriage to my daughter, and you're not going to live with your wife a moment longer either. That will teach you to accept what you're offered."

At these words all Masistes said was: "You haven't yet killed me, master." Then he walked out of the room.

In the mean time, during this conversation between Xerxes and his brother, Amestris had sent for Xerxes' personal guards and with their help had mutilated Masistes' wife. She cut off her breasts and threw them to the dogs, cut off her nose, ears, lips, and tongue, and then sent her back home, totally disfigured.

Did Amestris, having gotten her sister-in-law in her clutches, speak to her? Did she hurl insults at her while slowly, piece by piece (because the sharpness of steel was still unknown), hacking off her breasts? Did she shake a fist at her, the same fist in which she gripped the bloody knife? Or did she just pant and hiss with hatred? How did the guards behave, obliged to firmly hold down the victim? She must have screamed with pain, tossed about, tried to tear herself away. Did they ogle the breasts? Were they silent from terror? Did they giggle furtively? Or maybe the sister-in-law, slashed on her face, kept fainting, requiring them constantly to douse her with cold water? And what about her eyes? Did the king's wife gouge out her eyes? Herodotus says nothing about this. Did he forget? Or maybe Amestris forgot?

Masistes was still completely unaware of all this, but he was expecting something terrible to happen to him, so he ran back to his house. As soon as he saw how his wife had been maimed, he first sought the advice of his sons and then made his way to Bactria along with his sons and, of course, others as well, with the intention of stirring up revolt in the province of Bactria and doing the king as much harm as he could. And he would have succeeded in this, in my opinion, if he had managed to reach the Bactrians and the Sacae in time, because they were attached to him and he was the governor of Bactria. But Xerxes found out what he was up to; he dispatched an army to intercept him while he was on his way, and killed him, his sons, and all his troops. And that is the end of the story of Xerxes' desire and Masistes' death.

All this takes place at the pinnacle of imperial power. At the summit, and therefore in the most dangerous place, which time and again flows with blood. The king lives with his daughter-in-law; the enraged queen chops up her innocent sister-in-law. Later, the victim, her tongue cut out, will not even be able to denounce her. Good will be punished, defeated: a good man, Masistes, will be killed on his brother's orders, his sons will perish, his wife will be disfigured in the most horrible way possible. In the end, years later, Xerxes himself will be knifed to death. What happened to his queen? Did she perish, by revenge of the daughters of Masistes? Because the wheel of crime and punishment must have kept on turning. Did Shakespeare read Herodotus? Our Greek, after all, portrayed a world of the fiercest passions and royal murders two thousand years before the author of *Hamlet* and *Henry VIII* did.

III. The scene of revenge (the crucifixion)

In those days, Sestus and its environs are ruled by a satrap appointed by Xerxes, one Artayctes, *a Persian who was both cunning and corrupt. Once at Elaeus, during Xerxes' march towards Athens, he tricked him.* Herodotus faults him for stealing gold, silver, and all manner of other valuables, and also because *he used to have sex with women in the temple.*

The Greeks, chasing down the remnants of the Persian army and wishing to destroy the bridges over the Hellespont on which Xerxes' troops had crossed into Greece, reached Sestus, the best-fortified Persian city on the European side, and started to lay siege to it. At first, the city seemed impregnable. The discouraged Greek soldiers wanted to return home, but their commanders refused to allow it. Meantime, in Sestus, what was left of the supplies was running out and hunger was starting to decimate the besieged. *Inside the stronghold the situation was so utterly dire that they were boiling the leather straps from their beds and eating them. When there were not even any straps left, the Persians, including Artayctes . . . escaped from the town under cover of darkness by climbing down the most remote wall, where there were hardly any enemy troops.*

The Greeks threw themselves after him in pursuit. *Artayctes and his men . . . overtaken . . . resisted for a long time, but eventually were either killed or captured. The prisoners, who included Artayctes and his son, were bound by the Greeks and taken back to Sestus. . . . The Athenians took him down to the shore on which Xerxes' bridge across the straits had ended (or, in another version, to the hill which overlooks the town of Madytus), where they nailed him to a plank of wood and suspended him from it, and then stoned his son to death before his eyes.*

Herodotus does not say whether the crucified father is still alive when they split open his son's head with stones. Is the phrase "before his eyes" to be taken literally or metaphorically? It could be that Herodotus did not query witnesses about this sensitive and depressing detail. Or perhaps the witnesses themselves were unable to tell him, because they knew the story only from someone else's account?

IV. The flashback scene (should one seek a better country?)

Herodotus reminds us that an ancestor of the crucified Artayctes was a certain Artembares, who once submitted a proposition, widely supported by his countrymen, to the then ruling Persian king, Cyrus the Great. It went as follows: *"Since Zeus has given sovereignty to the Persians and to you in particular, Cyrus, ... let's emigrate from the country we currently own, which is small and rugged, and take over somewhere better. ... Will we ever have a better opportunity than now, when we rule over so many peoples and the whole of Asia?"*

Cyrus was not impressed with the proposal. He told them to go ahead—but he also advised them to be prepared, in that case, to become subjects instead of rulers, on the grounds that soft lands tend to breed soft men. It is impossible, he said, for one and the same country to produce remarkable crops and good fighting men. So the Persians admitted the truth of his argument and took their leave. Cyrus' point of view had proved more convincing than their own, and they chose to live in a harsh land and rule rather than to cultivate fertile plains and be others' slaves.

I read that final sentence of the book and put it down on the table. Abdou's aromatic enchantments had long ceased working, and swarms of pesky flies, mosquitoes, and moths once again swirled all about. They were even more aggressive now. I surrendered and fled from the terrace.

In the morning I went to the post office to send home some dispatches. A telegram was waiting for me at the window. My kind, protective boss, Michał Hofman, was suggesting that unless there was something extraordinary taking place in Africa, it would behoove me to come back to Warsaw to talk. I stayed in Dakar for a few days more, then bade goodbye to Mariem and Abdou, walked through the narrow, winding streets of Goree, and flew home.

HERODOTUS'S DISCOVERY

A friend came to visit me one evening before I left Goree, a Czech correspondent, Jarda, whom I had met once in Cairo. He, too, had come to Dakar for the festival of black art. We walked for hours through the exhibits, trying to puzzle out the meaning and purpose of the masks and sculptures of the Bambara, Makonde, and Ife. We understood how, seen at night in the flickering lights of fires and torches, they could come to life, arouse fear and dread.

We talked that evening on my terrace about the difficulties of writing about African art in a short article, in so few words. Visiting the exhibits, we were face-to-face with an alien, unknown world, our familiar concepts and vocabulary utterly inadequate for conveying its reality. We were aware of these problems, yet helpless before them.

If Jarda and I had lived in Herodotus's times, we would have been Scythians—they had inhabited our part of Europe. We would have cavorted through forests and fields on the swift horses that so delighted our Greek, shooting arrows and drinking kumiss. Herodotus would have been very interested in us, would have asked about our customs and beliefs, about what we ate and what we wore. Next, he would have described precisely how, having drawn the Persians into the winter trap of frigid temperatures, we had defeated their army, and how their great king, Darius, pursued by us, had barely escaped with his life.

As we talked, Jarda noticed Herodotus's book lying on the table. He asked how I had chanced upon it. I told him I had been given the book as a traveling companion, and how in the course of reading it I had in fact embarked on two journeys simultaneously— the first being the one I undertook while carrying out my reportorial assignments, and the second one following the expeditions of the author of *The Histories*. I quickly added that in my opinion the translated title, *The Histories*, misses the point. In Herodotus's days, the Greek word "history" meant something more like "investigation" or "inquiry," and either of those terms would have been better suited to the author's intentions and ambitions. He did not, after all, spend his time sitting in archives, and did not produce an academic text, as scholars for centuries after him did, but strove to find out, learn, and portray how history comes into being every day, how people create it, why its course often runs contrary to their efforts and expectations. Are the gods responsible for this, or is man, as a consequence of his flaws and limitations, unable to shape his own destiny wisely and rationally?

When I started reading this book, I told Jarda, I had asked myself the question, In what way did its author gather his material? There were no libraries back then, after all, no swollen archives, no files stuffed with newspaper clippings, none of the countless data banks now at our disposal. But Herodotus addresses my question on the very first pages, writing, for instance, *According to learned Persians* . . . Or *The Phoenicians say that* . . . , and adding: *So this is what the Persians and Phoenicians say. I am not going to come down in favour of this or that account of events, but I will talk about the man who, to my certain knowledge, first undertook criminal acts of aggression against the Greeks. I will show who it was who did this, and then proceed with the rest of the account. I will cover minor and major human settlements equally, because most of those which were important in the past have diminished in significance by now, and those which were great in my own time were small in times past. I will mention both equally because I know that human happiness never remains long in the same place.*

But how could Herodotus, a Greek, know what the faraway Persians or Phoenicians are saying, or the inhabitants of Egypt or Libya? It was because he traveled to where they were, asked, observed, and collected his information from what he himself saw and what others told him. His first act, therefore, was the journey. But is that not the case for all reporters? Is not our first thought to go on the road? The road is our source, our vault of treasures, our wealth. Only on the road does the reporter feel like himself, at home.

What set him into motion? Made him act? Compelled him to undertake the hardships of travel, to subject himself to the hazards of one expedition after another? I think that it was simply curiosity about the world. The desire to be there, to see it at any cost, to experience it no matter what.

It is actually a seldom encountered passion. Man is by nature a sedentary creature; from the moment he began cultivating the land and left behind the perilous and uncertain existence of a hunter or gatherer, he settled down happily, naturally, on his particular patch of earth and fenced himself off from others with a wall or a ditch, prepared to shed blood, even give his life to defend what was his. If he moved, it was only under duress, because he was driven by hunger, disease, or war, or by the search for better work, or for professional reasons—because he was a sailor, an itinerant merchant, leader of a caravan. But to traverse the world for years on end of his own free will, in order to get to know it, to plumb it, to understand it? And then, later, to put all his findings into words? Such people have always been uncommon.

Where did this passion of Herodotus's come from? Perhaps from the question that arose in a child's mind, the one about where ships come from. Children playing in the sand at the edge of a bay can see a ship suddenly appear far away on the horizon line and grow larger and larger as it sails toward them. Where did it originate? Most children do not ask themselves this question. But one, making castles out of sand, suddenly might. Where did this ship come from? That line between the sky and sea, very, very far away, had always seemed the end of the world; could it be that there is another world beyond that line? And then another one beyond that? What kind of world might it be? The child starts to seek answers. Later, when he grows up, he may have the freedom to seek even more persistently.

The road itself offers some relief. Motion. Travel. Herodotus's book arose from travel; it is world literature's first great work of reportage. Its author has reportorial instincts, a journalistic eye and ear. He is indefatigable; he sails over the sea, traverses the steppe, ventures deep into the desert—we have his accounts of all this. He astonishes us with his relentlessness, never complains of exhaustion. Nothing discourages him, and not once does he say that he is afraid.

What propelled him, fearless and tireless as he was, to throw himself into this great adventure? I think that it was an optimistic faith, one that we men lost long ago: faith in the possibility and value of truly describing the world.

Herodotus absorbed me from the start. I opened his book frequently, returning time and again to it, to him, to the scenes he depicted, to his dozens of stories, his countless digressions. I kept trying to enter his universe, find my way around it, familiarize myself with it.

This was not difficult to do, to judge by the way he saw and portrayed people and events. There is no anger in him, no animus. He tries to understand everything, find out why someone behaves in one way and not another. He does not blame the human being, but blames the system; it is not the individual who is by nature evil, depraved, villainous—it is the social arrangement in which he happens to live that is evil. That is why Herodotus is a passionate advocate of freedom and democracy and a foe of despotism, authoritarianism, and tyranny—he believes that only under the former circumstances does man have a chance to act with dignity, to be himself, to be human. Look, Herodotus seems to be saying, a small handful of Greek states defeated a great eastern power only because the Greeks felt free and for that freedom were willing to sacrifice everything.

But while maintaining the superiority of his fellow countrymen, Herodotus is not uncritical of them. He understands how the laudable principle of open discussion and freedom of speech can easily lead to pointless and destructive quarreling. He shows us that the free-speaking Greeks can bicker even on the field of battle, with the enemy poised to strike. Seeing that Xerxes' soldiers are advancing on them, that they are already letting their first arrows fly and are reaching for their swords, the Greeks start to argue about which Persians to attack first—the ones coming from the left, or the ones threatening from the right? Was this propensity to disputatiousness not one reason why the Greeks were never able to form a single, common state?

The insect brigades, which earlier had only me to attack, now, because there is also Jarda, have divided and formed two great buzzing and belligerent squadrons. Unable to cope with them, exhausted by their unflagging incursions, we call on Abdou for help, who like an ancient priest drives back with his fragrant incense the forces of evil, which in this case have assumed a bloodthirsty airborne guise.

Leaving for later the conversation about the current situation in Africa (a subject with which we must occupy ourselves daily), we stay on Herodotus. Jarda, who read the Greek long ago and says that he remembers little, asks what struck me most about this book.

I answer that it is its tragic dimension. Herodotus was the con-temporary of the greatest Greek tragedians—Aeschylus, Sopho-cles (with whom he may have been personally acquainted), and Euripides. His times were the golden age of theater (as well as much else), and stage art in those days was influenced by myster-ies, folk rituals, national festivals, religious services, Dionysian rites. This affected how Greeks wrote, how Herodotus wrote. He explains the history of the world through the fortunes of individ-uals. The pages of his book, whose goal is the recording of human history, are full of flesh-and-blood people, specific human beings with specific names, who are either powerful or weak, kind or cruel, triumphant or despondent. Under different appellations and in ever-changing contexts and situations, here are Antigones and Medeas, Cassandras and the servants of Clytemnestra, the Ghost of Darius and the lance-bearing knights of Aegisthus. Myths blend with reality, legends with facts. Herodotus tries to separate one from the other, without neglecting either or presum-ing to establish hierarchy. He knows to what great degree a man's way of thinking and his decision-making are determined by an inner realm of spirits, dreams, anxieties, and premonitions. He understands that the phantom which the king sees in his sleep can decide the fate of his nation and millions of his subjects. He knows how weak a human being is, how defenseless, in the face of terrors born of his own imagination.

At the same time, Herodotus sets himself a most ambitious task: to record the history of the world. No one before him ever attempted this. He is the first to have hit upon the idea. Constantly gathering material for his work and interrogating witnesses, bards, and priests, he finds that each of them remembers something different—different and differently. Moreover, many centuries before us, he discovers an important yet treacherous and complicating trait of human memory: people remember what they want to remember, not what actually happened. Everyone colors events after his fashion, brews up his own mélange of reminiscences. Therefore getting through to the past itself, the past as it really was, is impossible. What are available to us are only its various versions, more or less credible, one or another of them suiting us better at any given time. The past does not exist. There are only infinite renderings of it.

Herodotus is abundantly aware of this complication, yet he perseveres—he keeps conducting his investigations, citing various opinions about an incident or else rejecting them all outright as being absurd and contrary to common sense. He won't be a passive listener and chronicler, but wants to participate actively in the creation of this marvelous drama that is history—of today, yesterday, and times more distant still.

In any event, it was not only the accounts of witnesses to what once was that influenced and helped create the image of the world that he bequeathed to us. His contemporaries also had a hand in it. In those days before the advent of publishing and the solitary author, a writer lived in close, immediate contact with his audience. There were no books, after all, so he simply presented to the public what he had written and they would listen, reacting and commenting on the spot. Their responses would have likely been an important indicator for him of whether he was going in an apt direction, whether his manner of telling was favorable.

Herodotus's travels would not have been possible without the institution of the *proxenos*—"the guest's friend." The *proxenos*, or, abbreviated, proxen, was a type of consul. Voluntarily or for a fee, he took care of visitors who hailed from his native city. Feeling at home and well connected in his adoptive city, he took under his wing fellow countrymen who were newcomers there, as a fixer, a source of useful information and new contacts. The role of the proxen was particular to this extraordinary world in which gods lived among people and frequently could not be distinguished from them. One had to demonstrate genuine hospitality to a new arrival, because one could never be certain whether this wanderer asking for food and a roof over his head was merely a man, or in fact a god who had assumed human form.

Other valuable sources of material for Herodotus were all types of ubiquitous guardians of memory, self-taught historians, itinerant fiddlers. To this day in western Africa one can encounter and hear a griot, who walks around villages and marketplaces recounting the legends, myths, and stories of his people, tribe, or clan. In exchange for a small payment, or for a humble meal and a cup of cool water, the old griot, a man of great wisdom and exuberant imagination, will relate for you the history of your country, what happened there once upon a time, what accidents, events, and marvels occurred. And whether what he says is the truth or not, no one can say, and it's best not to look too closely.

Herodotus travels in order to satisfy a child's question: Where do the ships on the horizon come from? And is what we see with our own eyes not the edge of the world? No. So there are still other worlds? What kind? When the child grows up, he will want to get to know them. But it would be better if he didn't grow up completely, if he stayed always in some small measure a child. Only children pose important questions and truly want to discover things.

Herodotus learns about his worlds with the rapturous enthusiasm of a child. His most important discovery? That there are many worlds. And that each is different.

Each is important.

And that one must learn about them, because these other worlds, these other cultures, are mirrors in which we can see ourselves, thanks to which we understand ourselves better—for we cannot define our own identity until having confronted that of others, as comparison.

And that is why Herodotus, having made this discovery—that the cultures of others are a mirror in which we can examine ourselves in order to understand ourselves better—every morning, tirelessly, again and again, sets out on his journey.

WE STAND IN DARKNESS,
SURROUNDED BY LIGHT

Herodotus did not always accompany me. Frequently, my departures happened so suddenly that I had neither the time nor the presence of mind to think about the Greek. Even when I brought the book along, I often had so much work that I lacked the strength and the will to reread yet again that momentous conversation between Otanes, Megabyzus, and Darius, or to remind myself what the Ethiopians with whom Xerxes set out on his conquest of Greece looked like. *The Ethiopians were dressed in leopard skins and lion pelts, and were armed with bows made out of palm fronds. These bows were long, at least four cubits in length, and their arrows were short and tipped not with iron but with a head made from sharpened stone . . . They carried spears as well, whose heads were made out of gazelles' horns sharpened like the head of a lance, and also studded clubs. When they go into battle they paint half of their bodies with chalk and half with ochre.*

But even without reaching for the book, I could easily recall the epilogue to the war between the Greeks and the Amazons, which I had read on several previous occasions: *So the story goes that after their victory over the Amazons at the battle of Thermodon, the Greeks sailed away in three ships, taking with them all the Amazons that they had been able to capture alive. When they were out at sea, the women set upon the men and killed them, but they did not know anything about ships or how to use the rudders, sails, or oars; consequently, having done away with the men, they began to drift at the mercy of the waves and winds. They fetched up in Lake Maeetis, at the place called Cremni, which is in country inhabited by the free Scythians. The Amazons went ashore there and made their way to inhabited territory. The first thing they came across was a herd of horses, which they promptly seized, and then they began to ride about on these horses robbing the Scythians of their property.*

The Scythians could not understand what was going on. They could not make out the newcomers' nationality from their unfamiliar language and clothing; in short, they were puzzled as to where they had come from. Taking them to be young men, however, they fought against them. After the battle, the Scythians were left in possession of the corpses, and so they realized that they were women.

They decided that instead of killing more women, they would send in young Scythian men instead, in a number corresponding to that of the Amazons, and have them set up camp in the women's vicinity. *The point of the Scythians' plan was that they wanted to have children by the women.*

So the detachment of young men carried out their orders. When the Amazons realized that they had not come to harm them, they let them be, and day by day the distance between the two camps grew less. . . .

In the middle of every day the Amazons used to split up into ones or twos and go some way apart from one another in order to relieve themselves. When the Scythians noticed this, they did the same thing. One of them approached one of the women who was all alone, and the Amazon did not repulse him, but let him have intercourse with her. She could not speak to him, because they did not understand each other, but she used gestures to tell him to return the next day to the same place and bring someone else with him; she made it clear to him that there should be two of them, and that she would bring another woman with her too. The young man returned to his camp and told the others the news. He kept the appointment the next day, taking someone else along too, and found another Amazon there as well, waiting for them. When the other young men found out, they joined in and tamed the remaining Amazons.

After that the two sides joined forces and lived together . . .

Even when I had not opened *The Histories* for years, I never forgot about Herodotus. He had been a living, breathing man once, then was forgotten for two millennia, and now, after many centuries, lived anew—at least for me. I endowed him with the appearance and traits I wished him to have. He was now my Herodotus, near and dear to me, someone with whom I shared a common language and with whom I could communicate, or at least commune, almost without speaking.

I imagined him approaching me as I stood at the edge of the sea, putting down his cane, shaking the sand out of his sandals, and falling at once into conversation. He was probably one of those chatterboxes who prey upon helpless listeners, who must have them, who indeed wither and cannot live without them; one of those unwearying and perpetually excited intermediaries, who see something, hear something, and must immediately pass it on to others, constitutionally incapable of keeping things even briefly to themselves. To be a conduit is their passion: therein lies their life's mission. To walk, ride, find out—and proclaim it at once to the world.

There aren't many such enthusiasts born. The average person is not especially curious about the world. He is alive, and being somehow obliged to deal with this condition, feels the less effort it requires, the better. Whereas learning about the world is labor, and a great, all-consuming one at that. Most people develop quite antithetical talents, in fact—to look without seeing, to listen without hearing, mainly to preserve oneself within oneself. So when someone like Herodotus comes along—a man possessed by a craving, a bug, a mania for knowledge, and endowed, furthermore, with intellect and powers of written expression—it's not so surprising that his rare existence should outlive him.

Creatures like him are insatiable, spongelike organisms, absorbing everything easily and just as easily parting with it. They do not keep anything inside for long, and because nature abhors a vacuum, they constantly need to ingest something new, replenish themselves, multiply, augment. Herodotus's mind is incapable of stopping at one event or one country. Something always propels him forward, drives him on without rest. A fact that he discovered and ascertained today no longer fascinates him tomorrow, and so he must walk (or ride) elsewhere, further away.

Such people, while useful, even agreeable, to others, are, if truth be told, frequently unhappy—lonely in fact. Yes, they seek out others, and it may even seem to them that in a certain country or city they have managed to find true kindred and fellowship, having come to know and learn about a people; but they wake up one day and suddenly feel that nothing actually binds them to these people, that they can leave here at once. They realize that another country, some other people, have now beguiled them, and that yesterday's most riveting event now pales and loses all meaning and significance.

For all intents and purposes, they do not grow attached to anything, do not put down deep roots. Their empathy is sincere, but superficial. If asked which of the countries they have visited they like best, they are embarrassed—they do not know how to answer. Which one? In a certain sense—all of them. There is something compelling about each. To which country would they like to return once more? Again, embarrassment—they had never asked themselves such a question. The one certainty is that they would like to be back on the road, going somewhere. To be on their way again—that is the dream.

We do not really know what draws a human being out into the world. Is it curiosity? A hunger for experience? An addiction to wonderment? The man who ceases to be astonished is hollow, possessed of an extinguished heart. If he believes that everything has already happened, that he has seen it all, then something most precious has died within him—the delight in life. Herodotus is the antithesis of this spirit. A vivacious, fascinated, unflagging nomad, full of plans, ideas, theories. Always traveling. Even at home (but where is his home?), he has either just returned from an expedition, or is preparing for the next one. Travel is his vital exertion, his self-justification is the delving into, the struggle to learn—about life, the world, perhaps ultimately oneself.

He carries in his mind a map of the world—actually, he is creating it as he goes along, amending it, filling it in. It is a living image, a turning kaleidoscope, a flickering screen. A thousand things take place on it. The Egyptians are building pyramids, the Scythians are hunting big game, the Phoenicians are kidnapping young women, and the queen of the Cyreneans, Pheretime, is dying a dreadful death: *She became infested with a mass of worms while still alive* ...

Greece and Crete feature on Herodotus's map, as well as Persia and the Caucasus, Arabia and the Red Sea. There is no China, or either of the two Americas, or the Pacific. He is unclear as to Europe's shape, and also puzzles over the origins of its name. *No one knows for certain whether or not there is sea either to the east or to the north of Europe; it is known, however, that lengthwise it is equal to the other continents together. . . . Nor can I find out the names of those who decided upon these boundaries or how the continents got their names.*

He does not concern himself with the future, for the future is simply another today. He is interested in yesterday, in the past that is vanishing, and in peril of fading from memory, of being lost to us forever—a prospect that fills him with panic. We are human because we recount stories and myths; the past—that is what

269

differentiates us from animals. Shared histories and legends strengthen community, and man can exist only as part of a community, only by virtue of it. Individualism, modernity's unalloyed good, had not yet been conceived in Herodotus's time, nor egocentrism, nor any Freudian notion—such thoughts will not occur for another two thousand years. For now, people gather in the evenings at the long, communal table, by the fire, beneath the old tree. Better if the sea is nearby. They eat, drink wine, talk. Tales are woven into those conversations, endlessly varied stories. If a visitor, a traveler, happens by, they will invite him to join them. He will sit and listen. In the morning, he will be on his way. In the next place he comes to, he will be similarly welcomed. The scenario of these ancient evenings repeats itself. If the traveler has a good memory—and Herodotus must have had a phenomenal one—he will over time amass a great many stories. That was one of the sources upon which our Greek drew. Another one was what he saw. Yet another—what he thought.

There were times when journeys into the past appealed to me more than my present-day journeys as correspondent and reporter. I felt this way especially in moments of fatigue with the present. Everything in the present kept repeating itself: politics—always perfidious, unclean games and lies; the life of the ordinary man—unrelenting poverty and hopelessness; the division of the world into East and West—eternal duality.

And just as I had once desired to cross a physical border, so now I was fascinated by crossing a temporal one.

I was afraid that I might fall into the trap of provincialism. We normally associate the concept of provincialism with geographic space. A provincial is one whose worldview is shaped by a certain marginal area to which he ascribes an undue importance, inaptly universalizing the particular. But T. S. Eliot cautions against another kind of provincialism—not of space, but of time. "In our age," he writes in a 1944 essay about Virgil, "when men seem more than ever prone to confuse wisdom with knowledge, and knowledge with information, and to try to solve problems of life in terms of engineering, there is coming into existence a new kind of provincialism which perhaps deserves a new name. It is a provincialism, not of space, but of time; one for which history is merely the chronicle of human devices which have served their turn and been scrapped, one for which the world is the property solely of the living, a property in which the dead hold no shares. The menace of this kind of provincialism is, that we can all, all the peoples on the globe, be provincials together; and those who are not content to be provincials, can only become hermits."

So there are spatial and temporal provincials. Every globe, every map of the world, shows the former how lost and blind they are in their provincialism; similarly, every history—including every page of Herodotus—demonstrates to the latter that the present existed always, that history is merely an uninterrupted progression of presents, that what for us are ancient events were for those who lived them immediate and present reality.

To protect myself from this temporal provincialism, I set off into Herodotus's world, the wise, experienced Greek as my guide. We wandered together for years. And although one travels best alone, I do not think we disturbed each other—we were separated by twenty-five hundred years and also by distance of another kind, born of my feelings of respect. For although Herodotus was always straightforward, kind, and gentle in relation to others, there was always with me the feeling of rubbing shoulders undeservedly, perhaps presumptuously, but always thankfully, with a giant.

Did I do the right thing, trying to escape into history? Did this ambition make any sense? After all, we encounter in historical accounts the very same things such as we thought we could flee in our time.

Herodotus is entangled in a rather insoluble dilemma: he devotes his life to preserving historic truth, *to prevent the traces of human events from being erased by time*; at the same time, however, his main source of research is not firsthand experience, but history as it was recounted by others, as it appeared to them, therefore as it was selectively remembered and later more or less intentionally presented. In short, not primary history, but history as his interlocutors would have had it. There is no way around this divergence of purpose and means. We can try to minimize or mitigate it, but we will never approach the objective ideal. The subjective factor, its deforming presence, will remain impossible to strain out. Herodotus expresses an awareness of this predicament, constantly qualifying what he reports: "as they tell me," "as they maintain," "they present this in various ways," etc. In fact, though, however evolved our methods, we are never in the presence of unmediated history, but of history recounted, presented, history as it appeared to someone, as he or she believes it to have been. This has been the nature of the enterprise always, and the folly may be to believe one can resist it.

This fact is perhaps Herodotus's greatest discovery.

From the island of Kos I sailed to Halicarnassus, where Herodotus was born, on a small ship. En route, the taciturn, aged sailor lowered the Greek flag on the mast and hoisted the Turkish one. Both were crumpled, faded, and frayed.

The town lay well inside the arc of the blue-green bay, on whose waters, in this autumnal time of year, many yachts were idling. The policeman whom I queried about the way to Halicarnassus corrected me—to Bodrum, he said, that is how the place is now known in Turkish. He was understanding and polite. The boy at the reception desk in the cheap little hotel near the shore had an acute case of periostitis, with a face so horribly swollen that I was afraid the pus would tear his cheek apart at any moment. Just in case, I maintained a certain judicious distance. In the shabby little room on the first floor nothing closed properly—not the doors, not the window, not the armoire—which made me feel right at home, as if in an environment I knew long and well. For breakfast I was given delicious Turkish coffee with cardamom, pita bread, a piece of goat cheese, some onion and olives.

I set out along the town's main street, planted with palm trees and fig and azalea bushes. In one spot, at the edge of the bay, fishermen were selling their morning catch at a long table dripping water. They grabbed the floundering fish that had been dumped onto the tabletop, smashed open their heads with a blunt object, gutted them with lightning speed, and with sweeping dexterity tossed the entrails into the bay. The waters were swarming with other fish feeding on the bloody scraps. At dawn the next day, the fishermen would gather another day's fresh catch into their nets and toss those fish now caught onto the slippery table—where each fell straight under the knife. In this way nature, devouring its own tail, fed both itself and humans.

Halfway down the road, on a hill on a promontory jutting out to sea, stands the castle of Saint Peter, built by the Crusaders. It houses the rather extraordinary Museum of Underwater Archeology, a collection of objects found by divers at the bottom of the Aegean. Especially striking is the large collection of amphorae.

Amphorae have existed for five thousand years. Slender, with swan-like necks, they combine an elegant shape with the strength and resilience of their material—fired clay and stone. They were used to transport olive oil and wine, honey and cheese, wheat and fruit, and circulated throughout the entire antique world—from the Pillars of Heracles to Colchis and India. The bottom of the Aegean is strewn with their shards, but there are also plenty of intact amphorae about, perhaps still filled with olive oil and honey, reposing on the shelves of underwater cliffs or buried in the sand, like lurking, motionless beasts.

What the divers brought up is but a fragment of the whole watery world, whose depths are as rich and variegated as is the realm above, which we inhabit. There are sunken islands down there, and on them sunken towns and villages, ports and harbors, temples and sanctuaries, altars and statues. There are sunken ships and a good many fishing boats. There are merchant ships and the pirate vessels awaiting discovery. Galleys of the Phoenicians lie beneath the surface and, at Salamis, the great Persian fleet, the pride of Xerxes. Countless teams of horses, flocks of goats and sheep. Forests and arable fields. Vineyards and olive groves.

The world that Herodotus knew.

What moved me most, however, was one of the museum's dark chambers, mysterious as a murky cave, in which, on tables, in display cabinets, and on shelves lie illuminated glass objects which had been pulled up from the depths—cups, bowls, pitchers, perfume flasks, goblets. They are not clearly visible at first, when the doors to the room are still open and daylight penetrates its interior. But when the doors close and it grows dark, the curator presses a switch turning on small lightbulbs inside the little vessels, bringing to life the fragile, matte pieces of glass, which start to sparkle, brighten, pulsate. We stand in deep, thick darkness, as if at the bottom of the sea, at a feast of Poseidon's, surrounded by goddesses each holding an olive oil lamp above her head.

We stand in darkness, surrounded by light.

I returned to the hotel. At reception, in place of the dolorous boy, stood a young black-eyed Turkish girl. When she saw me, she adjusted her facial expression so that the professional smile meant to invite and tempt tourists was tempered by tradition's injunction always to maintain a serious and indifferent mien toward a strange man.

PENGUIN HISTORY

THE CLASSICAL WORLD
ROBIN LANE FOX

The classical civilizations of Greece and Rome dominated the world some forty lifetimes before our own, and they continue to intrigue, inspire and enlighten us. From Greece in the eighth century BC to Rome at the time of Julius Caesar and Augustus in the first century BC, their art and architecture, drama and epics, philosophy and politics have been the foundation of much of what we value today. Their heroes, from Achilles to Alexander, are still powerfully evoked in our modern culture, films and writing.

The Classical World brilliantly describes the vast sweep of history in which these two great civilizations ruled – from the epic poems of Homer and the beginning of literacy through the foundation of Athenian democracy and the turbulent empire-building of Alexander the Great to the establishment of the Roman Republic, the rise of Christianity, and the challenges this new faith faced in the Roman imperial age.

For those who are new to this enthralling subject and for the many who continue to share his fascination with classical Greece and Rome, Robin Lane Fox's account is a wonderfully exciting historical tour of two of the greatest empires the world has ever seen.

Praise for Robin Lane Fox

Pagans and Christians

'Brilliant...it is readable and rereadable, even gripping' *Spectator*

'This open-hearted and learned book is one that any scholar of the ancient world and of early Christianity would be proud to have written... Lane Fox has opened his pages to let in an entirely new world' *The New York Review of Books*

'Here is richness indeed... a magisterial analysis' *The Times*

Penguin Politics

THE SHADOW OF THE SUN
RYSZARD KAPUŚCIŃSKI

'Written with love and longing, as sharp and life-enhancing as the sun that rises on an African morning' *Sunday Times*

'For more than forty years, Ryszard Kapuściński has been the definitive voice on all things African ... Almost every page in this book comes alive with his quick brilliance ... He brings the world to us as nobody else' Ian Jack, *Observer*

'One of the finest books I have ever read about Africa ... Kapuściński has been visiting Africa as a journalist since 1957 ... he has avoided "official routes, important personages and high-level politics" ... it is here, in the margins, that Kapuściński has achieved something no other commentator I know of has done' Justin Cartwright, *Daily Mail*

'He has V. S. Naipaul's gift for characterization and Isaac Babel's openness to life-threatening experience ... *The Shadow of the Sun* is an indispensable book for anyone interested in great humanitarian writing about an indefinable continent' Russell Celyn Jones, *The Times*

He just wanted a decent book to read ...

Not too much to ask, is it? It was in 1935 when Allen Lane, Managing Director of Bodley Head Publishers, stood on a platform at Exeter railway station looking for something good to read on his journey back to London. His choice was limited to popular magazines and poor-quality paperbacks – the same choice faced every day by the vast majority of readers, few of whom could afford hardbacks. Lane's disappointment and subsequent anger at the range of books generally available led him to found a company – and change the world.

'We believed in the existence in this country of a vast reading public for intelligent books at a low price, and staked everything on it'
Sir Allen Lane, 1902–1970, founder of Penguin Books

The quality paperback had arrived – and not just in bookshops. Lane was adamant that his Penguins should appear in chain stores and tobacconists, and should cost no more than a packet of cigarettes.

Reading habits (and cigarette prices) have changed since 1935, but Penguin still believes in publishing the best books for everybody to enjoy. We still believe that good design costs no more than bad design, and we still believe that quality books published passionately and responsibly make the world a better place.

So wherever you see the little bird – whether it's on a piece of prize-winning literary fiction or a celebrity autobiography, political tour de force or historical masterpiece, a serial-killer thriller, reference book, world classic or a piece of pure escapism – you can bet that it represents the very best that the genre has to offer.

Whatever you like to read – trust Penguin.